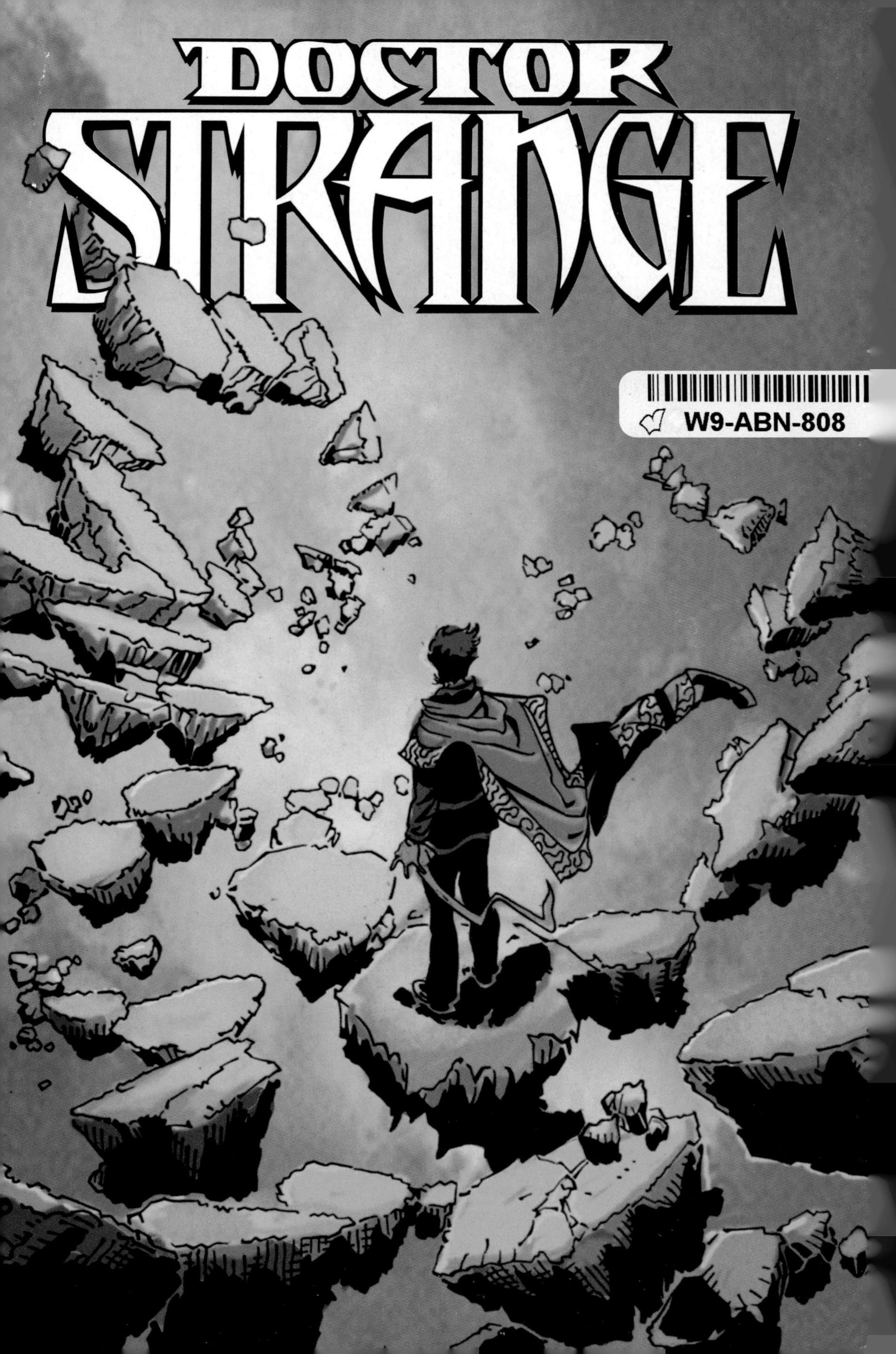
DOCTOR
STRANGE

COLLECTION EDITOR: **JENNIFER GRÜNWALD**
ASSOCIATE MANAGING EDITOR: **KATERI WOODY**
ASSOCIATE EDITOR: **SARAH BRUNSTAD**
EDITOR, SPECIAL PROJECTS: **MARK D. BEAZLEY**
VP PRODUCTION & SPECIAL PROJECTS: **JEFF YOUNGQUIST**
SVP PRINT, SALES & MARKETING: **DAVID GABRIEL**
BOOK DESIGNER: **JAY BOWEN**

EDITOR IN CHIEF: **AXEL ALONSO**
CHIEF CREATIVE OFFICER: **JOE QUESADA**
PUBLISHER: **DAN BUCKLEY**
EXECUTIVE PRODUCER: **ALAN FINE**

**DOCTOR STRANGE VOL. 1: THE WAY OF THE WEIRD.** Contains material originally published in magazine form as DOCTOR STRANGE #1-5. First printing 2016. ISBN# 978-0-7851-9932-8. Published by MARVEL WORLDWIDE, INC., a subsidiar of MARVEL ENTERTAINMENT, LLC. OFFICE OF PUBLICATION: 135 West 50th Street, New York, NY 10020. Copyright © 2016 MARVEL No similarity between any of the names, characters, persons, and/or institutions in this magazine wit those of any living or dead person or institution is intended, and any such similarity which may exist is purely coincidental. **Printed in the U.S.A.** ALAN FINE, President, Marvel Entertainment; DAN BUCKLEY, President, TV, Publishing & Bran Management; JOE QUESADA, Chief Creative Officer; TOM BREVOORT, SVP of Publishing; DAVID BOGART, SVP of Business Affairs & Operations. Publishing & Partnership; C.B. CEBULSKI, VP of Brand Management & Development, Asia; DAVII GABRIEL, SVP of Sales & Marketing, Publishing; JEFF YOUNGQUIST, VP of Production & Special Projects; DAN CARR, Executive Director of Publishing Technology; ALEX MORALES. Director of Publishing Operations; SUSAN CRESPI, Productio Manager; STAN LEE, Chairman Emeritus. For information regarding advertising in Marvel Comics or on Marvel.com, please contact Vit DeBellis, Integrated Sales Manager, at vdebellis@marvel.com. For Marvel subscription inquiries, pleas call 888-511-5480. **Manufactured between 10/14/2016 and 11/21/2016 by LSC COMMUNICATIONS INC., SALEM, VA, USA.**

10 9 8 7 6 5 4 3 2 1

# DOCTOR STRANGE

## The Way of the Weird

### Jason Aaron
WRITER

### Chris Bachalo
PENCILER/COLORIST

### Tim Townsend, Al Vey, Mark Irwin, John Livesay, Wayne Faucher, Victor Olazaba & Jaime Mendoza
INKERS

### "The Coming Slaughter"

#### Kevin Nowlan
ARTIST/COLORIST

### VC's Cory Petit
LETTERER

### Chris Bachalo & Tim Townsend (#1-3) and Kevin Nowlan (#4-5)
COVER ART

### Charles Beacham
ASSISTANT EDITOR

### Nick Lowe
EDITOR

DOCTOR STRANGE CREATED BY
STAN LEE & STEVE DITKO

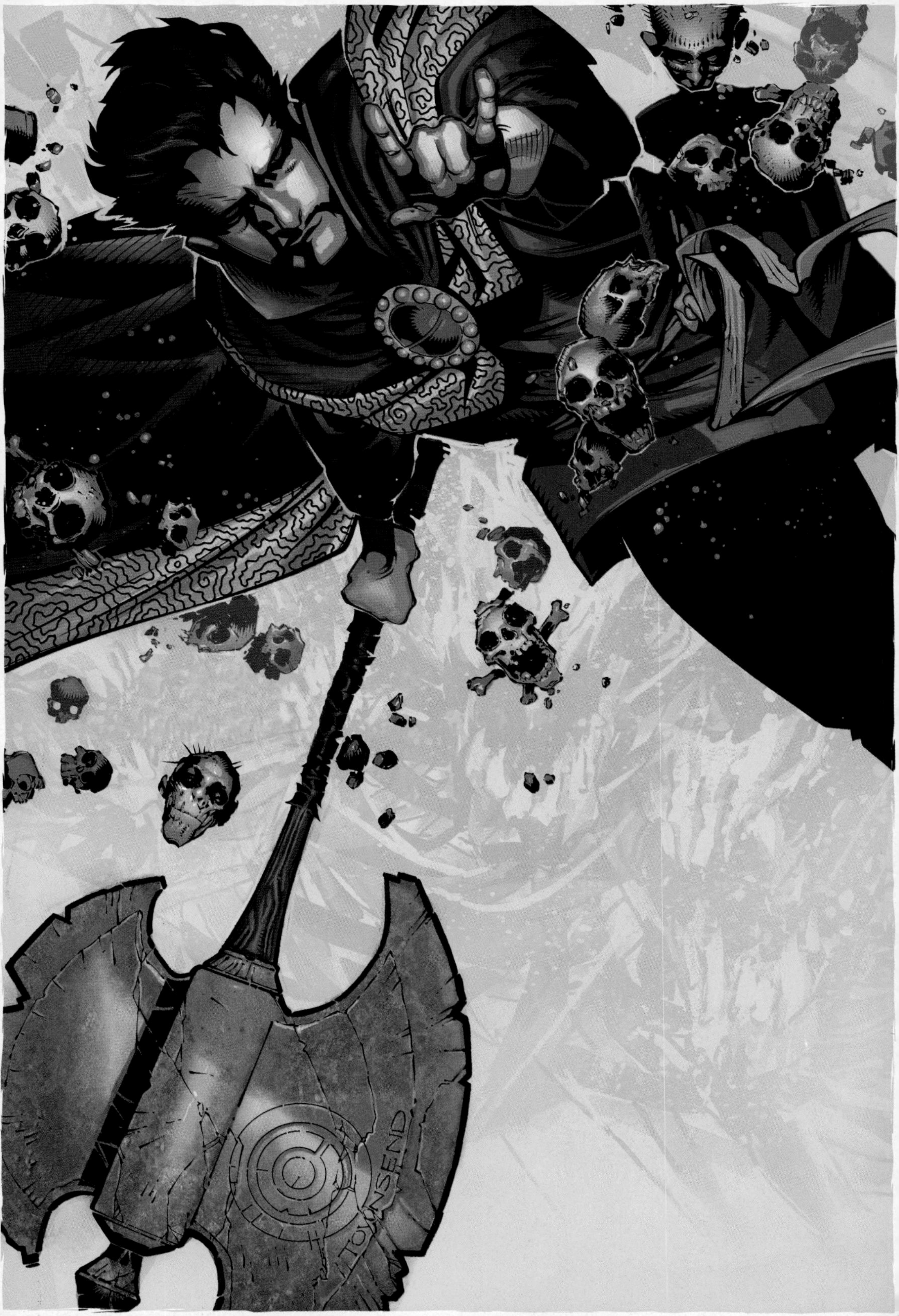
TOWNSEND

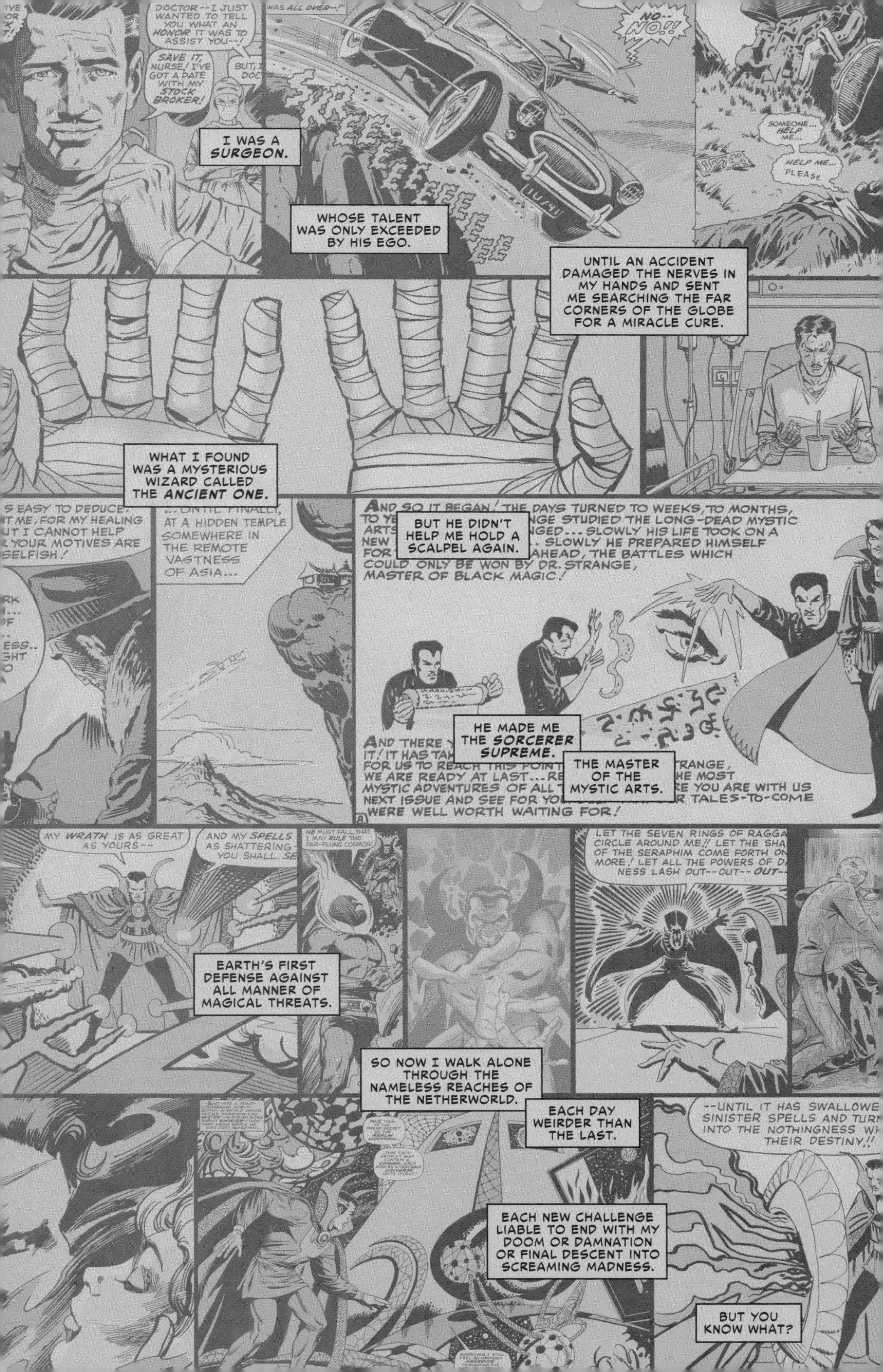
DOCTOR--I JUST WANTED TO TELL YOU WHAT AN HONOR IT WAS TO ASSIST YOU--!
SAVE IT, NURSE! I'VE GOT A DATE WITH MY STOCK BROKER!
I WAS A SURGEON.
NO--NO!!
WHOSE TALENT WAS ONLY EXCEEDED BY HIS EGO.
SOMEONE... HELP ME...
HELP ME... PLEASE
UNTIL AN ACCIDENT DAMAGED THE NERVES IN MY HANDS AND SENT ME SEARCHING THE FAR CORNERS OF THE GLOBE FOR A MIRACLE CURE.
WHAT I FOUND WAS A MYSTERIOUS WIZARD CALLED THE ANCIENT ONE.
...UNTIL FINALLY, AT A HIDDEN TEMPLE SOMEWHERE IN THE REMOTE VASTNESS OF ASIA...
BUT HE DIDN'T HELP ME HOLD A SCALPEL AGAIN.
HE MADE ME THE SORCERER SUPREME.
THE MASTER OF THE MYSTIC ARTS.
MY WRATH IS AS GREAT AS YOURS--
AND MY SPELLS AS SHATTERING--
HE MUST FALL, THAT I MAY RULE THE FAR-FLUNG COSMOS!
EARTH'S FIRST DEFENSE AGAINST ALL MANNER OF MAGICAL THREATS.
SO NOW I WALK ALONE THROUGH THE NAMELESS REACHES OF THE NETHERWORLD.
EACH DAY WEIRDER THAN THE LAST.
EACH NEW CHALLENGE LIABLE TO END WITH MY DOOM OR DAMNATION OR FINAL DESCENT INTO SCREAMING MADNESS.
BUT YOU KNOW WHAT?

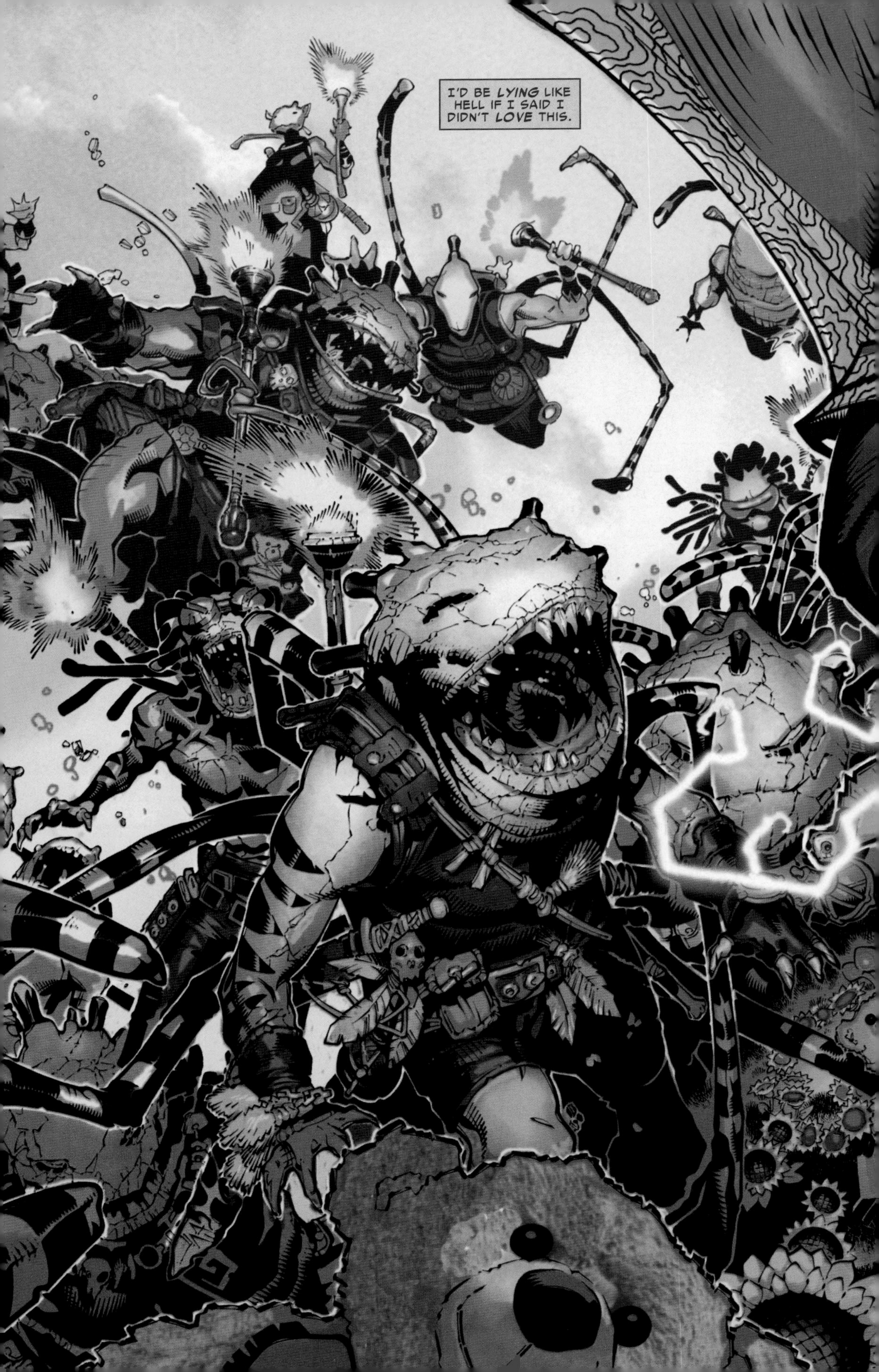
I'D BE LYING LIKE HELL IF I SAID I DIDN'T LOVE THIS.

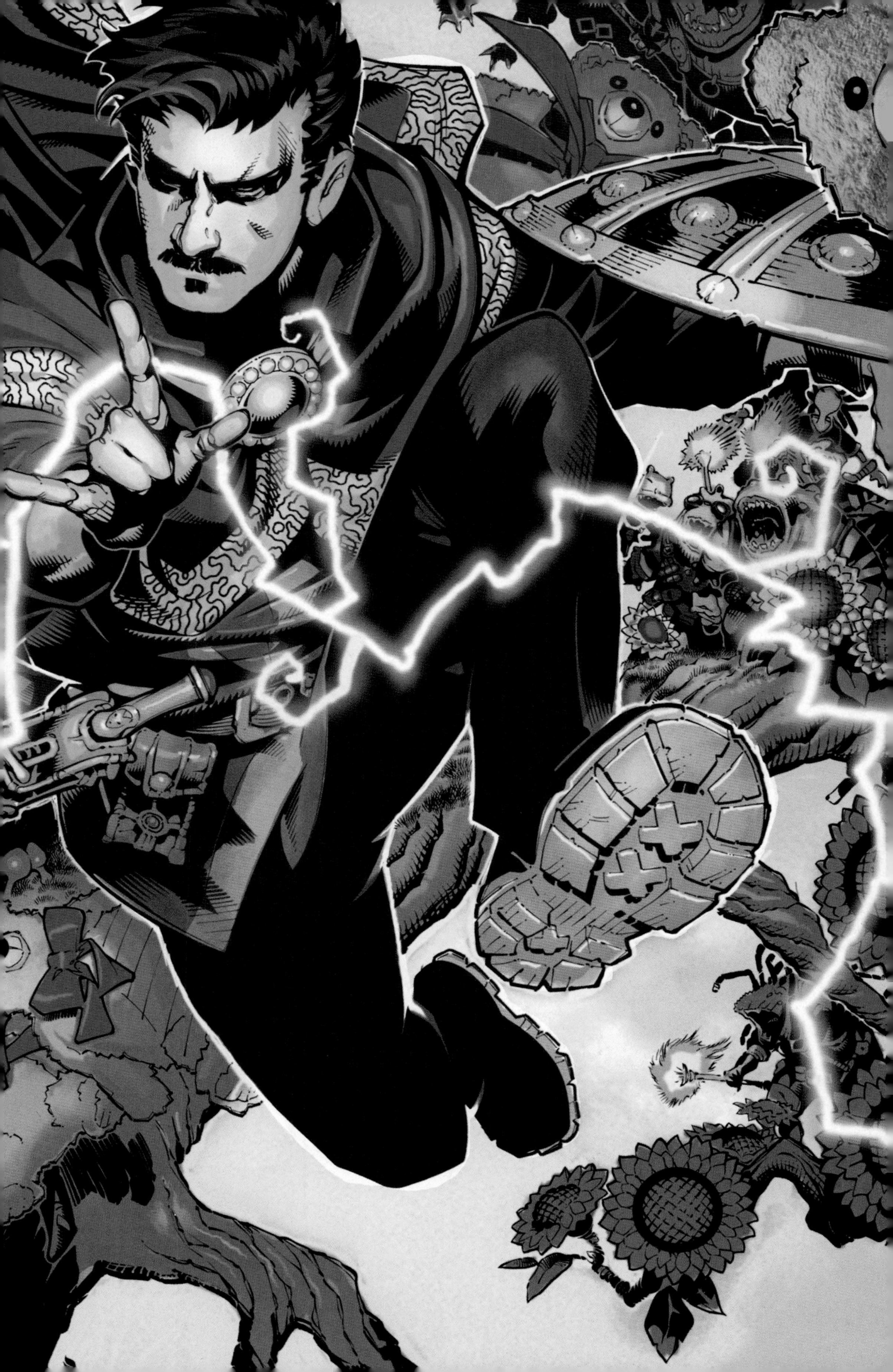

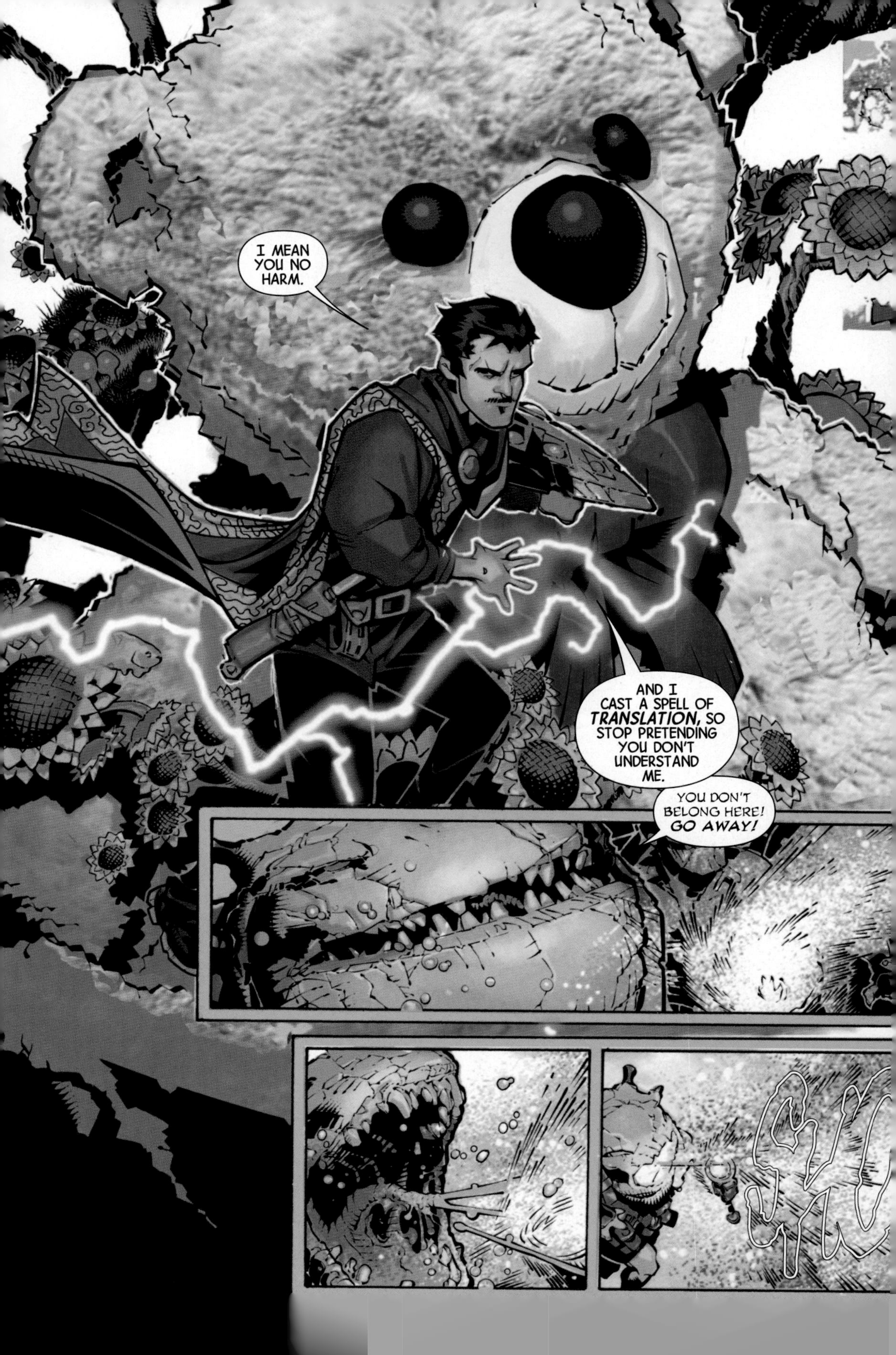
I MEAN YOU NO HARM.
AND I CAST A SPELL OF TRANSLATION, SO STOP PRETENDING YOU DON'T UNDERSTAND ME.
YOU DON'T BELONG HERE! GO AWAY!

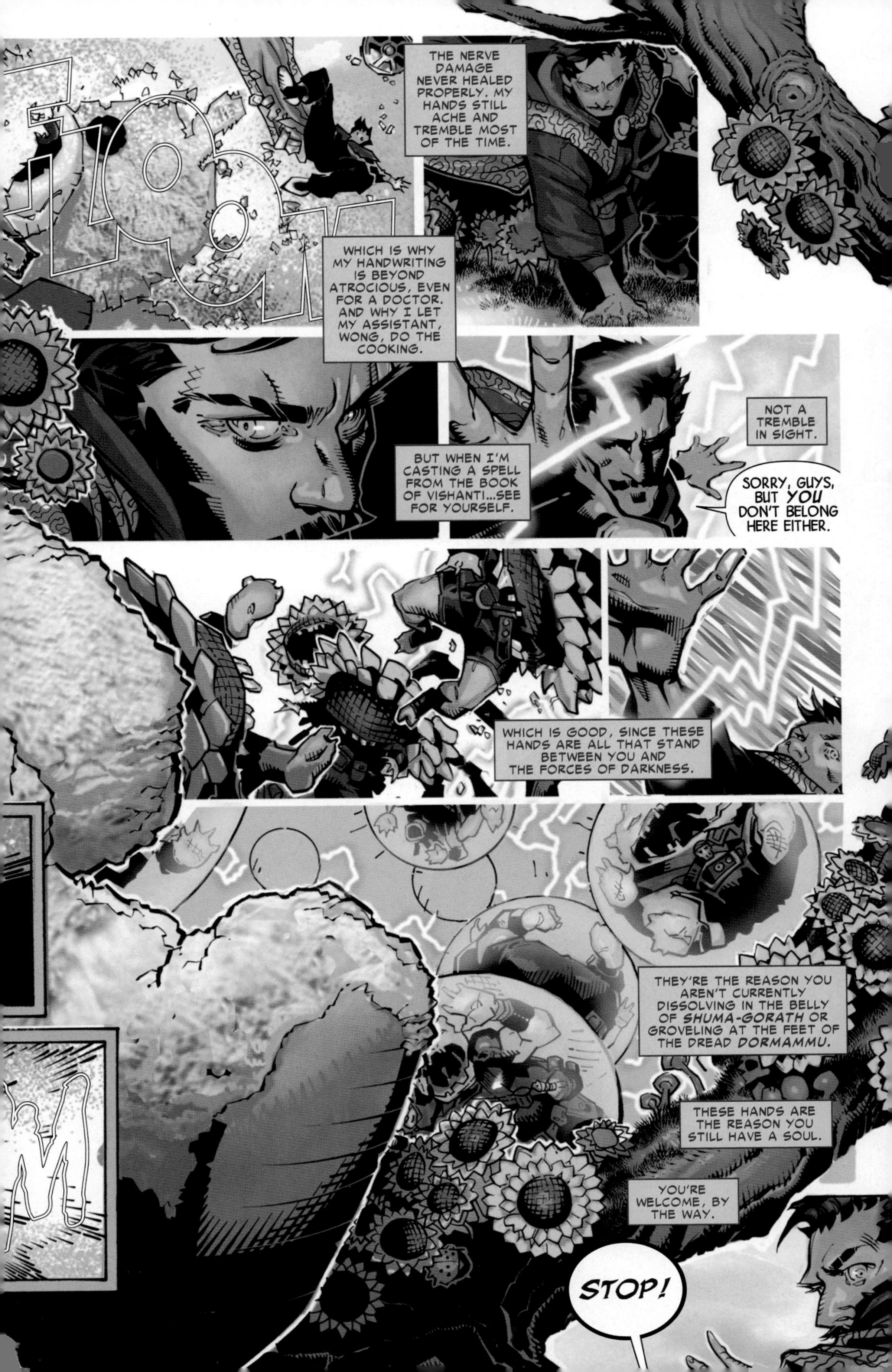
THE NERVE DAMAGE NEVER HEALED PROPERLY. MY HANDS STILL ACHE AND TREMBLE MOST OF THE TIME.
WHICH IS WHY MY HANDWRITING IS BEYOND ATROCIOUS, EVEN FOR A DOCTOR. AND WHY I LET MY ASSISTANT, WONG, DO THE COOKING.
BUT WHEN I'M CASTING A SPELL FROM THE BOOK OF VISHANTI...SEE FOR YOURSELF.
NOT A TREMBLE IN SIGHT.
SORRY, GUYS, BUT YOU DON'T BELONG HERE EITHER.
WHICH IS GOOD, SINCE THESE HANDS ARE ALL THAT STAND BETWEEN YOU AND THE FORCES OF DARKNESS.
THEY'RE THE REASON YOU AREN'T CURRENTLY DISSOLVING IN THE BELLY OF SHUMA-GORATH OR GROVELING AT THE FEET OF THE DREAD DORMAMMU.
THESE HANDS ARE THE REASON YOU STILL HAVE A SOUL.
YOU'RE WELCOME, BY THE WAY.
STOP!

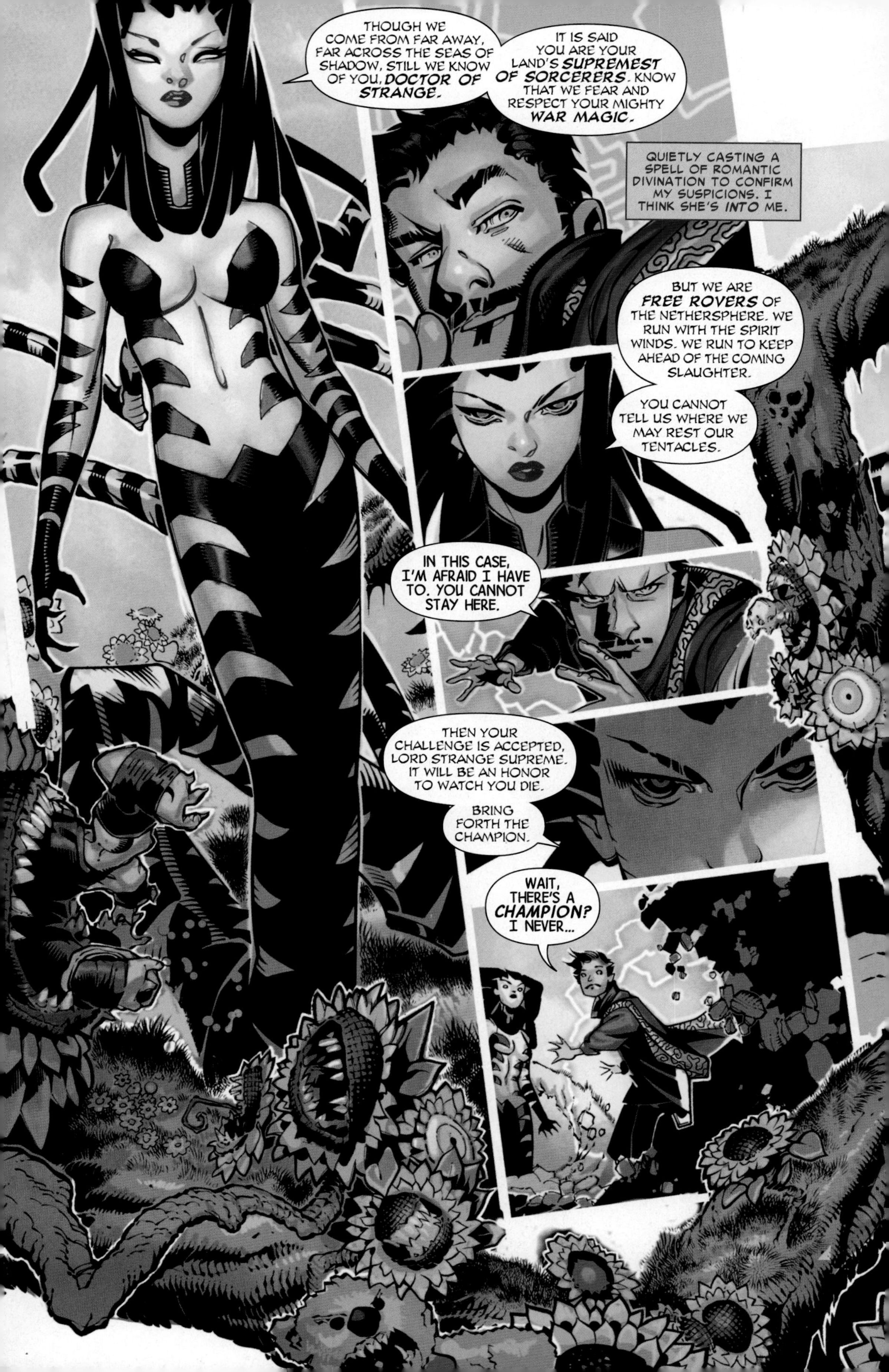
THOUGH WE COME FROM FAR AWAY, FAR ACROSS THE SEAS OF SHADOW, STILL WE KNOW OF YOU, DOCTOR OF STRANGE.
IT IS SAID YOU ARE YOUR LAND'S SUPREMEST OF SORCERERS. KNOW THAT WE FEAR AND RESPECT YOUR MIGHTY WAR MAGIC.
QUIETLY CASTING A SPELL OF ROMANTIC DIVINATION TO CONFIRM MY SUSPICIONS. I THINK SHE'S INTO ME.
BUT WE ARE FREE ROVERS OF THE NETHERSPHERE. WE RUN WITH THE SPIRIT WINDS. WE RUN TO KEEP AHEAD OF THE COMING SLAUGHTER.
YOU CANNOT TELL US WHERE WE MAY REST OUR TENTACLES.
IN THIS CASE, I'M AFRAID I HAVE TO. YOU CANNOT STAY HERE.
THEN YOUR CHALLENGE IS ACCEPTED, LORD STRANGE SUPREME. IT WILL BE AN HONOR TO WATCH YOU DIE.
BRING FORTH THE CHAMPION.
WAIT, THERE'S A CHAMPION? I NEVER...

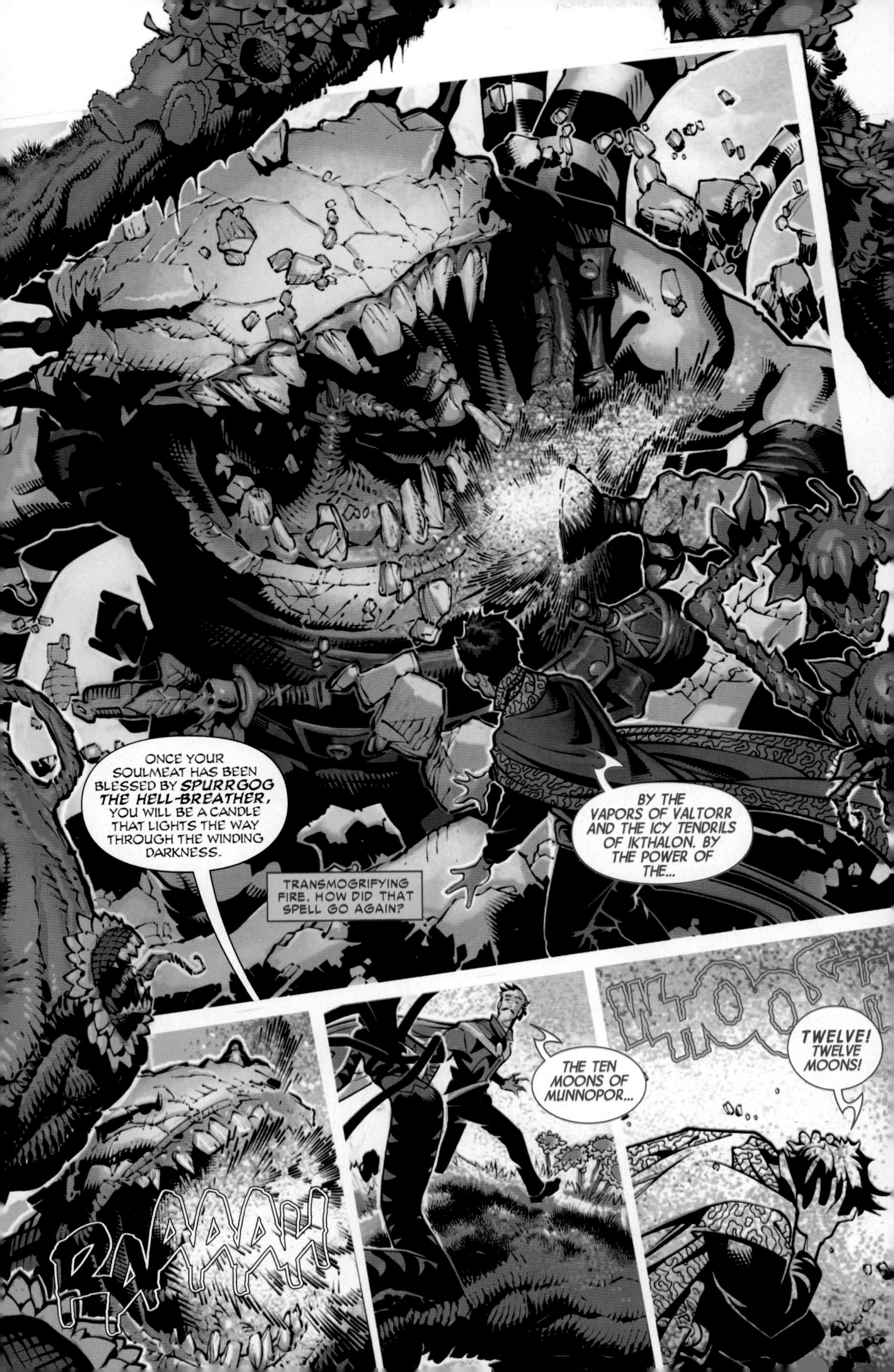
ONCE YOUR SOULMEAT HAS BEEN BLESSED BY SPURRGOG THE HELL-BREATHER, YOU WILL BE A CANDLE THAT LIGHTS THE WAY THROUGH THE WINDING DARKNESS.
BY THE VAPORS OF VALTORR AND THE ICY TENDRILS OF IKTHALON. BY THE POWER OF THE...
TRANSMOGRIFYING FIRE. HOW DID THAT SPELL GO AGAIN?
THE TEN MOONS OF MUNNOPOR...
TWELVE! TWELVE MOONS!

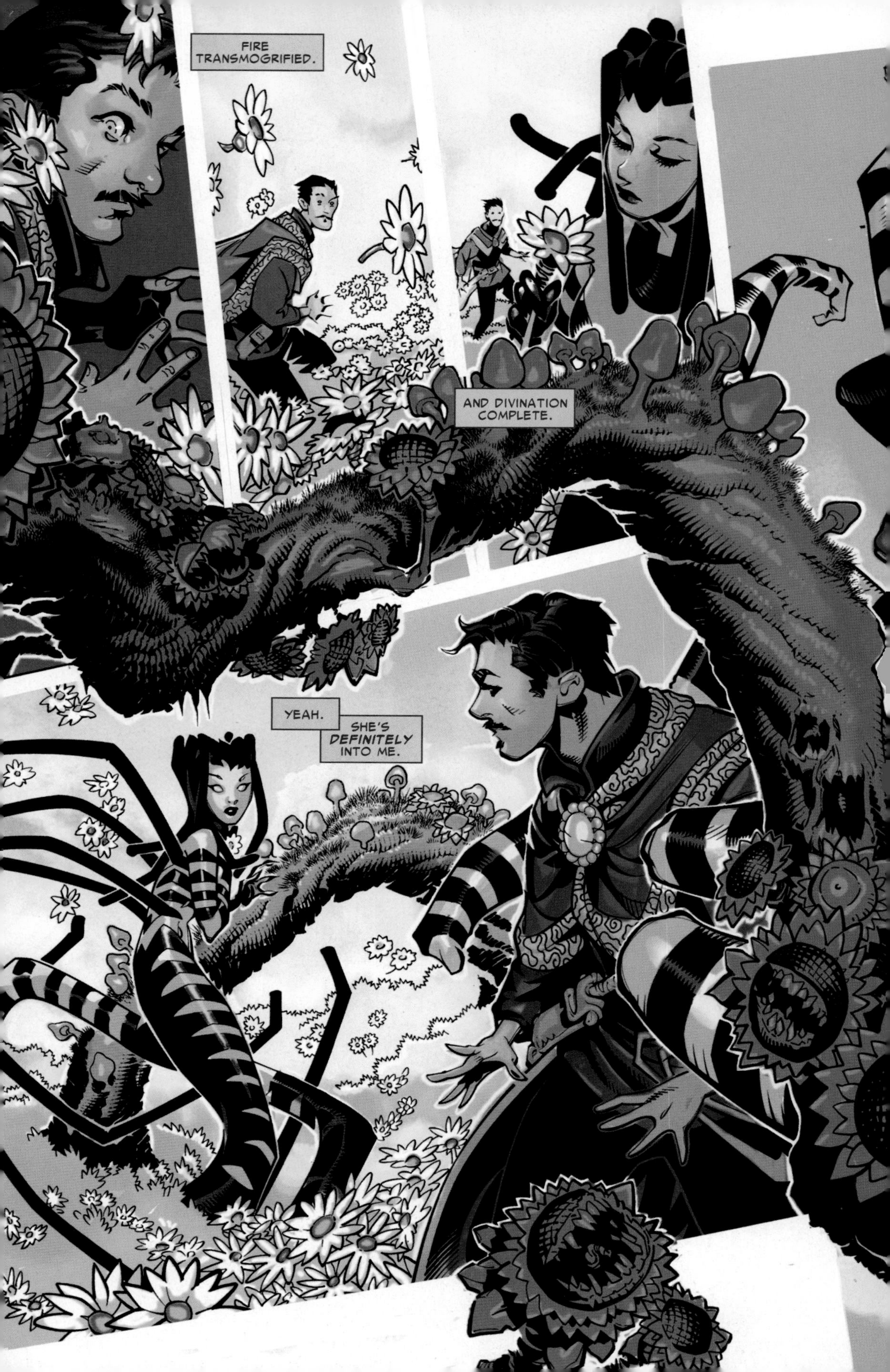
FIRE TRANSMOGRIFIED.
AND DIVINATION COMPLETE.
YEAH.
SHE'S *DEFINITELY* INTO ME.

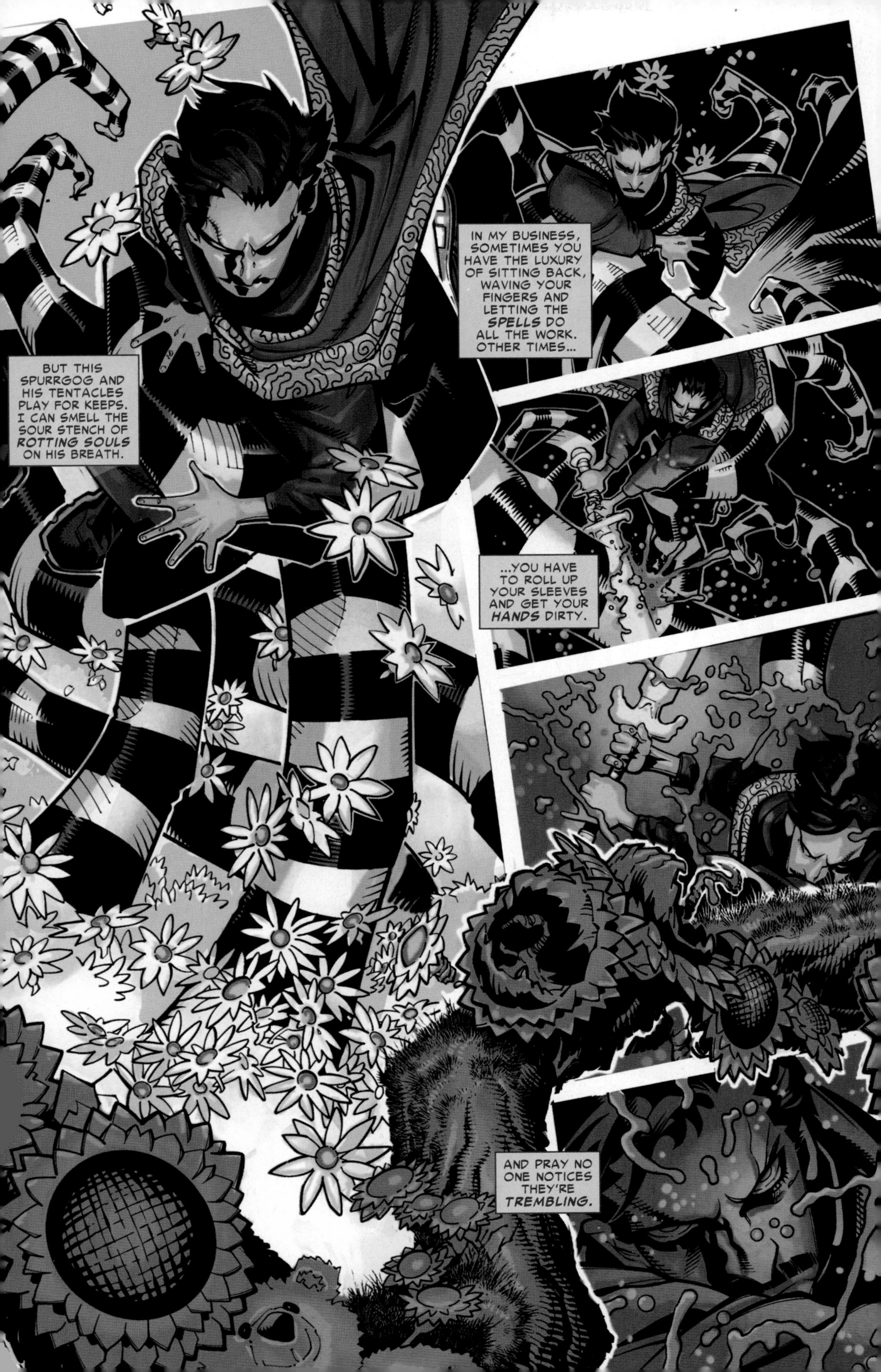
IN MY BUSINESS, SOMETIMES YOU HAVE THE LUXURY OF SITTING BACK, WAVING YOUR FINGERS AND LETTING THE SPELLS DO ALL THE WORK. OTHER TIMES...
BUT THIS SPURRGOG AND HIS TENTACLES PLAY FOR KEEPS. I CAN SMELL THE SOUR STENCH OF ROTTING SOULS ON HIS BREATH.
...YOU HAVE TO ROLL UP YOUR SLEEVES AND GET YOUR HANDS DIRTY.
AND PRAY NO ONE NOTICES THEY'RE TREMBLING.

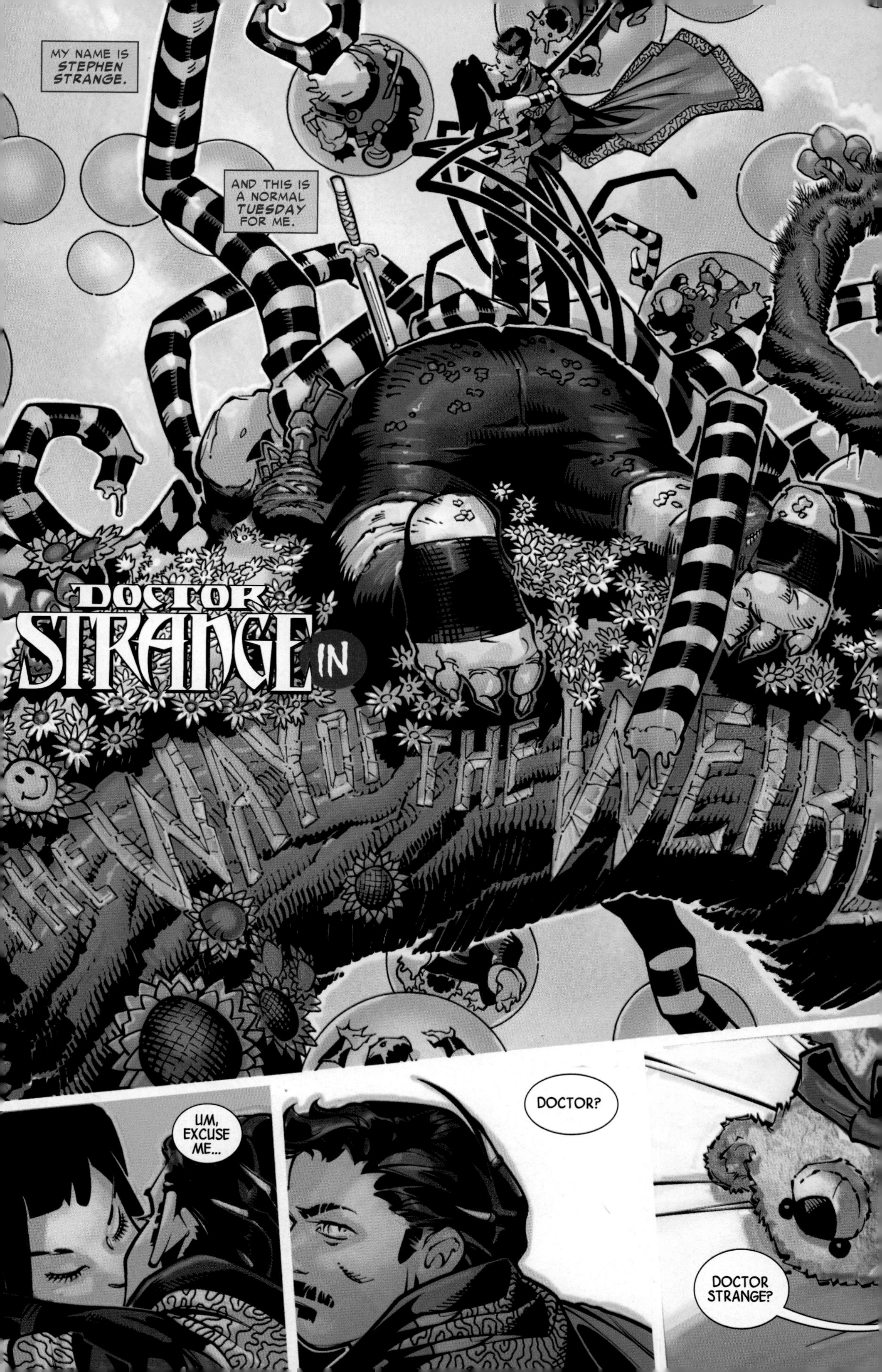

MY NAME IS STEPHEN STRANGE.
AND THIS IS A NORMAL TUESDAY FOR ME.
DOCTOR STRANGE IN
THE WAY OF THE WEIRD
UM, EXCUSE ME...
DOCTOR?
DOCTOR STRANGE?

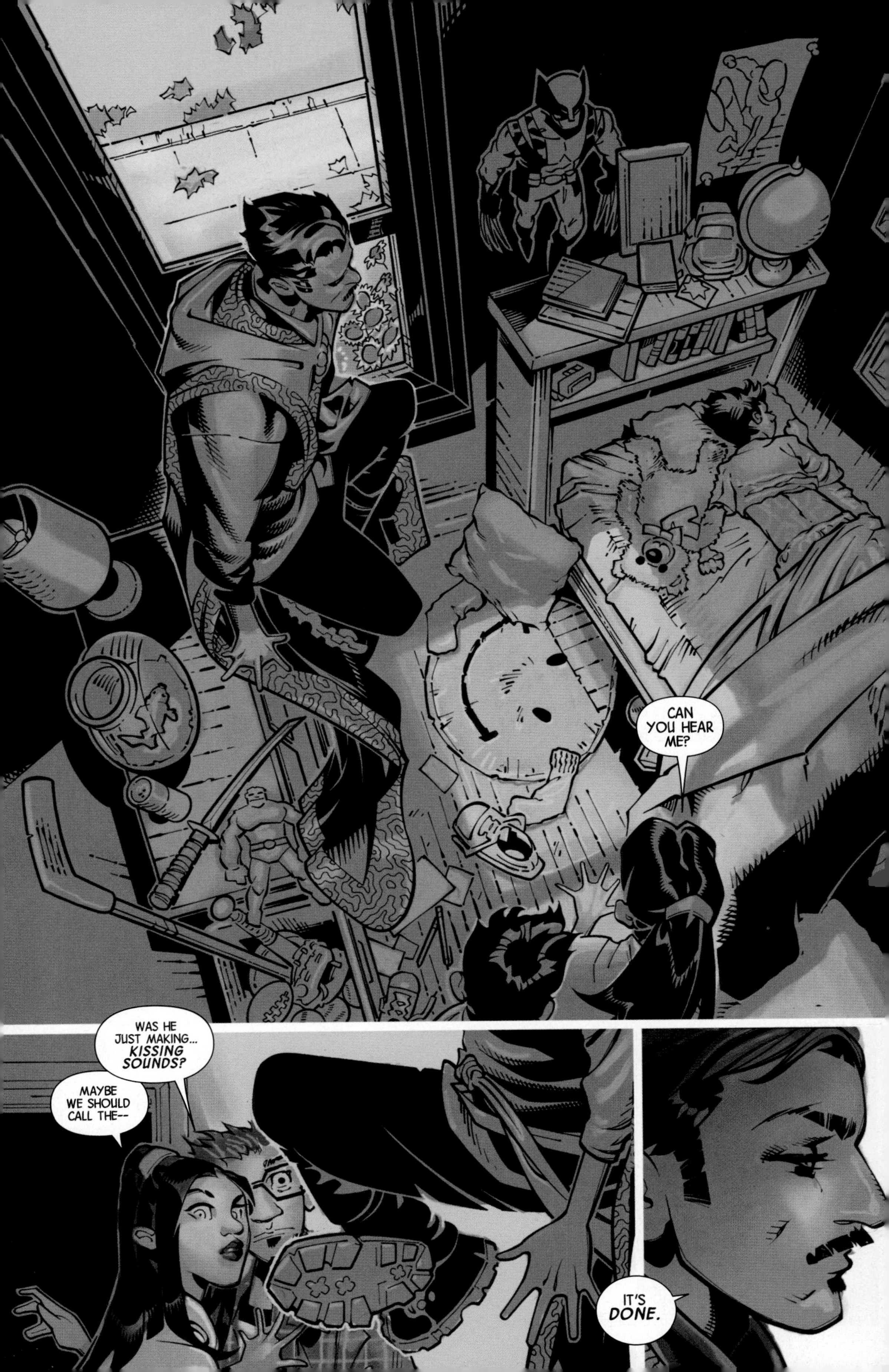
CAN YOU HEAR ME?
WAS HE JUST MAKING... *KISSING SOUNDS?*
MAYBE WE SHOULD CALL THE--
IT'S *DONE.*

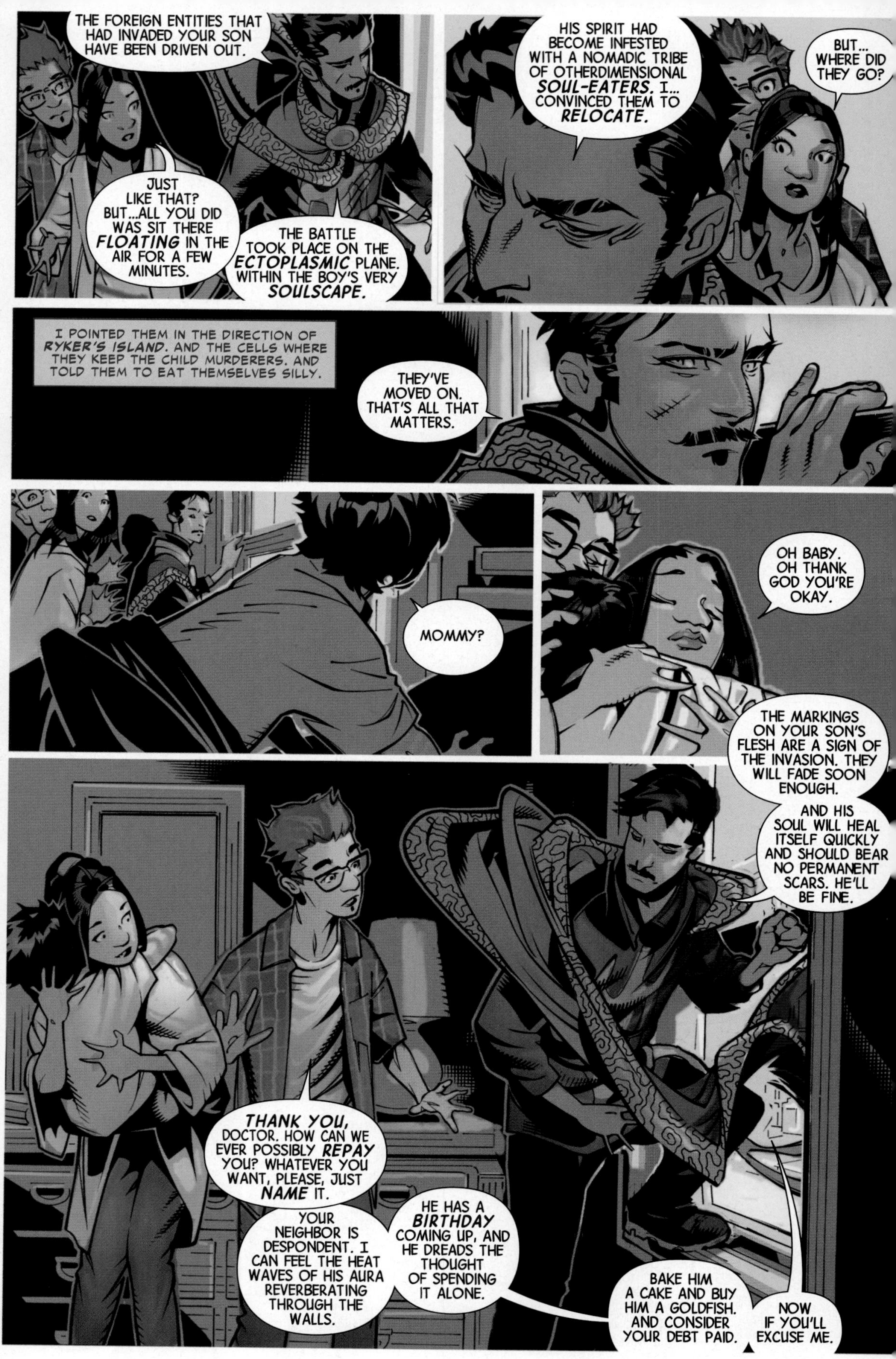
THE FOREIGN ENTITIES THAT HAD INVADED YOUR SON HAVE BEEN DRIVEN OUT.
JUST LIKE THAT? BUT...ALL YOU DID WAS SIT THERE FLOATING IN THE AIR FOR A FEW MINUTES.
THE BATTLE TOOK PLACE ON THE ECTOPLASMIC PLANE. WITHIN THE BOY'S VERY SOULSCAPE.
HIS SPIRIT HAD BECOME INFESTED WITH A NOMADIC TRIBE OF OTHERDIMENSIONAL SOUL-EATERS. I... CONVINCED THEM TO RELOCATE.
BUT... WHERE DID THEY GO?
I POINTED THEM IN THE DIRECTION OF RYKER'S ISLAND. AND THE CELLS WHERE THEY KEEP THE CHILD MURDERERS. AND TOLD THEM TO EAT THEMSELVES SILLY.
THEY'VE MOVED ON. THAT'S ALL THAT MATTERS.
MOMMY?
OH BABY. OH THANK GOD YOU'RE OKAY.
THE MARKINGS ON YOUR SON'S FLESH ARE A SIGN OF THE INVASION. THEY WILL FADE SOON ENOUGH.
AND HIS SOUL WILL HEAL ITSELF QUICKLY AND SHOULD BEAR NO PERMANENT SCARS. HE'LL BE FINE.
THANK YOU, DOCTOR. HOW CAN WE EVER POSSIBLY REPAY YOU? WHATEVER YOU WANT, PLEASE, JUST NAME IT.
YOUR NEIGHBOR IS DESPONDENT. I CAN FEEL THE HEAT WAVES OF HIS AURA REVERBERATING THROUGH THE WALLS.
HE HAS A BIRTHDAY COMING UP, AND HE DREADS THE THOUGHT OF SPENDING IT ALONE.
BAKE HIM A CAKE AND BUY HIM A GOLDFISH. AND CONSIDER YOUR DEBT PAID.
NOW IF YOU'LL EXCUSE ME.

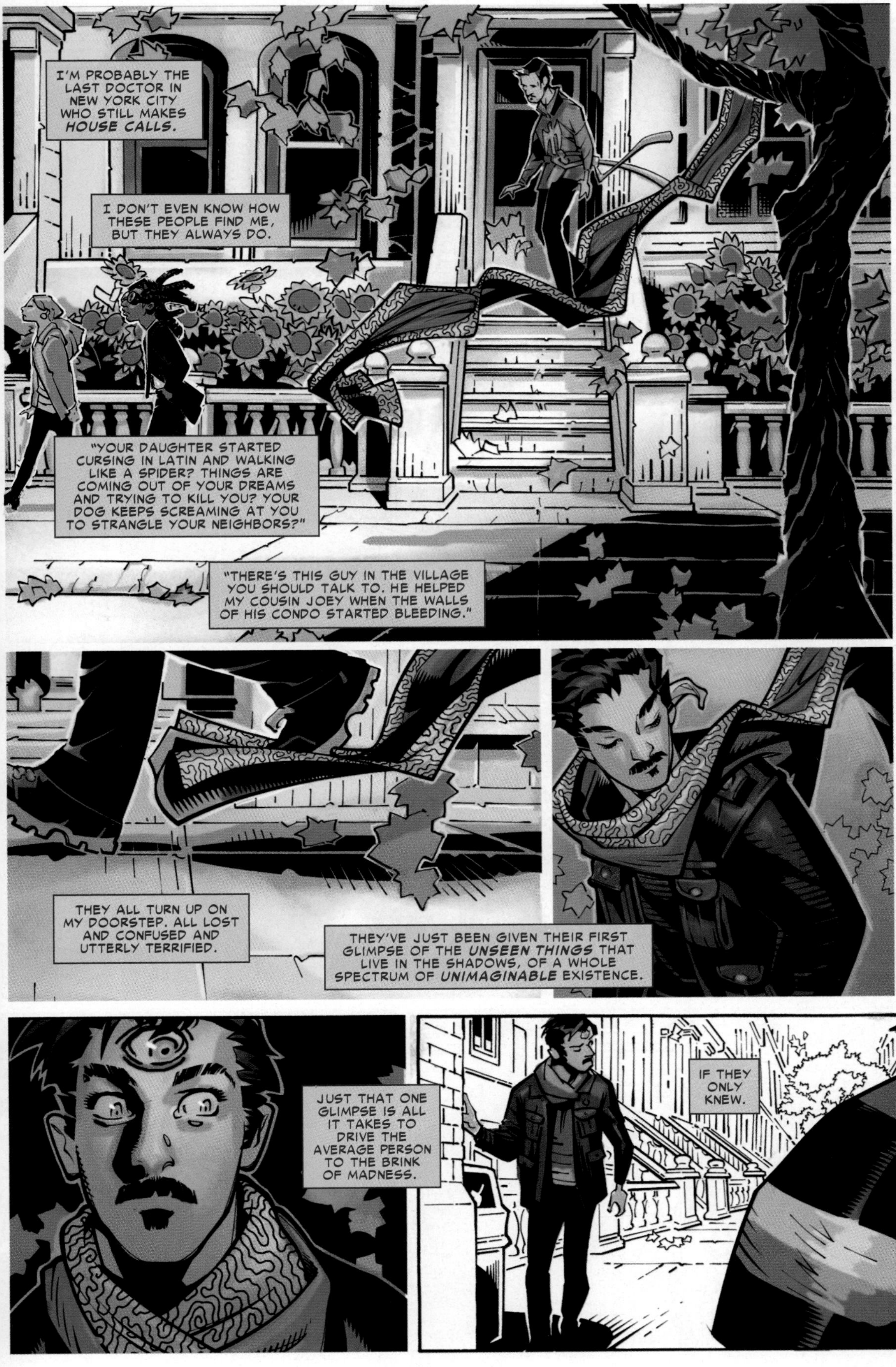
I'M PROBABLY THE LAST DOCTOR IN NEW YORK CITY WHO STILL MAKES *HOUSE CALLS.*
I DON'T EVEN KNOW HOW THESE PEOPLE FIND ME, BUT THEY ALWAYS DO.
"YOUR DAUGHTER STARTED CURSING IN LATIN AND WALKING LIKE A SPIDER? THINGS ARE COMING OUT OF YOUR DREAMS AND TRYING TO KILL YOU? YOUR DOG KEEPS SCREAMING AT YOU TO STRANGLE YOUR NEIGHBORS?"
"THERE'S THIS GUY IN THE VILLAGE YOU SHOULD TALK TO. HE HELPED MY COUSIN JOEY WHEN THE WALLS OF HIS CONDO STARTED BLEEDING."
THEY ALL TURN UP ON MY DOORSTEP. ALL LOST AND CONFUSED AND UTTERLY TERRIFIED.
THEY'VE JUST BEEN GIVEN THEIR FIRST GLIMPSE OF THE *UNSEEN THINGS* THAT LIVE IN THE SHADOWS, OF A WHOLE SPECTRUM OF *UNIMAGINABLE* EXISTENCE.
JUST THAT ONE GLIMPSE IS ALL IT TAKES TO DRIVE THE AVERAGE PERSON TO THE BRINK OF MADNESS.
IF THEY ONLY KNEW.

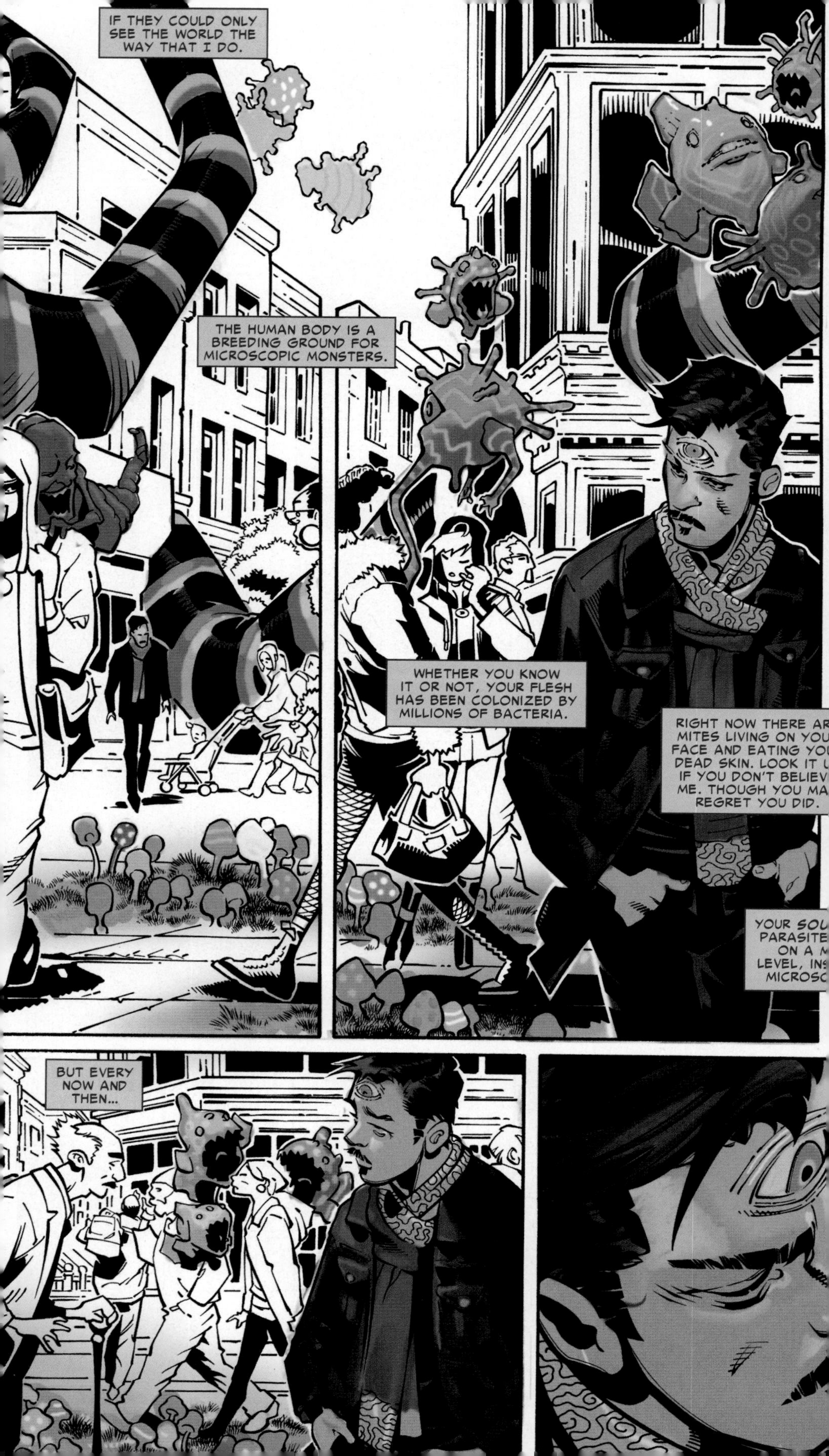
IF THEY COULD ONLY SEE THE WORLD THE WAY THAT I DO.
THE HUMAN BODY IS A BREEDING GROUND FOR MICROSCOPIC MONSTERS.
WHETHER YOU KNOW IT OR NOT, YOUR FLESH HAS BEEN COLONIZED BY MILLIONS OF BACTERIA.
RIGHT NOW THERE AR MITES LIVING ON YOU FACE AND EATING YOU DEAD SKIN. LOOK IT U IF YOU DON'T BELIEV ME. THOUGH YOU MA REGRET YOU DID.
YOUR SOU PARASITE ON A M LEVEL, INS MICROSC
BUT EVERY NOW AND THEN...

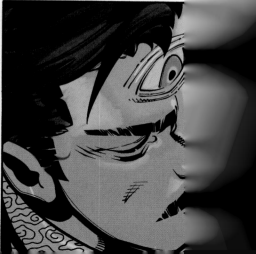

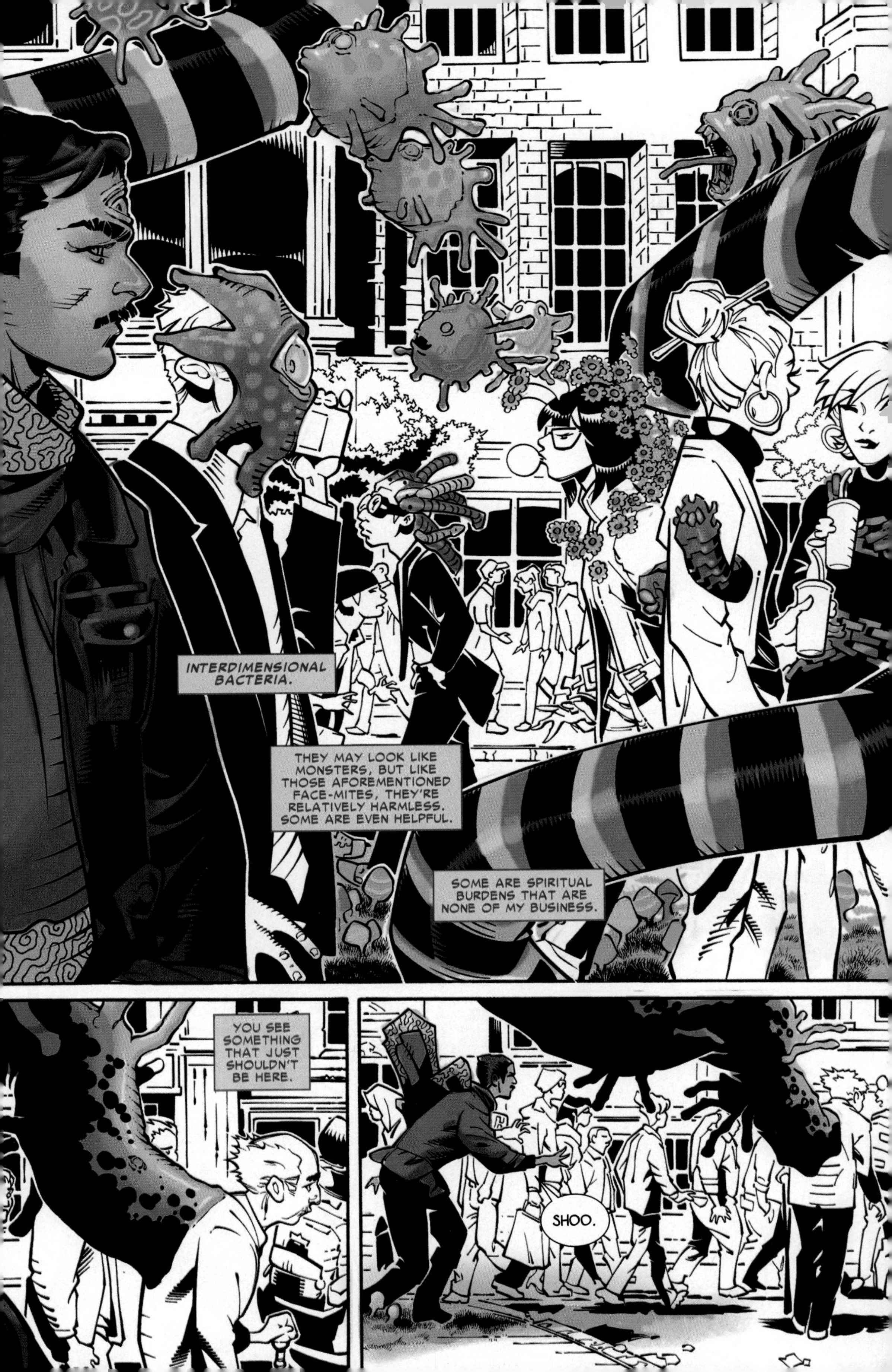
INTERDIMENSIONAL BACTERIA.
THEY MAY LOOK LIKE MONSTERS, BUT LIKE THOSE AFOREMENTIONED FACE-MITES, THEY'RE RELATIVELY HARMLESS. SOME ARE EVEN HELPFUL.
SOME ARE SPIRITUAL BURDENS THAT ARE NONE OF MY BUSINESS.
YOU SEE SOMETHING THAT JUST SHOULDN'T BE HERE.
SHOO.

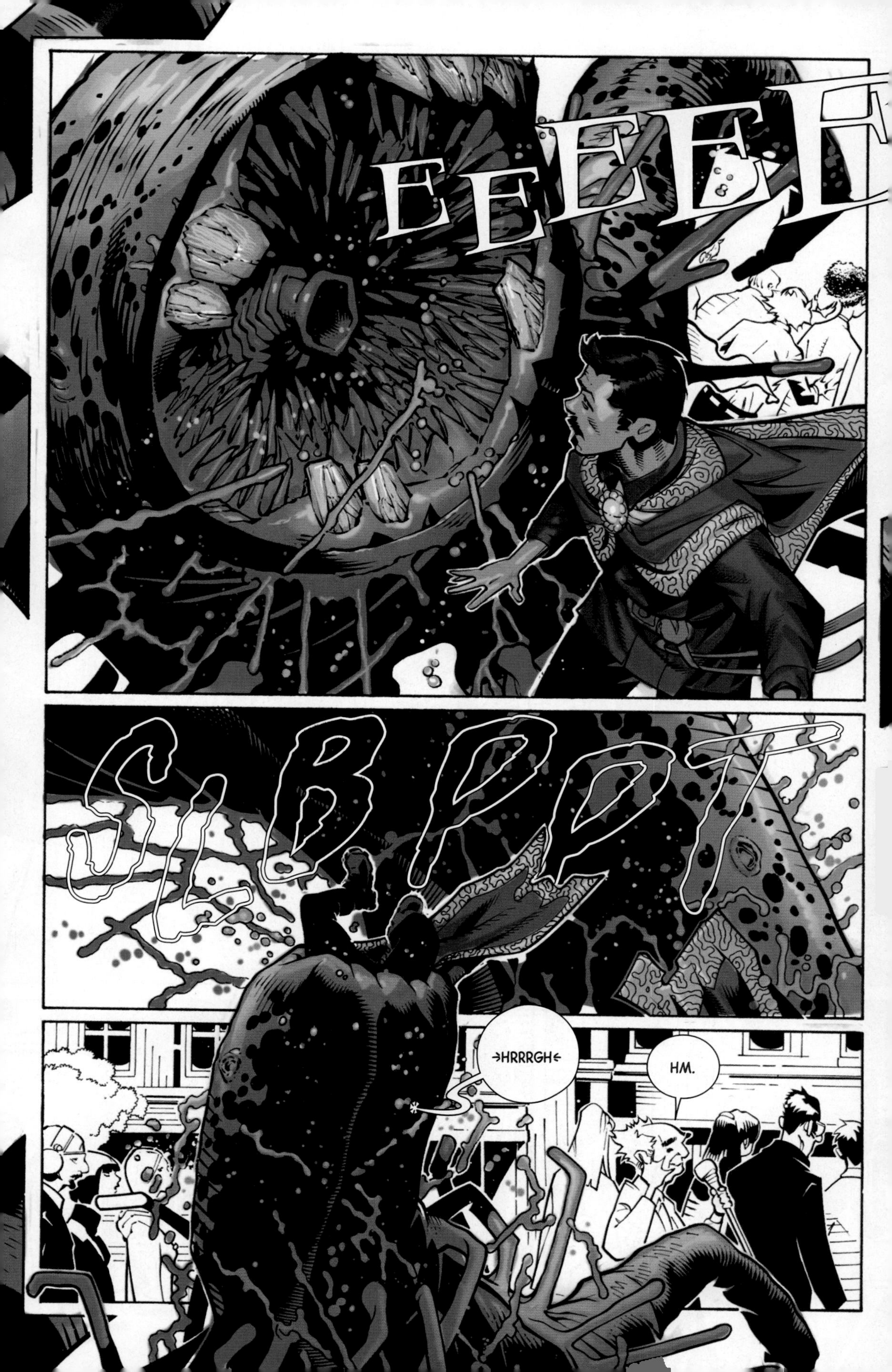
EEEEEE
SLRPPT
HRRRGH
HM.

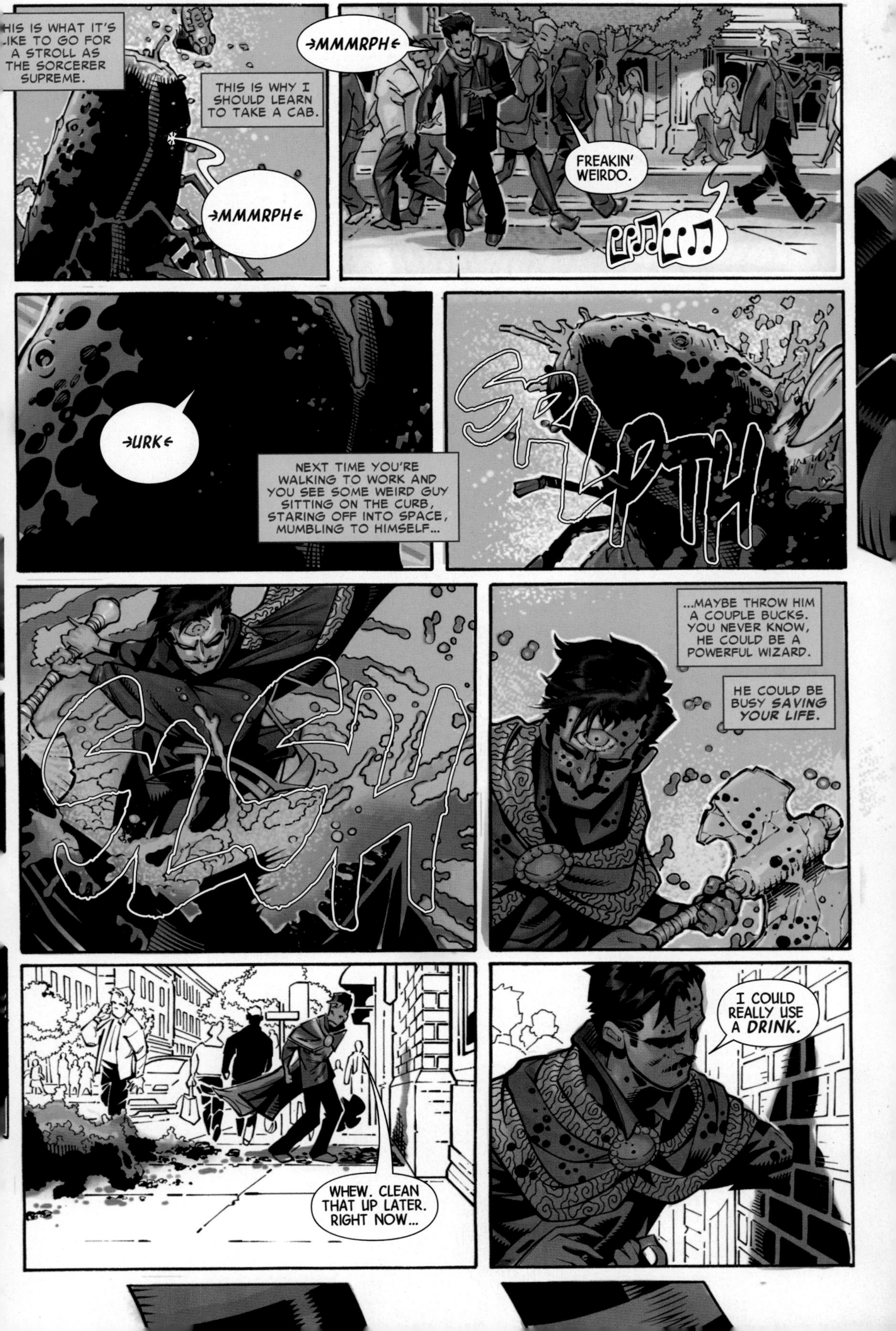

THIS IS WHAT IT'S LIKE TO GO FOR A STROLL AS THE SORCERER SUPREME.
THIS IS WHY I SHOULD LEARN TO TAKE A CAB.
MMMRPH
MMMRPH
FREAKIN' WEIRDO.
URK
NEXT TIME YOU'RE WALKING TO WORK AND YOU SEE SOME WEIRD GUY SITTING ON THE CURB, STARING OFF INTO SPACE, MUMBLING TO HIMSELF...
SPLPTH
SZSH
...MAYBE THROW HIM A COUPLE BUCKS. YOU NEVER KNOW, HE COULD BE A POWERFUL WIZARD.
HE COULD BE BUSY SAVING YOUR LIFE.
WHEW. CLEAN THAT UP LATER. RIGHT NOW...
I COULD REALLY USE A DRINK.

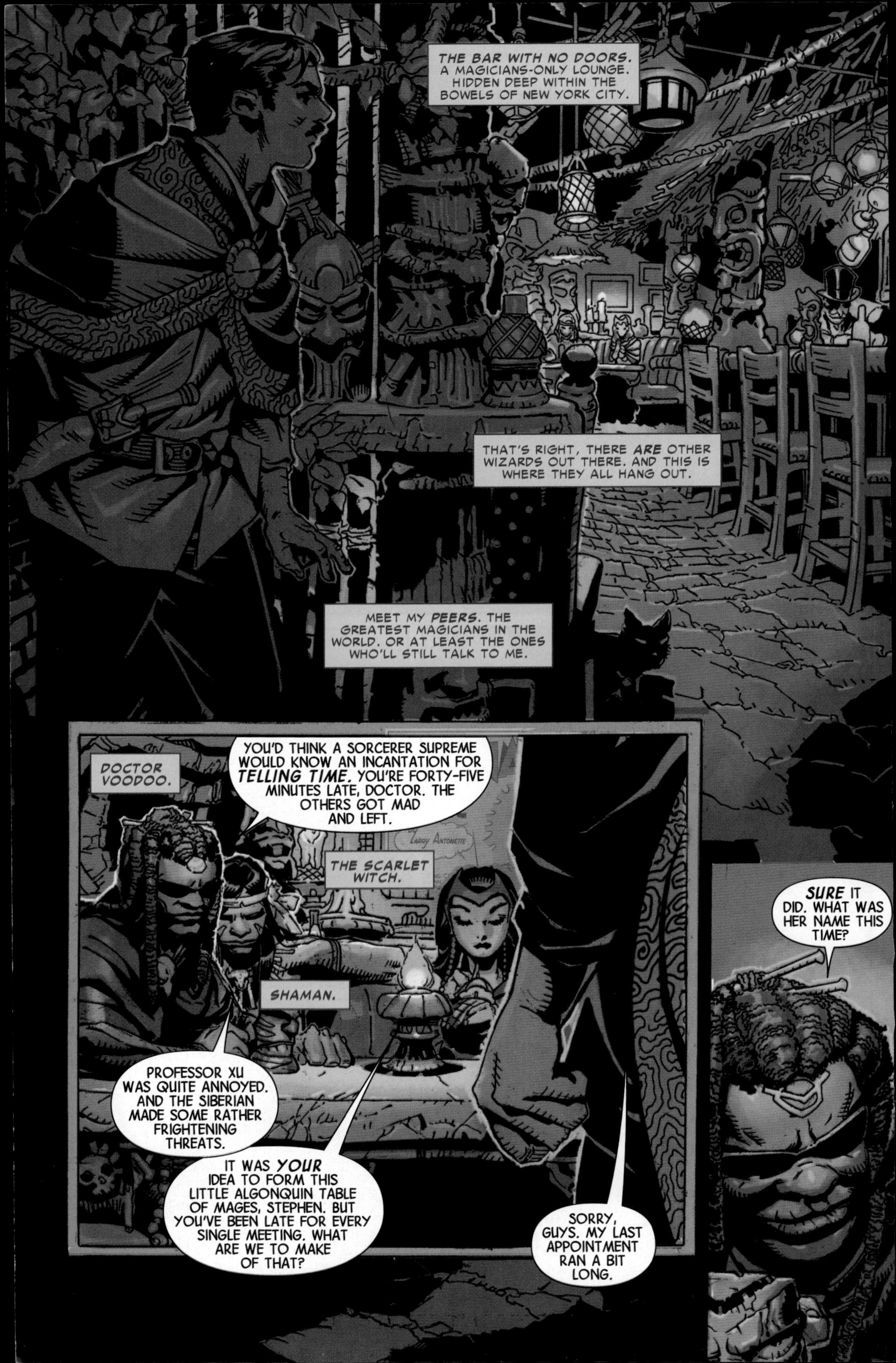
THE BAR WITH NO DOORS. A MAGICIANS-ONLY LOUNGE. HIDDEN DEEP WITHIN THE BOWELS OF NEW YORK CITY.
THAT'S RIGHT, THERE ARE OTHER WIZARDS OUT THERE. AND THIS IS WHERE THEY ALL HANG OUT.
MEET MY PEERS. THE GREATEST MAGICIANS IN THE WORLD. OR AT LEAST THE ONES WHO'LL STILL TALK TO ME.
DOCTOR VOODOO.
YOU'D THINK A SORCERER SUPREME WOULD KNOW AN INCANTATION FOR TELLING TIME. YOU'RE FORTY-FIVE MINUTES LATE, DOCTOR. THE OTHERS GOT MAD AND LEFT.
THE SCARLET WITCH.
SHAMAN.
PROFESSOR XU WAS QUITE ANNOYED. AND THE SIBERIAN MADE SOME RATHER FRIGHTENING THREATS.
IT WAS YOUR IDEA TO FORM THIS LITTLE ALGONQUIN TABLE OF MAGES, STEPHEN. BUT YOU'VE BEEN LATE FOR EVERY SINGLE MEETING. WHAT ARE WE TO MAKE OF THAT?
SORRY, GUYS. MY LAST APPOINTMENT RAN A BIT LONG.
SURE IT DID. WHAT WAS HER NAME THIS TIME?

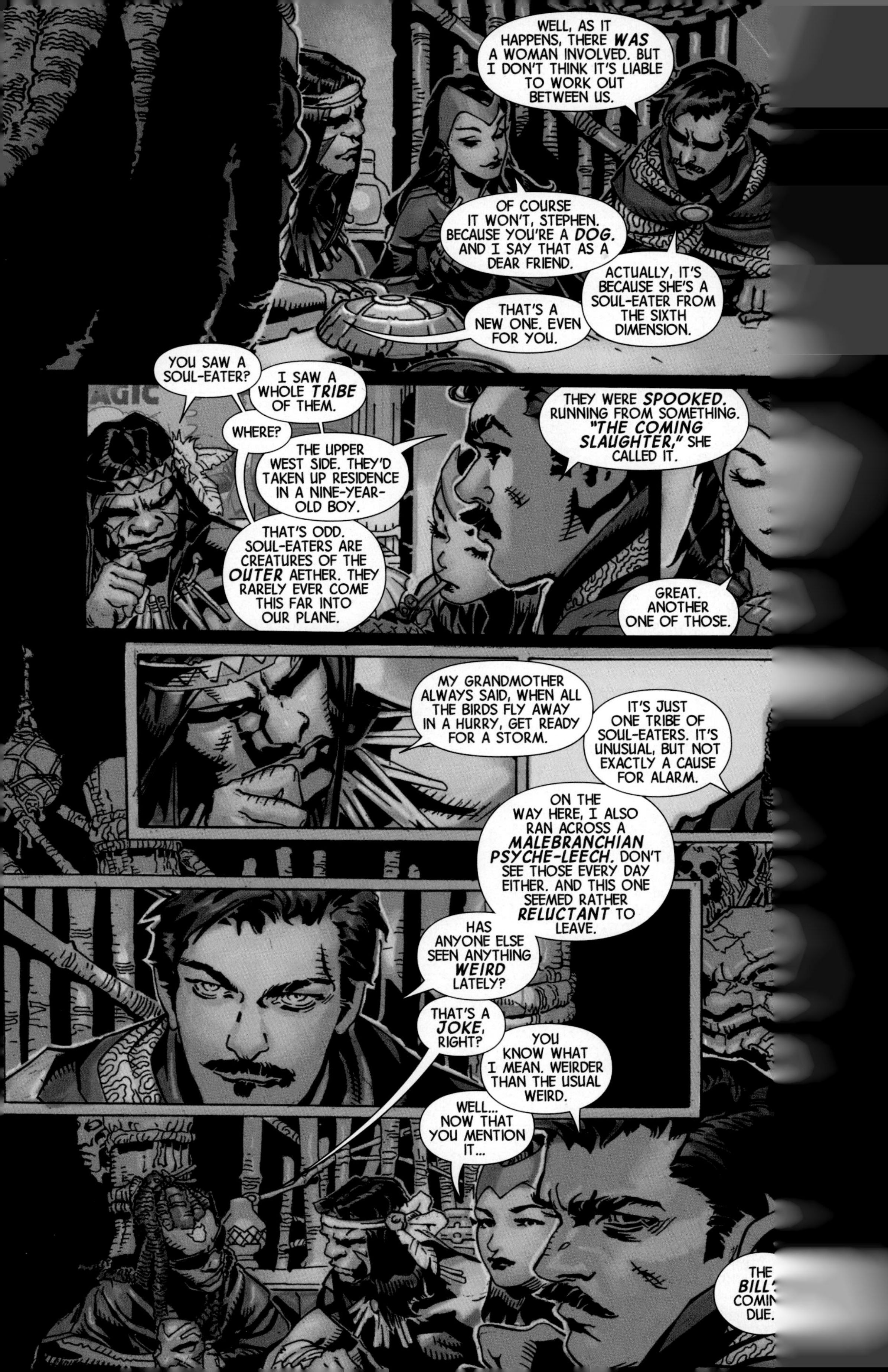

WELL, AS IT HAPPENS, THERE *WAS* A WOMAN INVOLVED. BUT I DON'T THINK IT'S LIABLE TO WORK OUT BETWEEN US.
OF COURSE IT WON'T, STEPHEN. BECAUSE YOU'RE A *DOG.* AND I SAY THAT AS A DEAR FRIEND.
ACTUALLY, IT'S BECAUSE SHE'S A SOUL-EATER FROM THE SIXTH DIMENSION.
THAT'S A NEW ONE. EVEN FOR YOU.
YOU SAW A SOUL-EATER?
I SAW A WHOLE *TRIBE* OF THEM.
WHERE?
THE UPPER WEST SIDE. THEY'D TAKEN UP RESIDENCE IN A NINE-YEAR-OLD BOY.
THEY WERE *SPOOKED.* RUNNING FROM SOMETHING. *"THE COMING SLAUGHTER,"* SHE CALLED IT.
THAT'S ODD. SOUL-EATERS ARE CREATURES OF THE *OUTER* AETHER. THEY RARELY EVER COME THIS FAR INTO OUR PLANE.
GREAT. ANOTHER ONE OF THOSE.
MY GRANDMOTHER ALWAYS SAID, WHEN ALL THE BIRDS FLY AWAY IN A HURRY, GET READY FOR A STORM.
IT'S JUST ONE TRIBE OF SOUL-EATERS. IT'S UNUSUAL, BUT NOT EXACTLY A CAUSE FOR ALARM.
ON THE WAY HERE, I ALSO RAN ACROSS A *MALEBRANCHIAN PSYCHE-LEECH.* DON'T SEE THOSE EVERY DAY EITHER. AND THIS ONE SEEMED RATHER *RELUCTANT* TO LEAVE.
HAS ANYONE ELSE SEEN ANYTHING *WEIRD* LATELY?
THAT'S A *JOKE,* RIGHT?
YOU KNOW WHAT I MEAN. WEIRDER THAN THE USUAL WEIRD.
WELL... NOW THAT YOU MENTION IT...
THE *BILL* COMIN DUE.

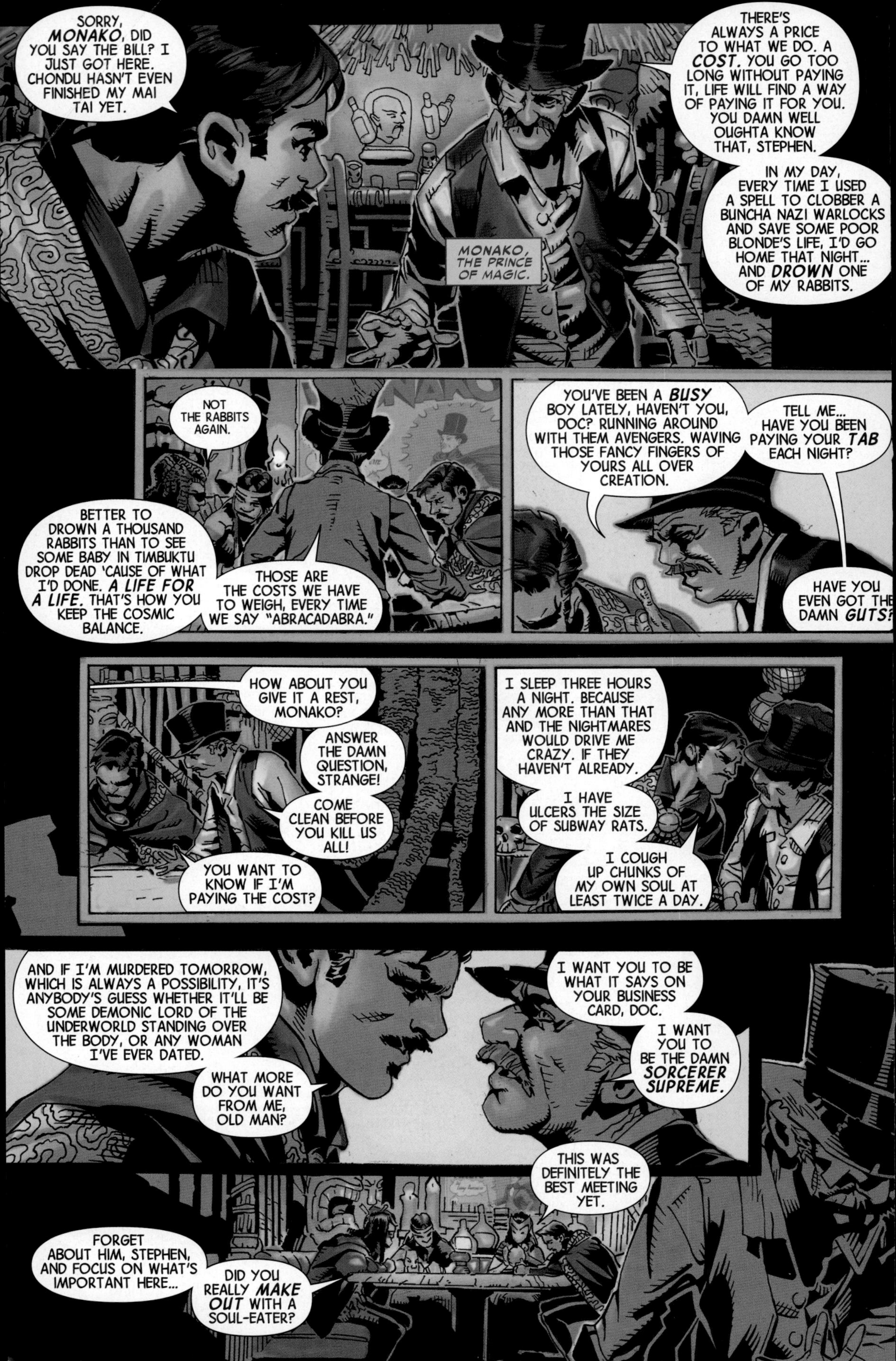
SORRY, MONAKO, DID YOU SAY THE BILL? I JUST GOT HERE. CHONDU HASN'T EVEN FINISHED MY MAI TAI YET.
THERE'S ALWAYS A PRICE TO WHAT WE DO. A COST. YOU GO TOO LONG WITHOUT PAYING IT, LIFE WILL FIND A WAY OF PAYING IT FOR YOU. YOU DAMN WELL OUGHTA KNOW THAT, STEPHEN.
IN MY DAY, EVERY TIME I USED A SPELL TO CLOBBER A BUNCHA NAZI WARLOCKS AND SAVE SOME POOR BLONDE'S LIFE, I'D GO HOME THAT NIGHT... AND DROWN ONE OF MY RABBITS.
MONAKO, THE PRINCE OF MAGIC.
NOT THE RABBITS AGAIN.
BETTER TO DROWN A THOUSAND RABBITS THAN TO SEE SOME BABY IN TIMBUKTU DROP DEAD 'CAUSE OF WHAT I'D DONE. A LIFE FOR A LIFE. THAT'S HOW YOU KEEP THE COSMIC BALANCE.
THOSE ARE THE COSTS WE HAVE TO WEIGH, EVERY TIME WE SAY "ABRACADABRA."
YOU'VE BEEN A BUSY BOY LATELY, HAVEN'T YOU, DOC? RUNNING AROUND WITH THEM AVENGERS. WAVING THOSE FANCY FINGERS OF YOURS ALL OVER CREATION.
TELL ME... HAVE YOU BEEN PAYING YOUR TAB EACH NIGHT?
HAVE YOU EVEN GOT THE DAMN GUTS?
HOW ABOUT YOU GIVE IT A REST, MONAKO?
ANSWER THE DAMN QUESTION, STRANGE!
COME CLEAN BEFORE YOU KILL US ALL!
YOU WANT TO KNOW IF I'M PAYING THE COST?
I SLEEP THREE HOURS A NIGHT. BECAUSE ANY MORE THAN THAT AND THE NIGHTMARES WOULD DRIVE ME CRAZY. IF THEY HAVEN'T ALREADY.
I HAVE ULCERS THE SIZE OF SUBWAY RATS.
I COUGH UP CHUNKS OF MY OWN SOUL AT LEAST TWICE A DAY.
AND IF I'M MURDERED TOMORROW, WHICH IS ALWAYS A POSSIBILITY, IT'S ANYBODY'S GUESS WHETHER IT'LL BE SOME DEMONIC LORD OF THE UNDERWORLD STANDING OVER THE BODY, OR ANY WOMAN I'VE EVER DATED.
WHAT MORE DO YOU WANT FROM ME, OLD MAN?
I WANT YOU TO BE WHAT IT SAYS ON YOUR BUSINESS CARD, DOC.
I WANT YOU TO BE THE DAMN SORCERER SUPREME.
THIS WAS DEFINITELY THE BEST MEETING YET.
FORGET ABOUT HIM, STEPHEN, AND FOCUS ON WHAT'S IMPORTANT HERE...
DID YOU REALLY MAKE OUT WITH A SOUL-EATER?

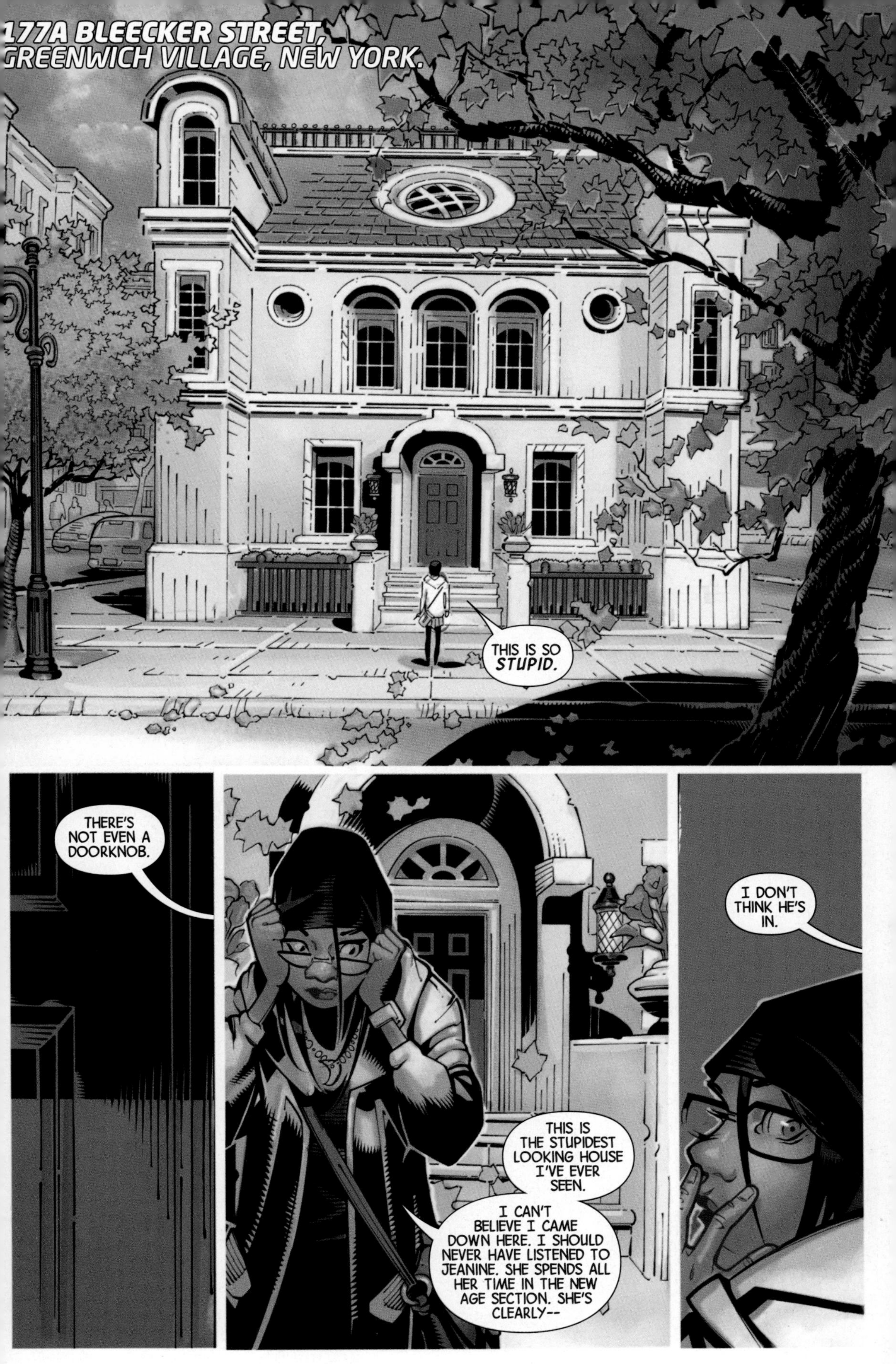
177A BLEECKER STREET, GREENWICH VILLAGE, NEW YORK.
THIS IS SO STUPID.
THERE'S NOT EVEN A DOORKNOB.
THIS IS THE STUPIDEST LOOKING HOUSE I'VE EVER SEEN.
I CAN'T BELIEVE I CAME DOWN HERE. I SHOULD NEVER HAVE LISTENED TO JEANINE. SHE SPENDS ALL HER TIME IN THE NEW AGE SECTION. SHE'S CLEARLY--
I DON'T THINK HE'S IN.

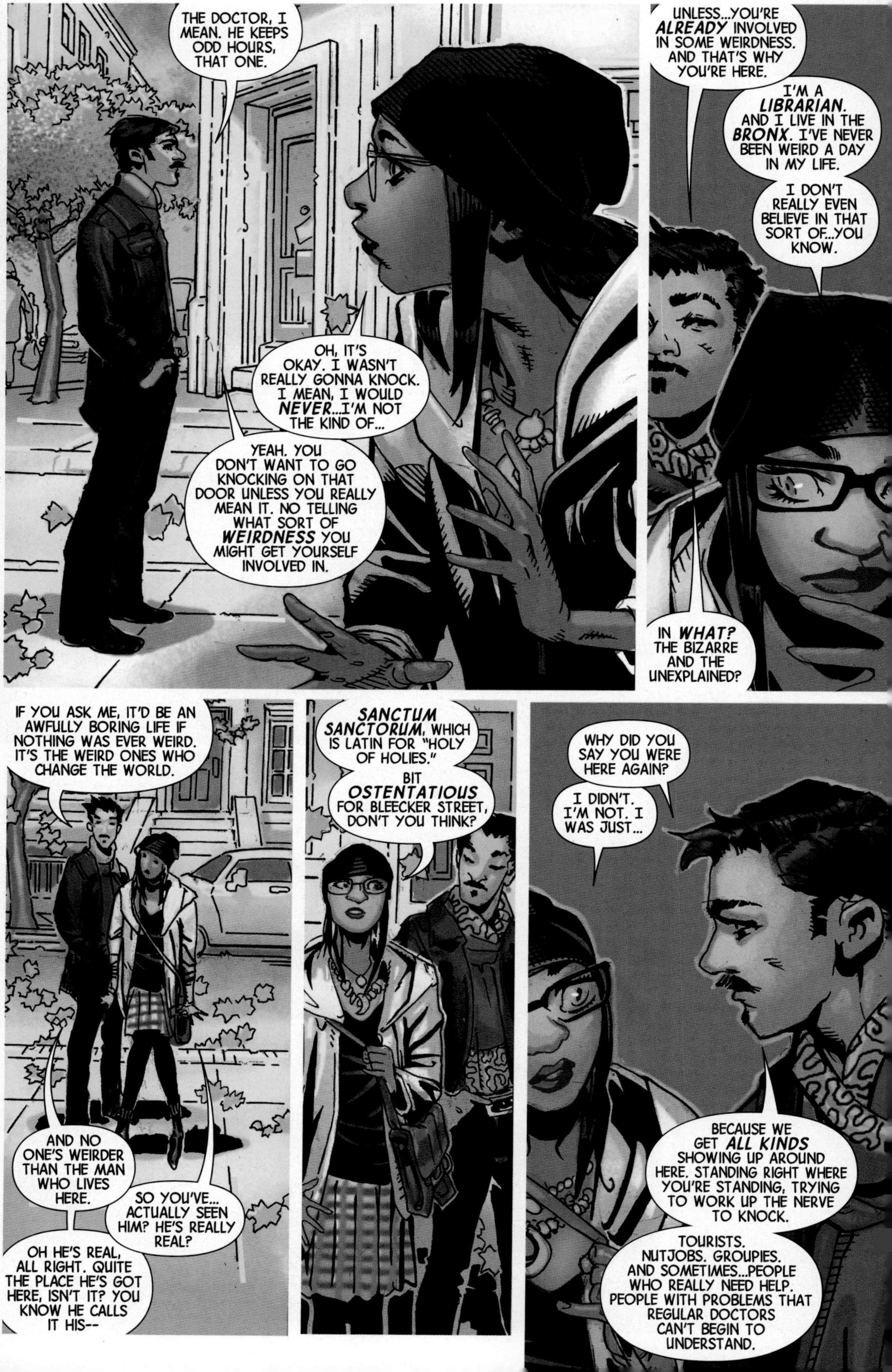
THE DOCTOR, I MEAN. HE KEEPS ODD HOURS, THAT ONE.
OH, IT'S OKAY. I WASN'T REALLY GONNA KNOCK. I MEAN, I WOULD NEVER...I'M NOT THE KIND OF...
YEAH. YOU DON'T WANT TO GO KNOCKING ON THAT DOOR UNLESS YOU REALLY MEAN IT. NO TELLING WHAT SORT OF WEIRDNESS YOU MIGHT GET YOURSELF INVOLVED IN.
UNLESS...YOU'RE ALREADY INVOLVED IN SOME WEIRDNESS. AND THAT'S WHY YOU'RE HERE.
I'M A LIBRARIAN. AND I LIVE IN THE BRONX. I'VE NEVER BEEN WEIRD A DAY IN MY LIFE.
I DON'T REALLY EVEN BELIEVE IN THAT SORT OF...YOU KNOW.
IN WHAT? THE BIZARRE AND THE UNEXPLAINED?
IF YOU ASK ME, IT'D BE AN AWFULLY BORING LIFE IF NOTHING WAS EVER WEIRD. IT'S THE WEIRD ONES WHO CHANGE THE WORLD.
AND NO ONE'S WEIRDER THAN THE MAN WHO LIVES HERE.
SO YOU'VE... ACTUALLY SEEN HIM? HE'S REALLY REAL?
OH HE'S REAL, ALL RIGHT. QUITE THE PLACE HE'S GOT HERE, ISN'T IT? YOU KNOW HE CALLS IT HIS--
SANCTUM SANCTORUM, WHICH IS LATIN FOR "HOLY OF HOLIES."
BIT OSTENTATIOUS FOR BLEECKER STREET, DON'T YOU THINK?
WHY DID YOU SAY YOU WERE HERE AGAIN?
I DIDN'T. I'M NOT. I WAS JUST...
BECAUSE WE GET ALL KINDS SHOWING UP AROUND HERE. STANDING RIGHT WHERE YOU'RE STANDING, TRYING TO WORK UP THE NERVE TO KNOCK.
TOURISTS. NUTJOBS. GROUPIES. AND SOMETIMES...PEOPLE WHO REALLY NEED HELP. PEOPLE WITH PROBLEMS THAT REGULAR DOCTORS CAN'T BEGIN TO UNDERSTAND.

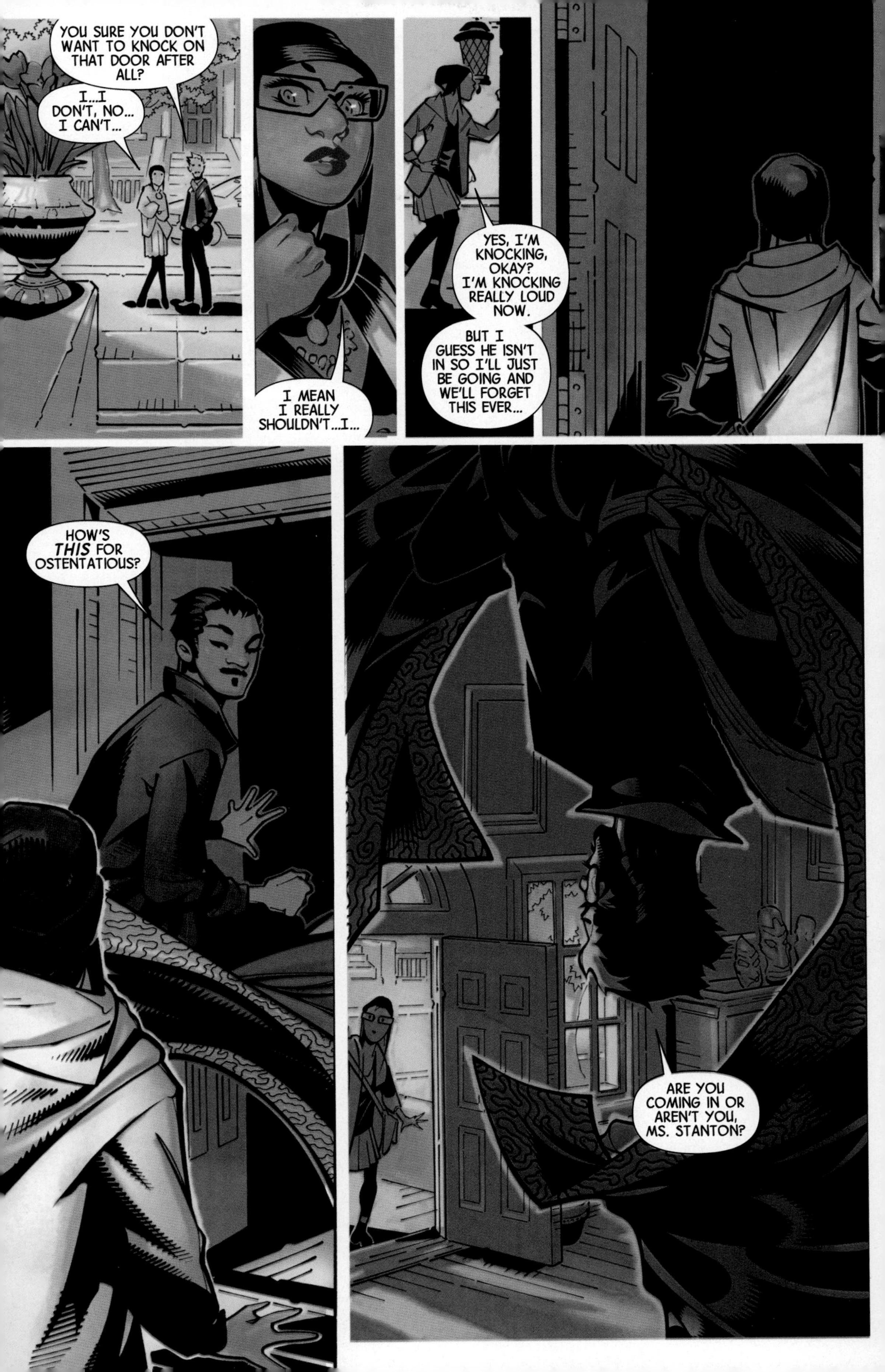
YOU SURE YOU DON'T WANT TO KNOCK ON THAT DOOR AFTER ALL?
I...I DON'T, NO... I CAN'T...
I MEAN I REALLY SHOULDN'T...I...
YES, I'M KNOCKING, OKAY? I'M KNOCKING REALLY LOUD NOW.
BUT I GUESS HE ISN'T IN SO I'LL JUST BE GOING AND WE'LL FORGET THIS EVER...
HOW'S *THIS* FOR OSTENTATIOUS?
ARE YOU COMING IN OR AREN'T YOU, MS. STANTON?

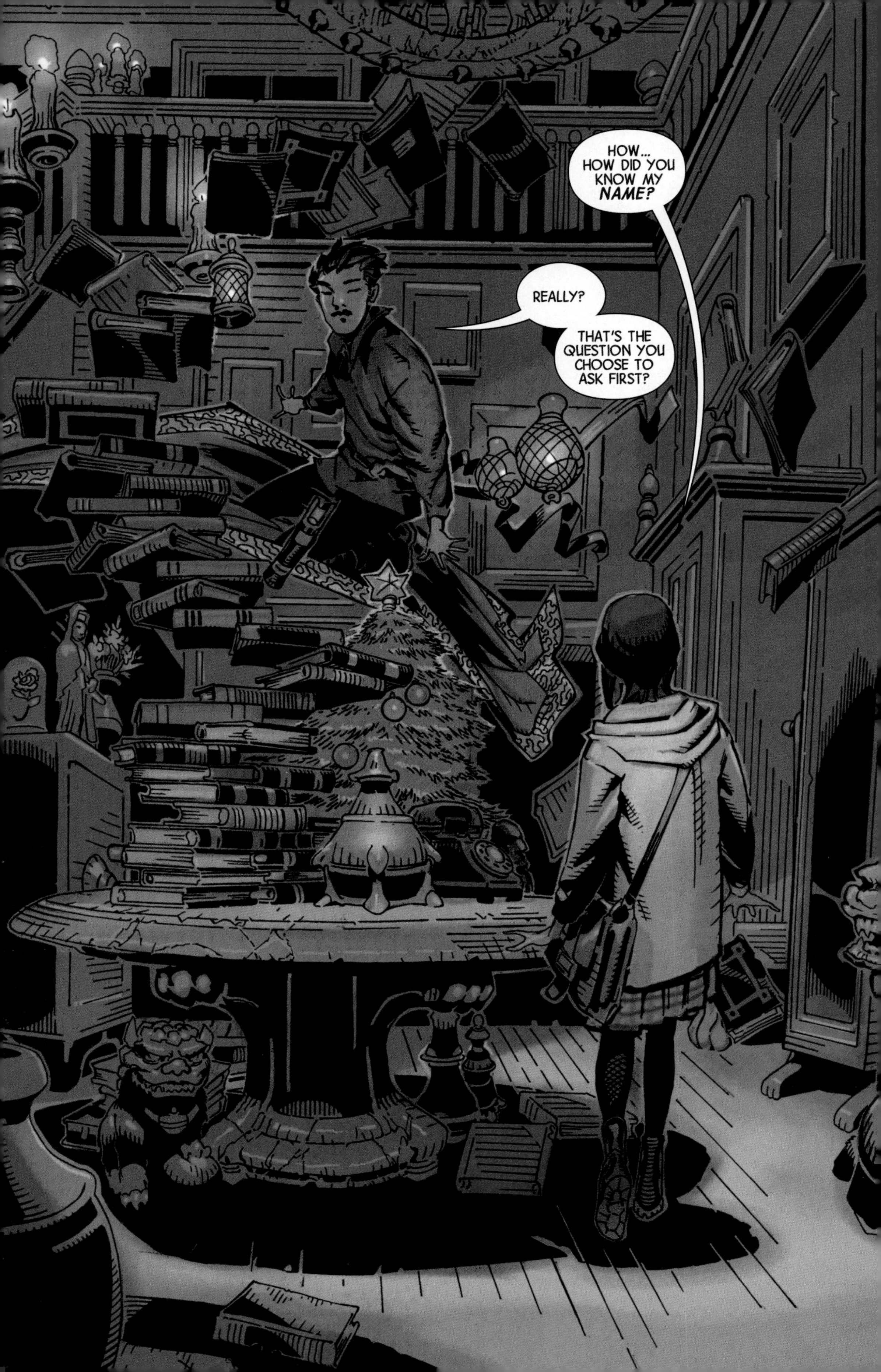
HOW... HOW DID YOU KNOW MY NAME?
REALLY?
THAT'S THE QUESTION YOU CHOOSE TO ASK FIRST?

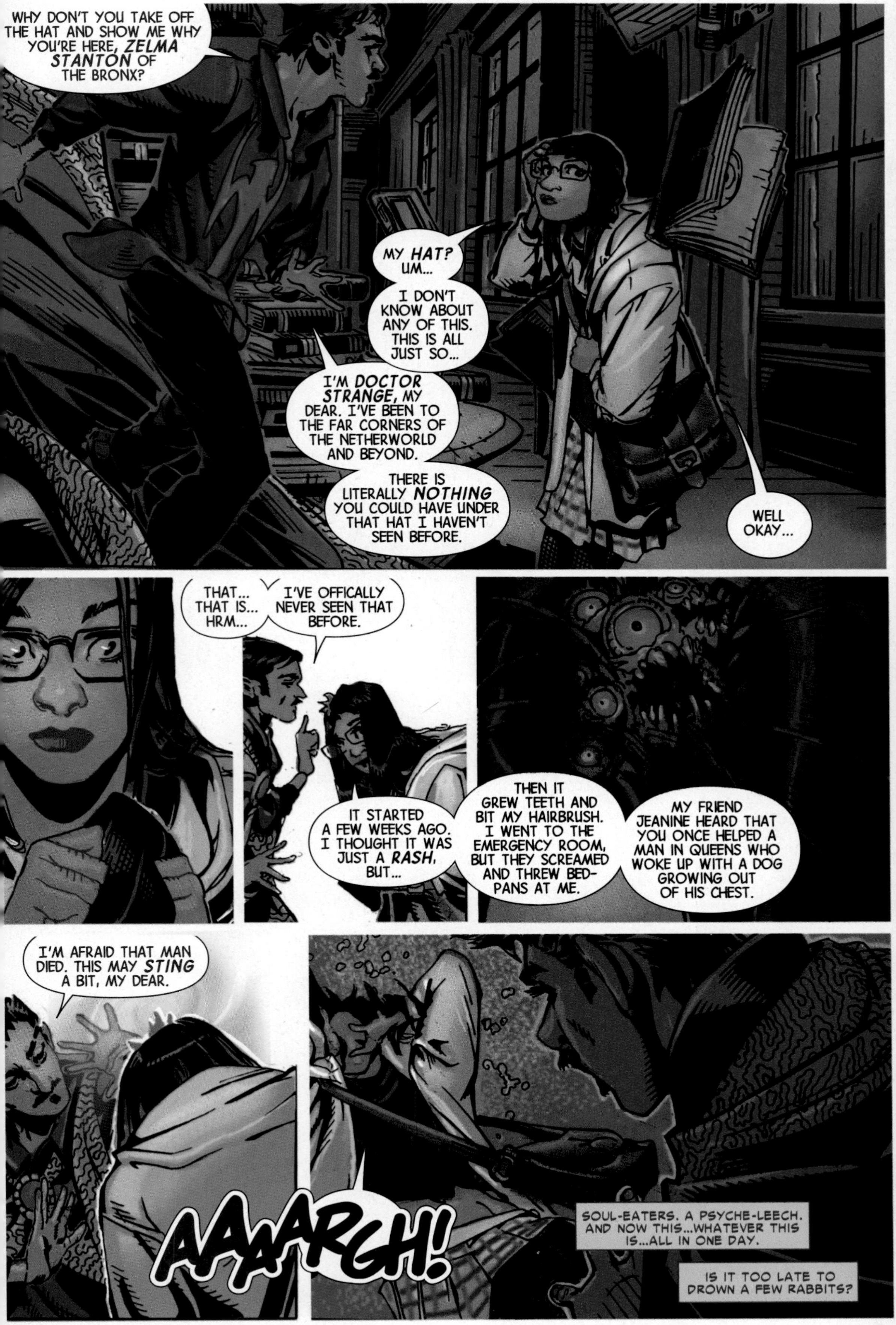
WHY DON'T YOU TAKE OFF THE HAT AND SHOW ME WHY YOU'RE HERE, ZELMA STANTON OF THE BRONX?
MY HAT? UM...
I DON'T KNOW ABOUT ANY OF THIS. THIS IS ALL JUST SO...
I'M DOCTOR STRANGE, MY DEAR. I'VE BEEN TO THE FAR CORNERS OF THE NETHERWORLD AND BEYOND.
THERE IS LITERALLY NOTHING YOU COULD HAVE UNDER THAT HAT I HAVEN'T SEEN BEFORE.
WELL OKAY...
THAT... THAT IS... HRM...
I'VE OFFICALLY NEVER SEEN THAT BEFORE.
IT STARTED A FEW WEEKS AGO. I THOUGHT IT WAS JUST A RASH, BUT...
THEN IT GREW TEETH AND BIT MY HAIRBRUSH. I WENT TO THE EMERGENCY ROOM, BUT THEY SCREAMED AND THREW BED-PANS AT ME.
MY FRIEND JEANINE HEARD THAT YOU ONCE HELPED A MAN IN QUEENS WHO WOKE UP WITH A DOG GROWING OUT OF HIS CHEST.
I'M AFRAID THAT MAN DIED. THIS MAY STING A BIT, MY DEAR.
AAAARGH!
SOUL-EATERS. A PSYCHE-LEECH. AND NOW THIS...WHATEVER THIS IS...ALL IN ONE DAY.
IS IT TOO LATE TO DROWN A FEW RABBITS?

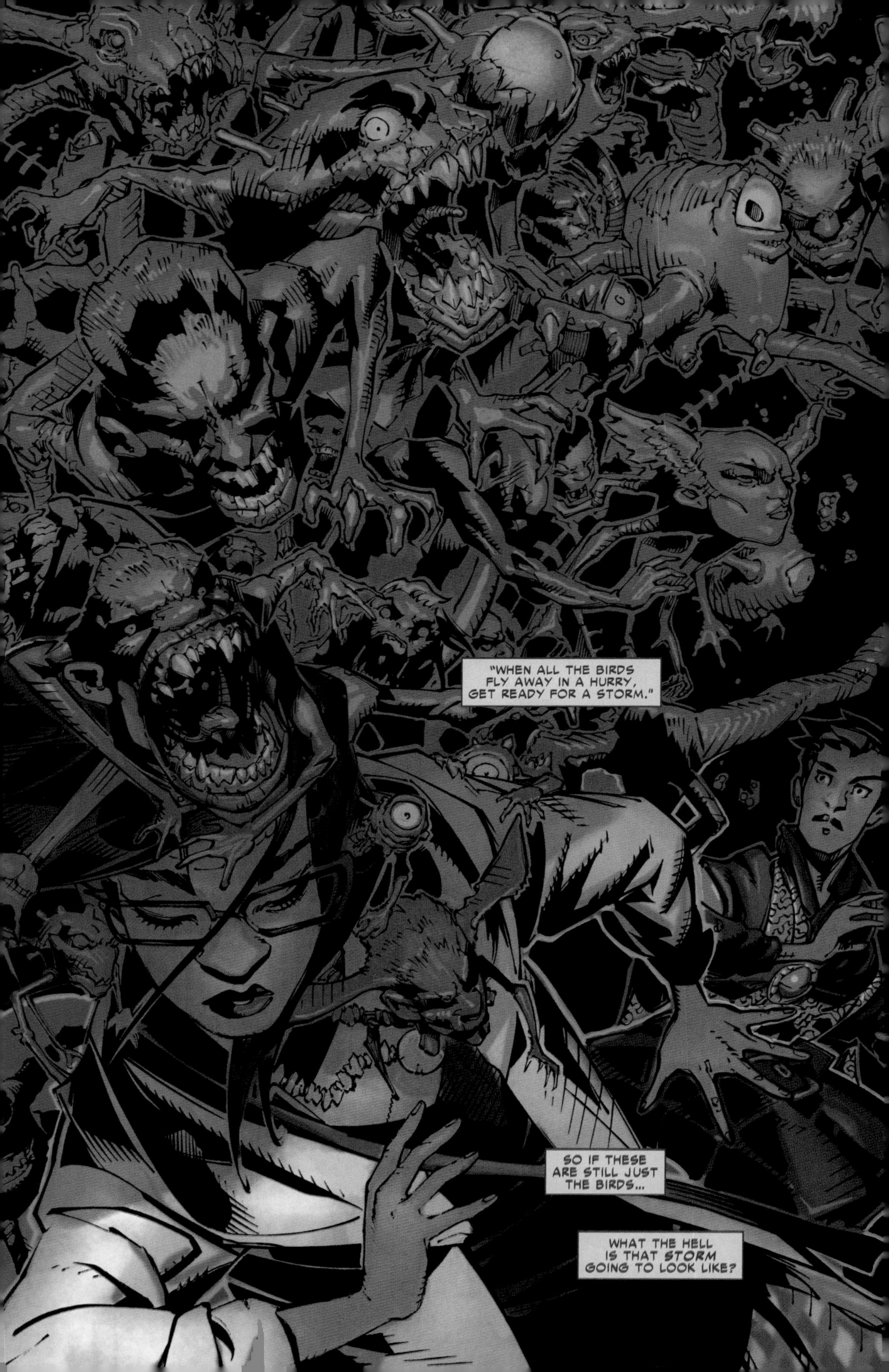
"WHEN ALL THE BIRDS FLY AWAY IN A HURRY, GET READY FOR A STORM."
SO IF THESE ARE STILL JUST THE BIRDS...
WHAT THE HELL IS THAT STORM GOING TO LOOK LIKE?

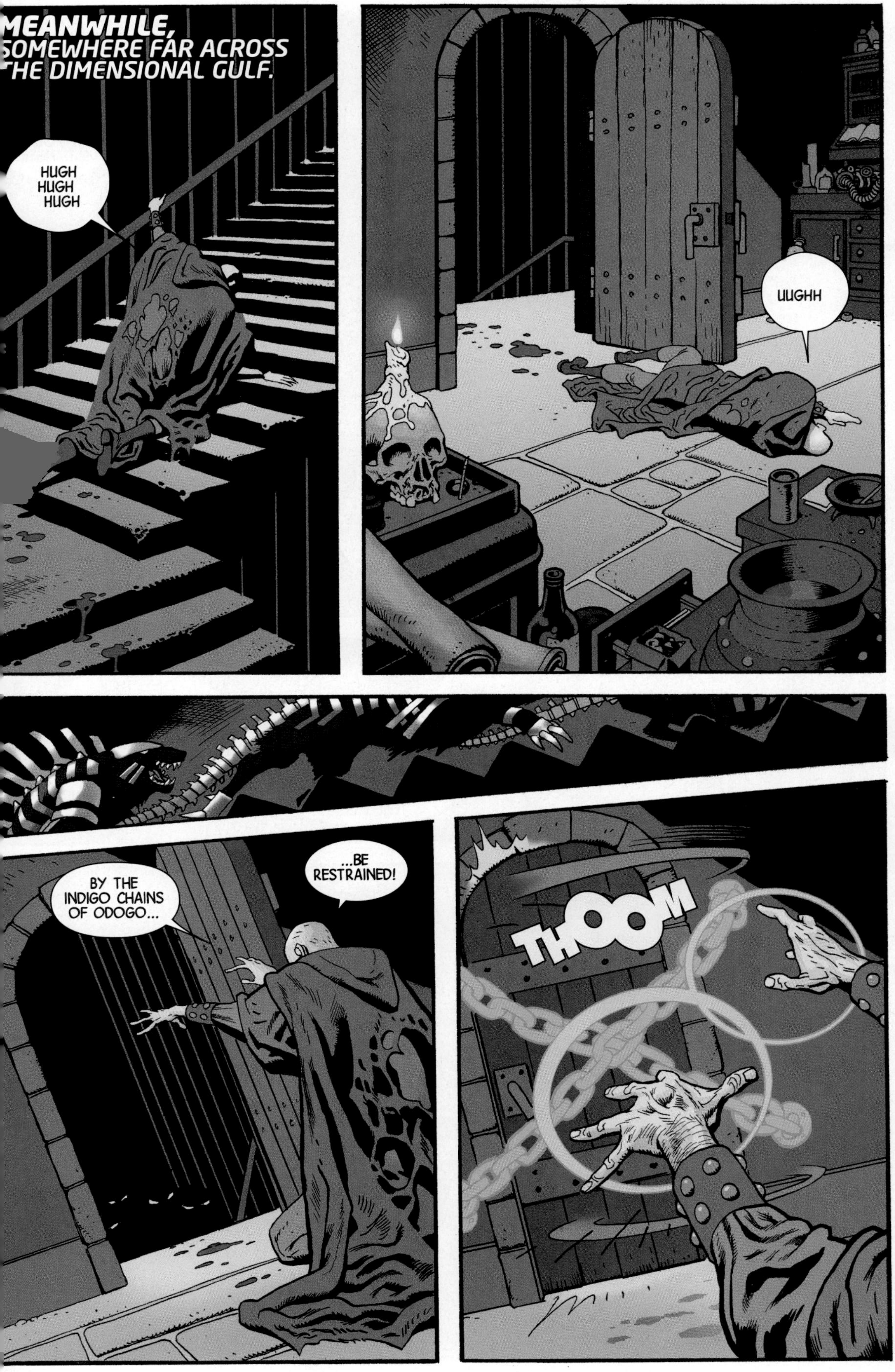
MEANWHILE, SOMEWHERE FAR ACROSS THE DIMENSIONAL GULF.
HUGH HUGH HUGH
UUGHH
BY THE INDIGO CHAINS OF ODOGO...
...BE RESTRAINED!
THOOM

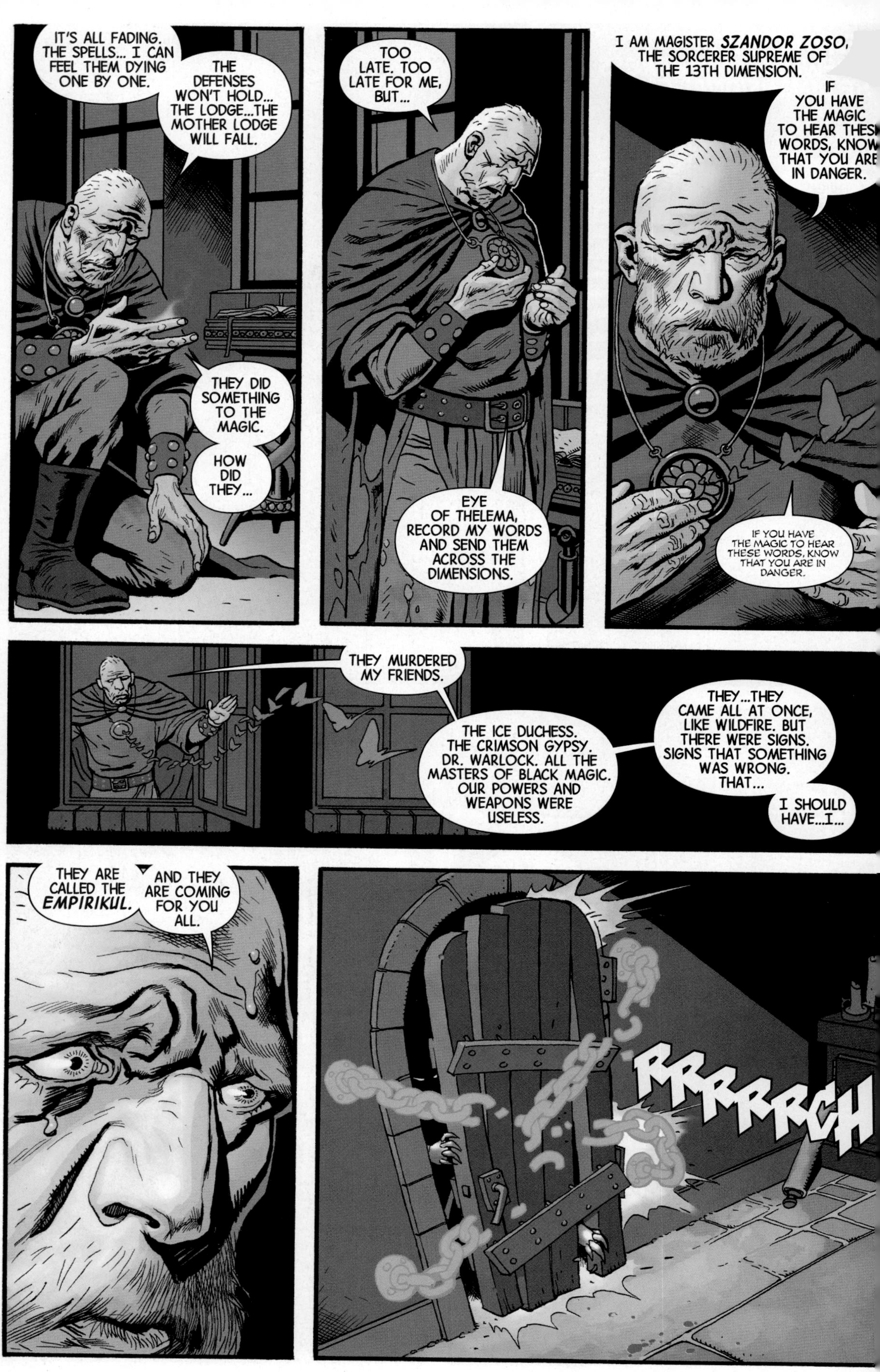

IT'S ALL FADING. THE SPELLS... I CAN FEEL THEM DYING ONE BY ONE.
THE DEFENSES WON'T HOLD... THE LODGE...THE MOTHER LODGE WILL FALL.
THEY DID SOMETHING TO THE MAGIC.
HOW DID THEY...
TOO LATE. TOO LATE FOR ME, BUT...
EYE OF THELEMA, RECORD MY WORDS AND SEND THEM ACROSS THE DIMENSIONS.
I AM MAGISTER SZANDOR ZOSO, THE SORCERER SUPREME OF THE 13TH DIMENSION.
IF YOU HAVE THE MAGIC TO HEAR THESE WORDS, KNOW THAT YOU ARE IN DANGER.
IF YOU HAVE THE MAGIC TO HEAR THESE WORDS, KNOW THAT YOU ARE IN DANGER.
THEY MURDERED MY FRIENDS.
THE ICE DUCHESS. THE CRIMSON GYPSY. DR. WARLOCK. ALL THE MASTERS OF BLACK MAGIC. OUR POWERS AND WEAPONS WERE USELESS.
THEY...THEY CAME ALL AT ONCE, LIKE WILDFIRE. BUT THERE WERE SIGNS. SIGNS THAT SOMETHING WAS WRONG. THAT...
I SHOULD HAVE...I...
THEY ARE CALLED THE EMPIRIKUL.
AND THEY ARE COMING FOR YOU ALL.
RRRRRRCH

THELEMA SAVE ME. THEY'RE--

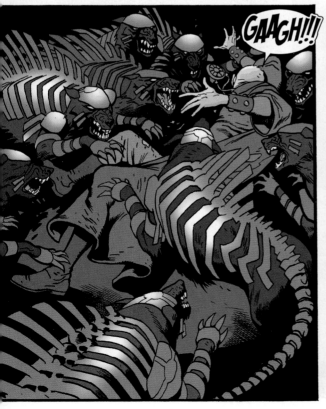

GAAGH!!!

AAAARRGH!

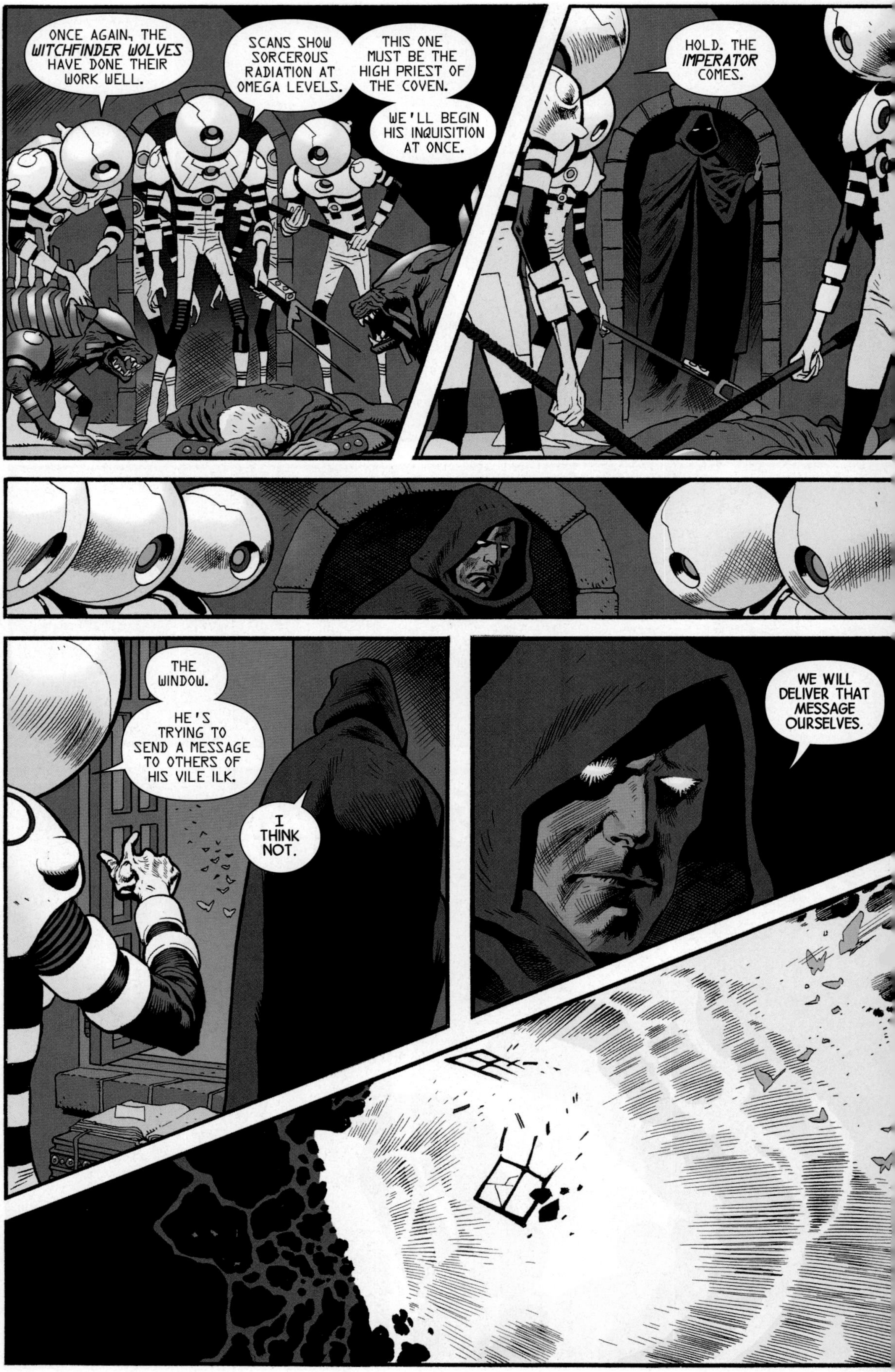
ONCE AGAIN, THE *WITCHFINDER WOLVES* HAVE DONE THEIR WORK WELL.
SCANS SHOW SORCEROUS RADIATION AT OMEGA LEVELS.
THIS ONE MUST BE THE HIGH PRIEST OF THE COVEN.
WE'LL BEGIN HIS INQUISITION AT ONCE.
HOLD. THE *IMPERATOR* COMES.
THE WINDOW.
HE'S TRYING TO SEND A MESSAGE TO OTHERS OF HIS VILE ILK.
I THINK NOT.
WE WILL DELIVER THAT MESSAGE OURSELVES.

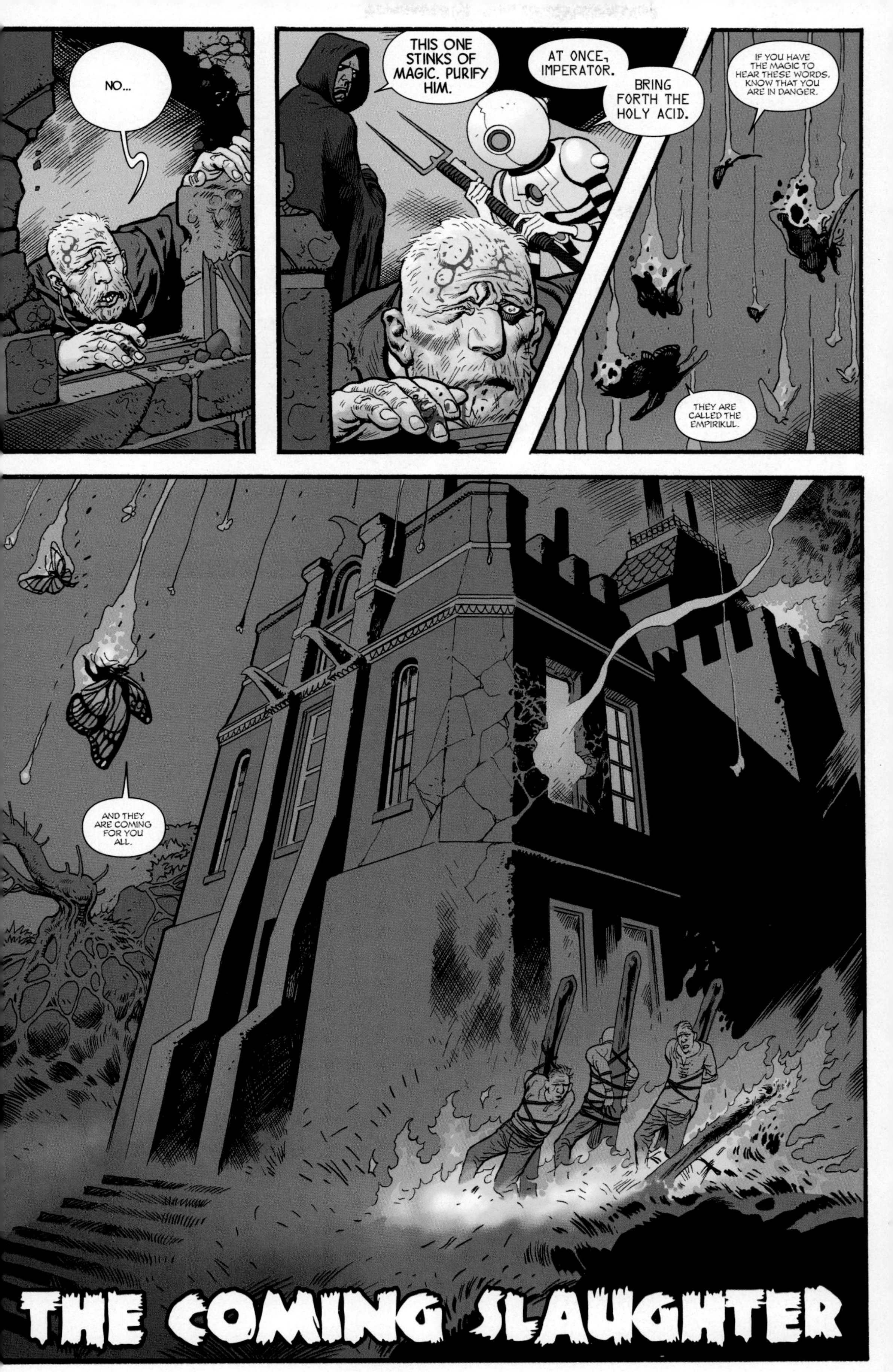
NO...
THIS ONE STINKS OF MAGIC. PURIFY HIM.
AT ONCE, IMPERATOR.
BRING FORTH THE HOLY ACID.
IF YOU HAVE THE MAGIC TO HEAR THESE WORDS, KNOW THAT YOU ARE IN DANGER.
THEY ARE CALLED THE EMPIRIKUL.
AND THEY ARE COMING FOR YOU ALL.
THE COMING SLAUGHTER

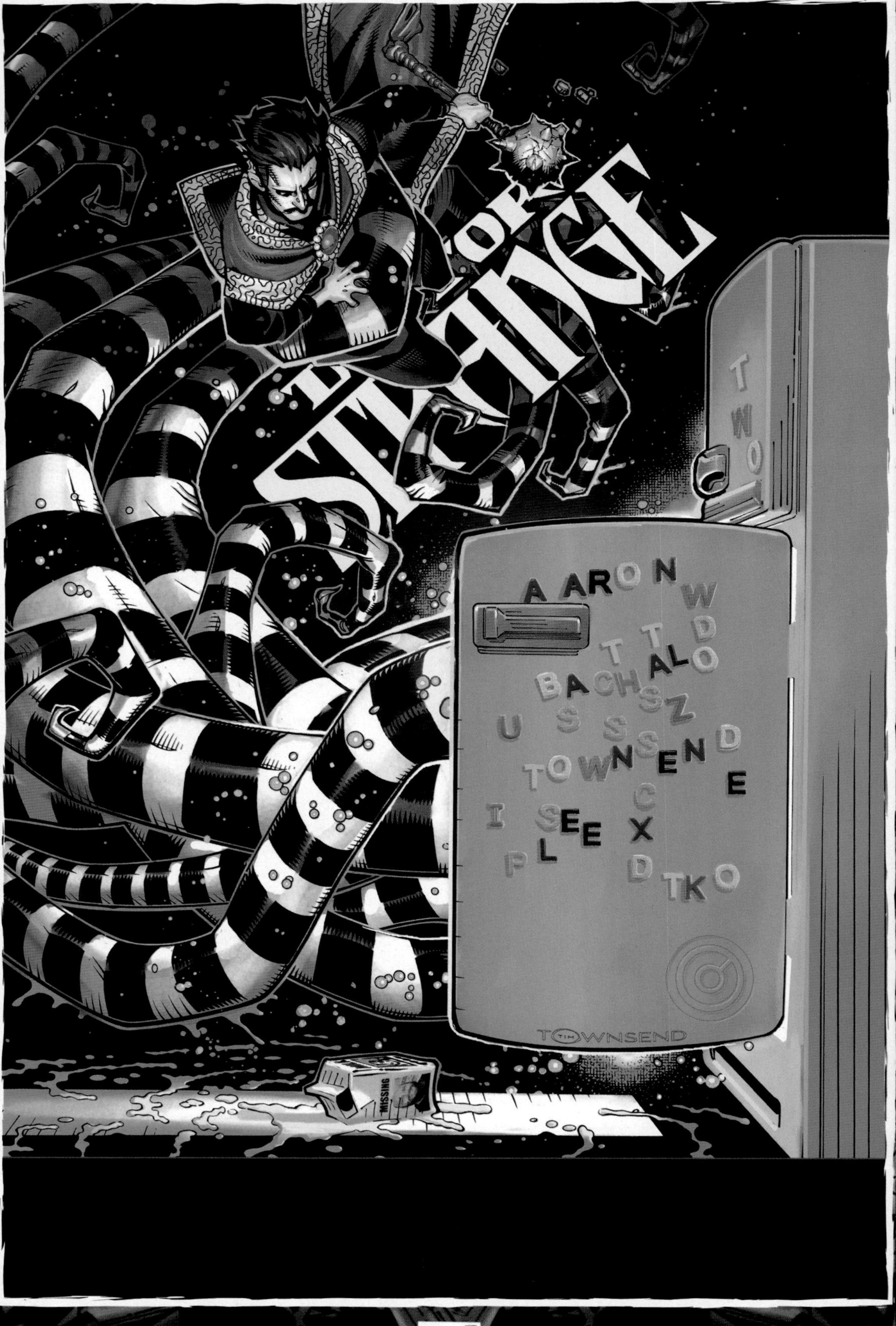
TWO
AARON
BACHALO
TOWNSEND
TIM TOWNSEND
MISSING

DOCTOR STRANGE THIS IS WHERE THINGS GET UNUSUAL

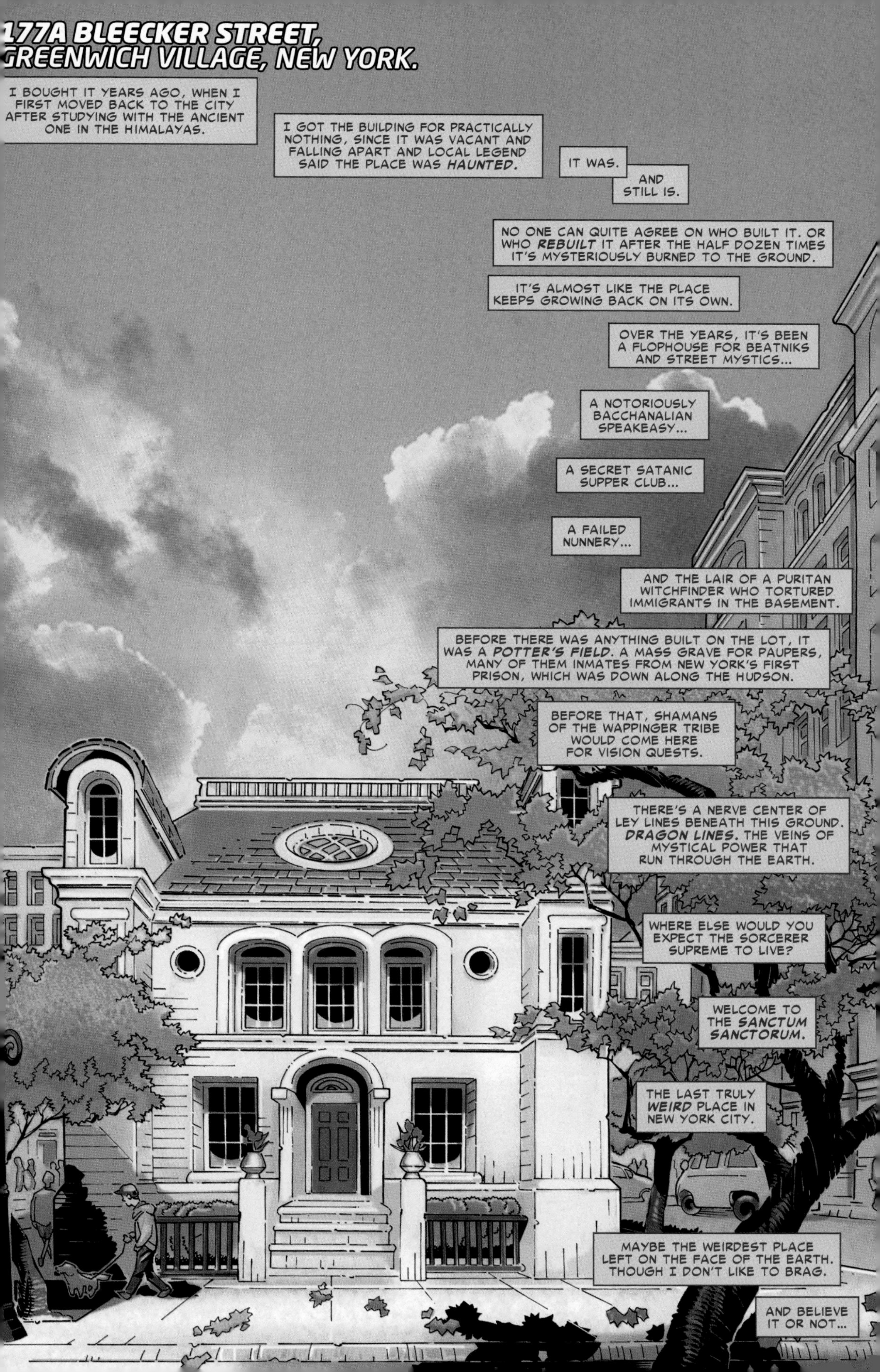
177A BLEECKER STREET, GREENWICH VILLAGE, NEW YORK.
I BOUGHT IT YEARS AGO, WHEN I FIRST MOVED BACK TO THE CITY AFTER STUDYING WITH THE ANCIENT ONE IN THE HIMALAYAS.
I GOT THE BUILDING FOR PRACTICALLY NOTHING, SINCE IT WAS VACANT AND FALLING APART AND LOCAL LEGEND SAID THE PLACE WAS *HAUNTED.*
IT WAS.
AND STILL IS.
NO ONE CAN QUITE AGREE ON WHO BUILT IT. OR WHO *REBUILT* IT AFTER THE HALF DOZEN TIMES IT'S MYSTERIOUSLY BURNED TO THE GROUND.
IT'S ALMOST LIKE THE PLACE KEEPS GROWING BACK ON ITS OWN.
OVER THE YEARS, IT'S BEEN A FLOPHOUSE FOR BEATNIKS AND STREET MYSTICS...
A NOTORIOUSLY BACCHANALIAN SPEAKEASY...
A SECRET SATANIC SUPPER CLUB...
A FAILED NUNNERY...
AND THE LAIR OF A PURITAN WITCHFINDER WHO TORTURED IMMIGRANTS IN THE BASEMENT.
BEFORE THERE WAS ANYTHING BUILT ON THE LOT, IT WAS A *POTTER'S FIELD*. A MASS GRAVE FOR PAUPERS, MANY OF THEM INMATES FROM NEW YORK'S FIRST PRISON, WHICH WAS DOWN ALONG THE HUDSON.
BEFORE THAT, SHAMANS OF THE WAPPINGER TRIBE WOULD COME HERE FOR VISION QUESTS.
THERE'S A NERVE CENTER OF LEY LINES BENEATH THIS GROUND. *DRAGON LINES*. THE VEINS OF MYSTICAL POWER THAT RUN THROUGH THE EARTH.
WHERE ELSE WOULD YOU EXPECT THE SORCERER SUPREME TO LIVE?
WELCOME TO THE *SANCTUM SANCTORUM*.
THE LAST TRULY *WEIRD* PLACE IN NEW YORK CITY.
MAYBE THE WEIRDEST PLACE LEFT ON THE FACE OF THE EARTH. THOUGH I DON'T LIKE TO BRAG.
AND BELIEVE IT OR NOT...

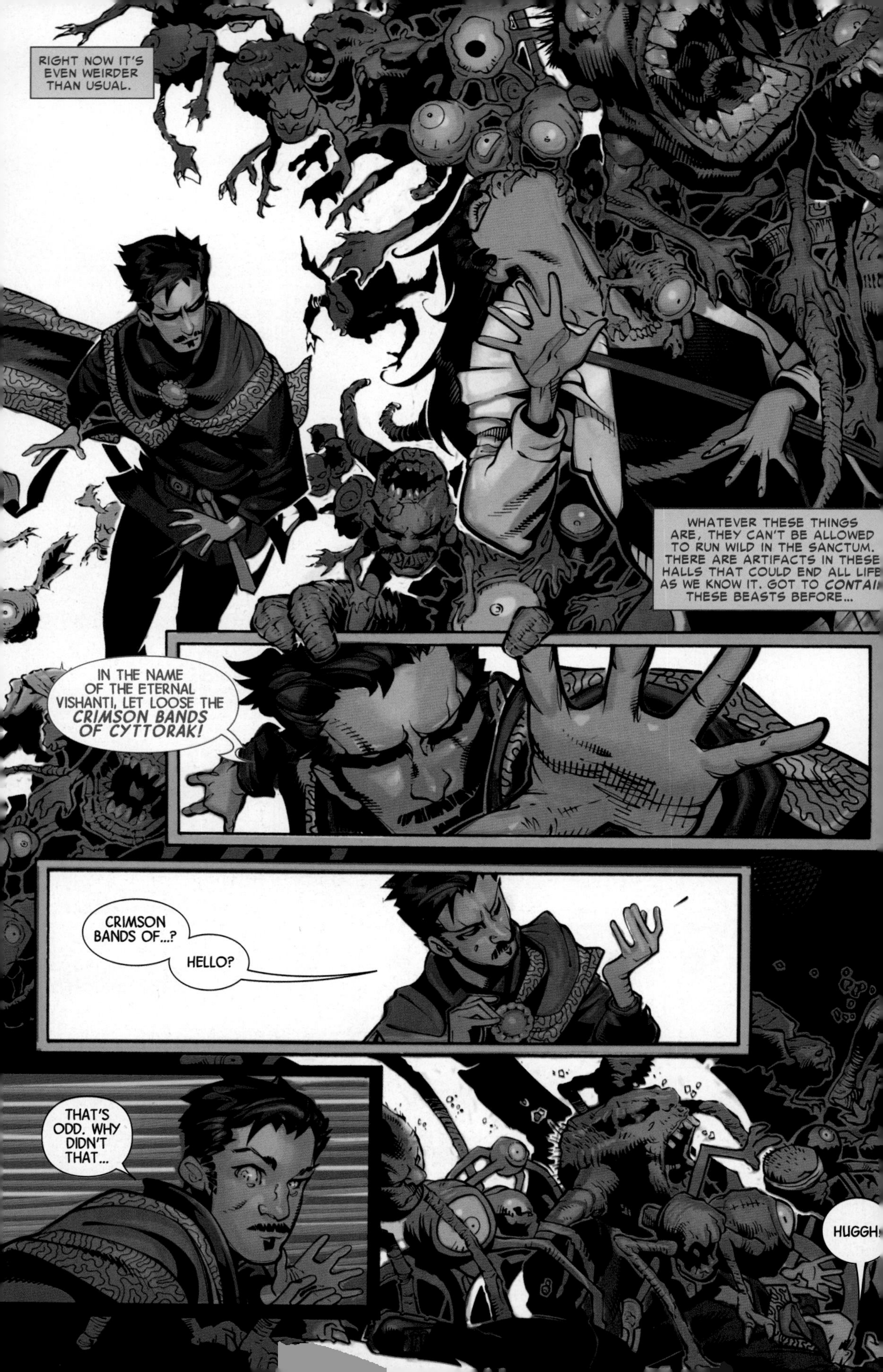
RIGHT NOW IT'S EVEN WEIRDER THAN USUAL.
WHATEVER THESE THINGS ARE, THEY CAN'T BE ALLOWED TO RUN WILD IN THE SANCTUM. THERE ARE ARTIFACTS IN THESE HALLS THAT COULD END ALL LIFE AS WE KNOW IT. GOT TO CONTAI THESE BEASTS BEFORE...
IN THE NAME OF THE ETERNAL VISHANTI, LET LOOSE THE *CRIMSON BANDS OF CYTTORAK!*
CRIMSON BANDS OF...?
HELLO?
THAT'S ODD. WHY DIDN'T THAT...
HUGGH

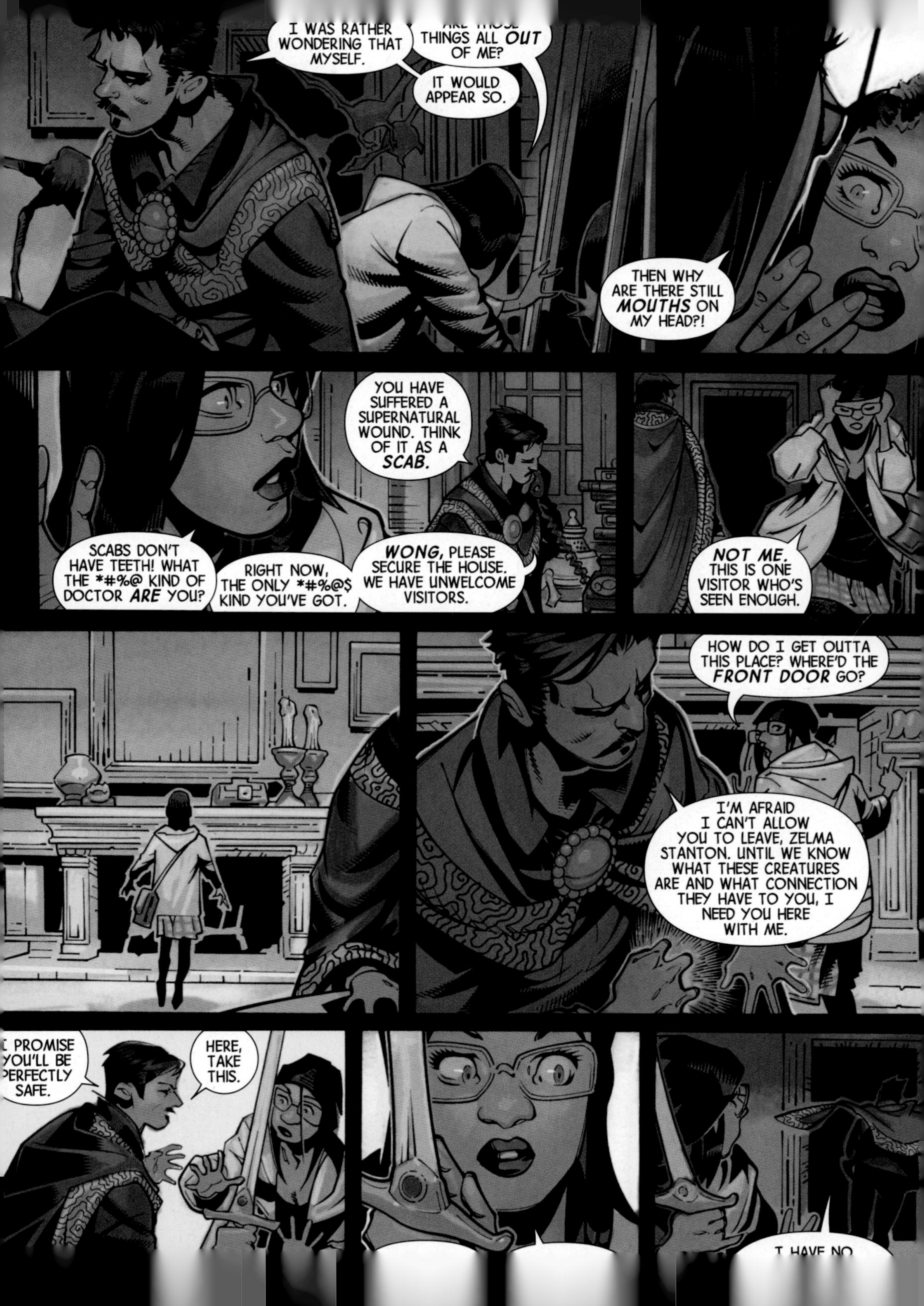
I WAS RATHER WONDERING THAT MYSELF.
THINGS ALL OUT OF ME?
IT WOULD APPEAR SO.
THEN WHY ARE THERE STILL MOUTHS ON MY HEAD?!
YOU HAVE SUFFERED A SUPERNATURAL WOUND. THINK OF IT AS A SCAB.
SCABS DON'T HAVE TEETH! WHAT THE *#%@ KIND OF DOCTOR ARE YOU?
RIGHT NOW, THE ONLY *#%@$ KIND YOU'VE GOT.
WONG, PLEASE SECURE THE HOUSE. WE HAVE UNWELCOME VISITORS.
NOT ME. THIS IS ONE VISITOR WHO'S SEEN ENOUGH.
HOW DO I GET OUTTA THIS PLACE? WHERE'D THE FRONT DOOR GO?
I'M AFRAID I CAN'T ALLOW YOU TO LEAVE, ZELMA STANTON. UNTIL WE KNOW WHAT THESE CREATURES ARE AND WHAT CONNECTION THEY HAVE TO YOU, I NEED YOU HERE WITH ME.
I PROMISE YOU'LL BE PERFECTLY SAFE.
HERE, TAKE THIS.

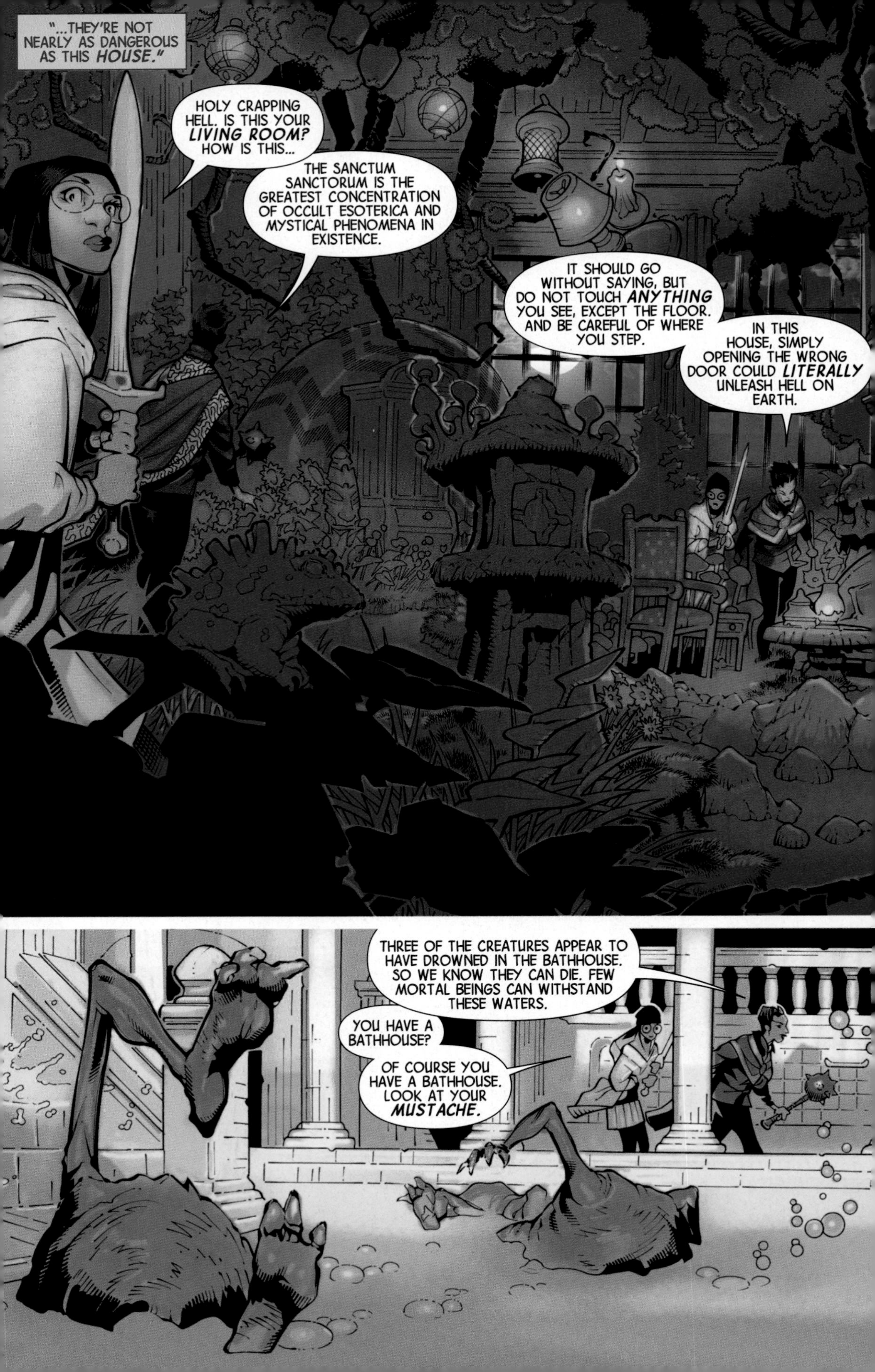
"...THEY'RE NOT NEARLY AS DANGEROUS AS THIS HOUSE."
HOLY CRAPPING HELL. IS THIS YOUR LIVING ROOM? HOW IS THIS...
THE SANCTUM SANCTORUM IS THE GREATEST CONCENTRATION OF OCCULT ESOTERICA AND MYSTICAL PHENOMENA IN EXISTENCE.
IT SHOULD GO WITHOUT SAYING, BUT DO NOT TOUCH ANYTHING YOU SEE, EXCEPT THE FLOOR. AND BE CAREFUL OF WHERE YOU STEP.
IN THIS HOUSE, SIMPLY OPENING THE WRONG DOOR COULD LITERALLY UNLEASH HELL ON EARTH.
THREE OF THE CREATURES APPEAR TO HAVE DROWNED IN THE BATHHOUSE. SO WE KNOW THEY CAN DIE. FEW MORTAL BEINGS CAN WITHSTAND THESE WATERS.
YOU HAVE A BATHHOUSE?
OF COURSE YOU HAVE A BATHHOUSE. LOOK AT YOUR MUSTACHE.

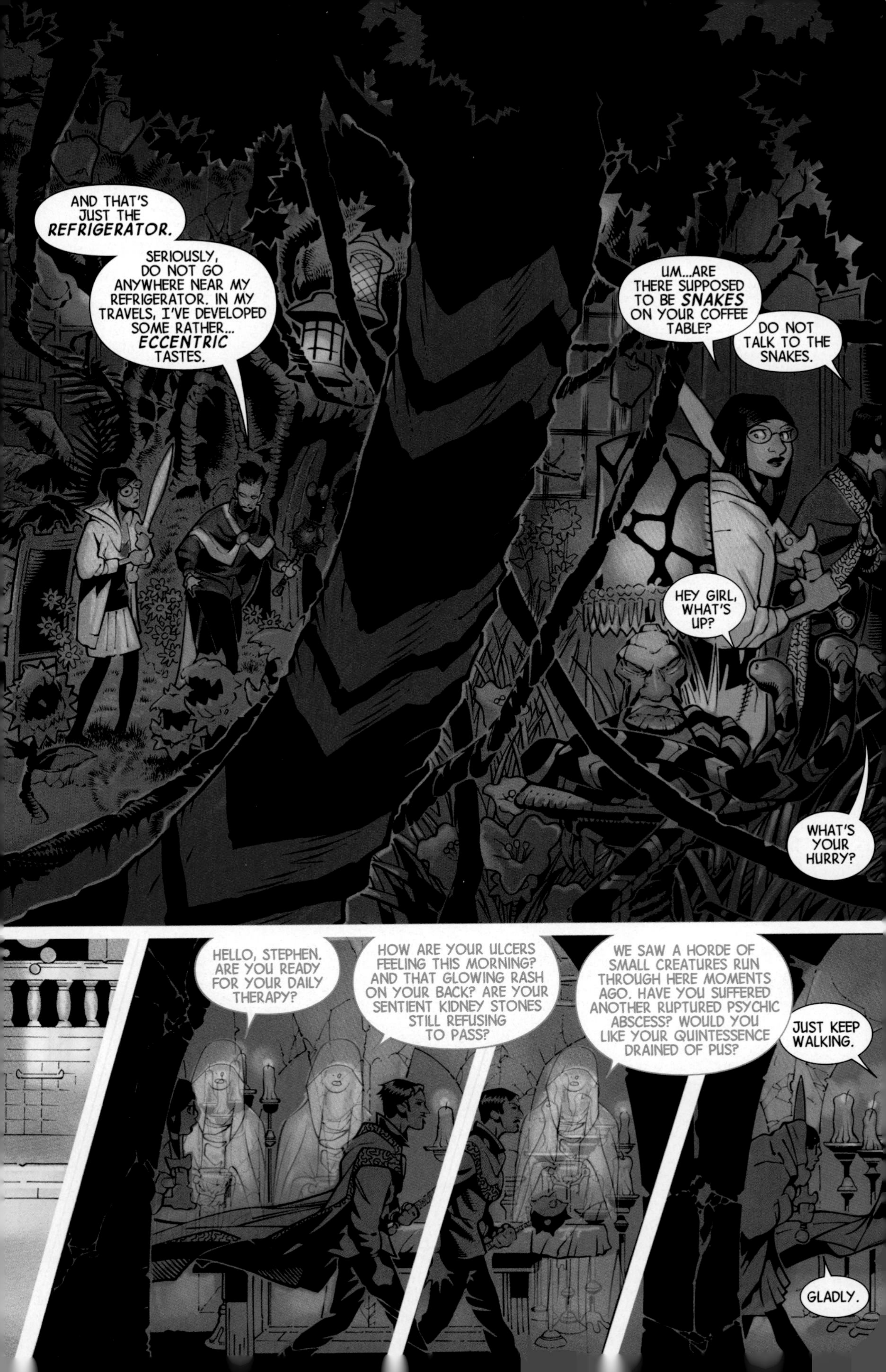
AND THAT'S JUST THE REFRIGERATOR.
SERIOUSLY, DO NOT GO ANYWHERE NEAR MY REFRIGERATOR. IN MY TRAVELS, I'VE DEVELOPED SOME RATHER... ECCENTRIC TASTES.
UM...ARE THERE SUPPOSED TO BE SNAKES ON YOUR COFFEE TABLE?
DO NOT TALK TO THE SNAKES.
HEY GIRL, WHAT'S UP?
WHAT'S YOUR HURRY?
HELLO, STEPHEN. ARE YOU READY FOR YOUR DAILY THERAPY?
HOW ARE YOUR ULCERS FEELING THIS MORNING? AND THAT GLOWING RASH ON YOUR BACK? ARE YOUR SENTIENT KIDNEY STONES STILL REFUSING TO PASS?
WE SAW A HORDE OF SMALL CREATURES RUN THROUGH HERE MOMENTS AGO. HAVE YOU SUFFERED ANOTHER RUPTURED PSYCHIC ABSCESS? WOULD YOU LIKE YOUR QUINTESSENCE DRAINED OF PUS?
JUST KEEP WALKING.
GLADLY.

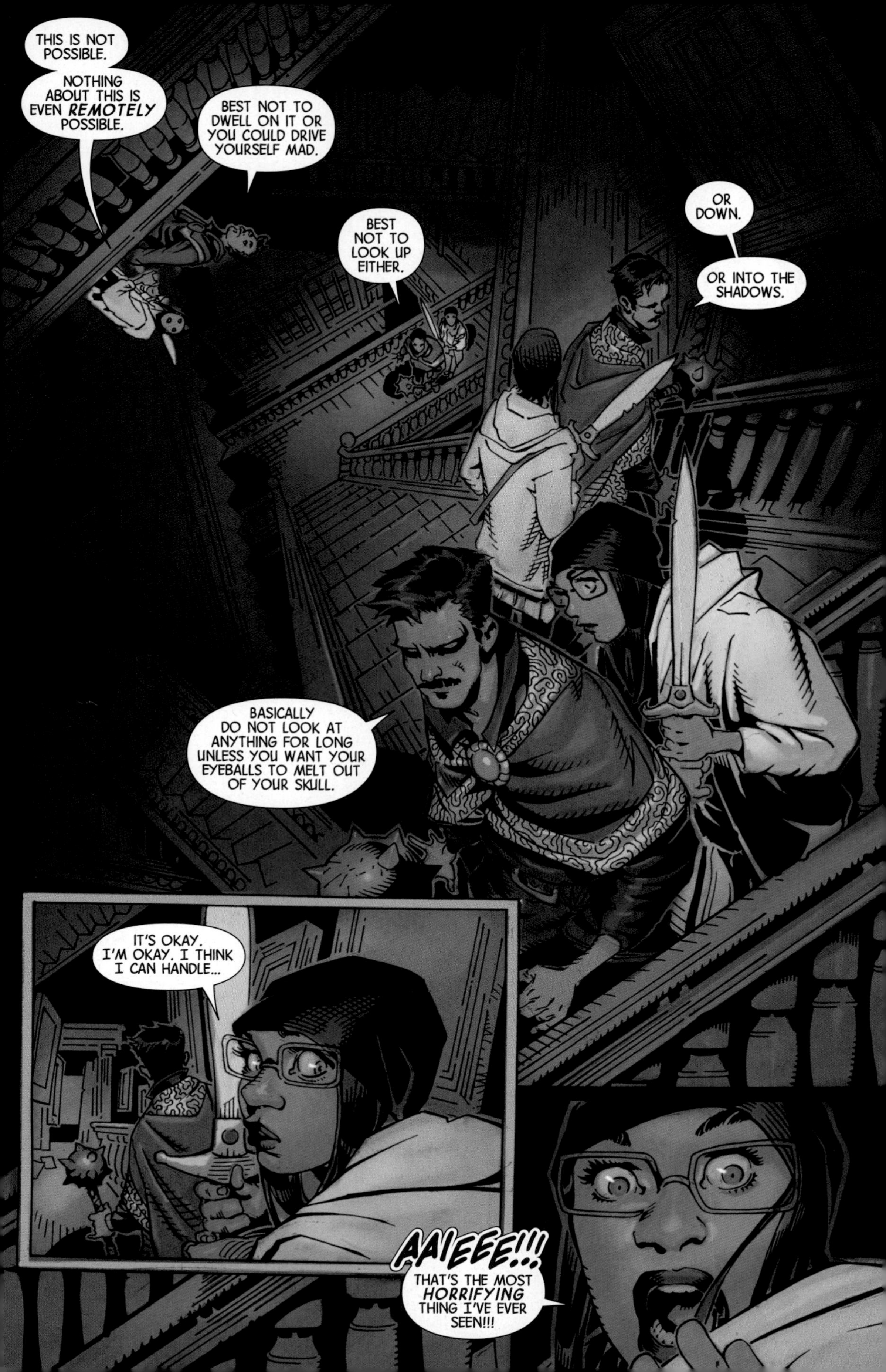
THIS IS NOT POSSIBLE.
NOTHING ABOUT THIS IS EVEN *REMOTELY* POSSIBLE.
BEST NOT TO DWELL ON IT OR YOU COULD DRIVE YOURSELF MAD.
BEST NOT TO LOOK UP EITHER.
OR DOWN.
OR INTO THE SHADOWS.
BASICALLY DO NOT LOOK AT ANYTHING FOR LONG UNLESS YOU WANT YOUR EYEBALLS TO MELT OUT OF YOUR SKULL.
IT'S OKAY. I'M OKAY. I THINK I CAN HANDLE...
AAIEEE!!!
THAT'S THE MOST *HORRIFYING* THING I'VE EVER SEEN!!!

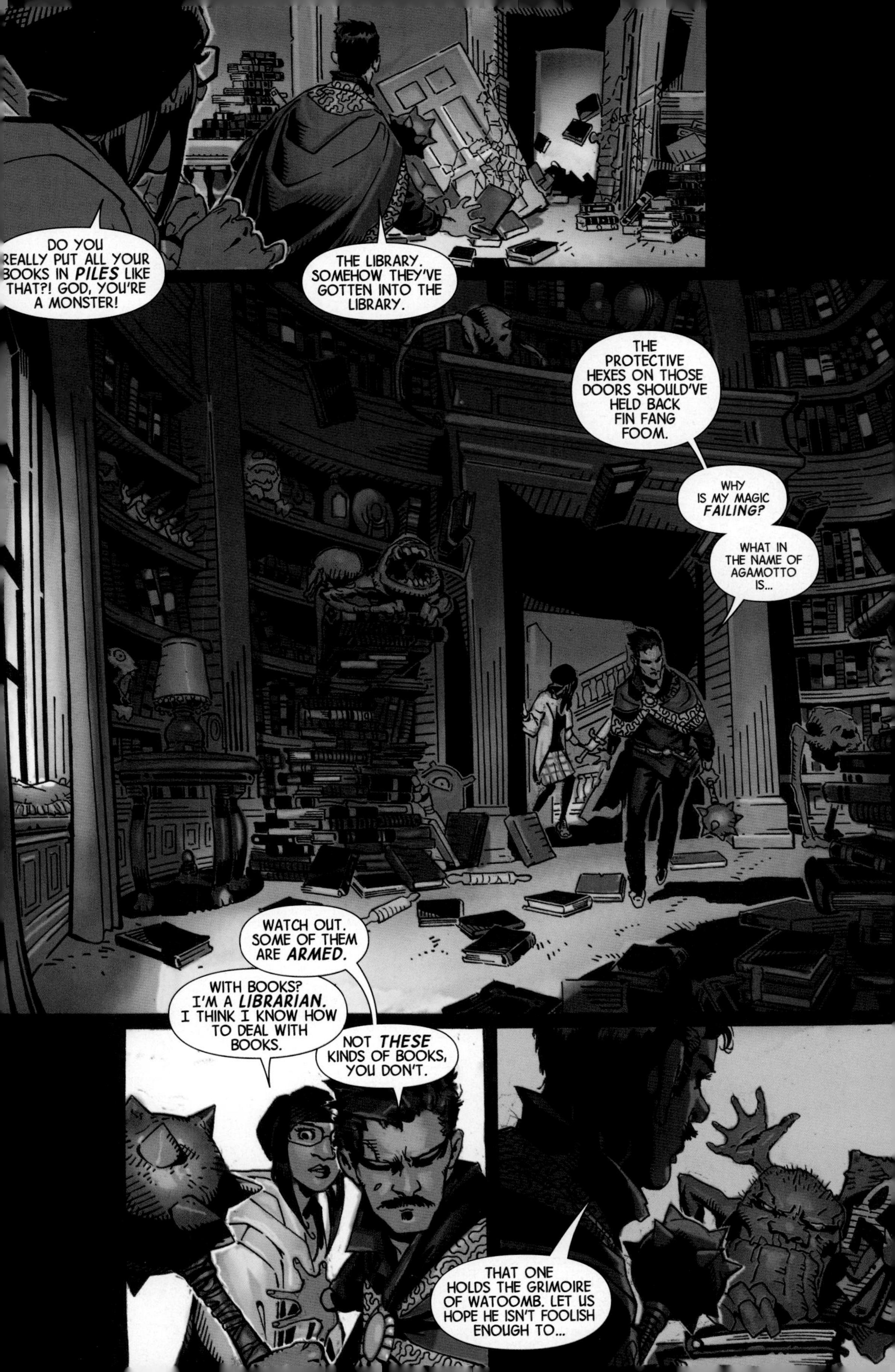
DO YOU REALLY PUT ALL YOUR BOOKS IN PILES LIKE THAT?! GOD, YOU'RE A MONSTER!
THE LIBRARY. SOMEHOW THEY'VE GOTTEN INTO THE LIBRARY.
THE PROTECTIVE HEXES ON THOSE DOORS SHOULD'VE HELD BACK FIN FANG FOOM.
WHY IS MY MAGIC FAILING?
WHAT IN THE NAME OF AGAMOTTO IS...
WATCH OUT. SOME OF THEM ARE ARMED.
WITH BOOKS? I'M A LIBRARIAN. I THINK I KNOW HOW TO DEAL WITH BOOKS.
NOT THESE KINDS OF BOOKS, YOU DON'T.
THAT ONE HOLDS THE GRIMOIRE OF WATOOMB. LET US HOPE HE ISN'T FOOLISH ENOUGH TO...

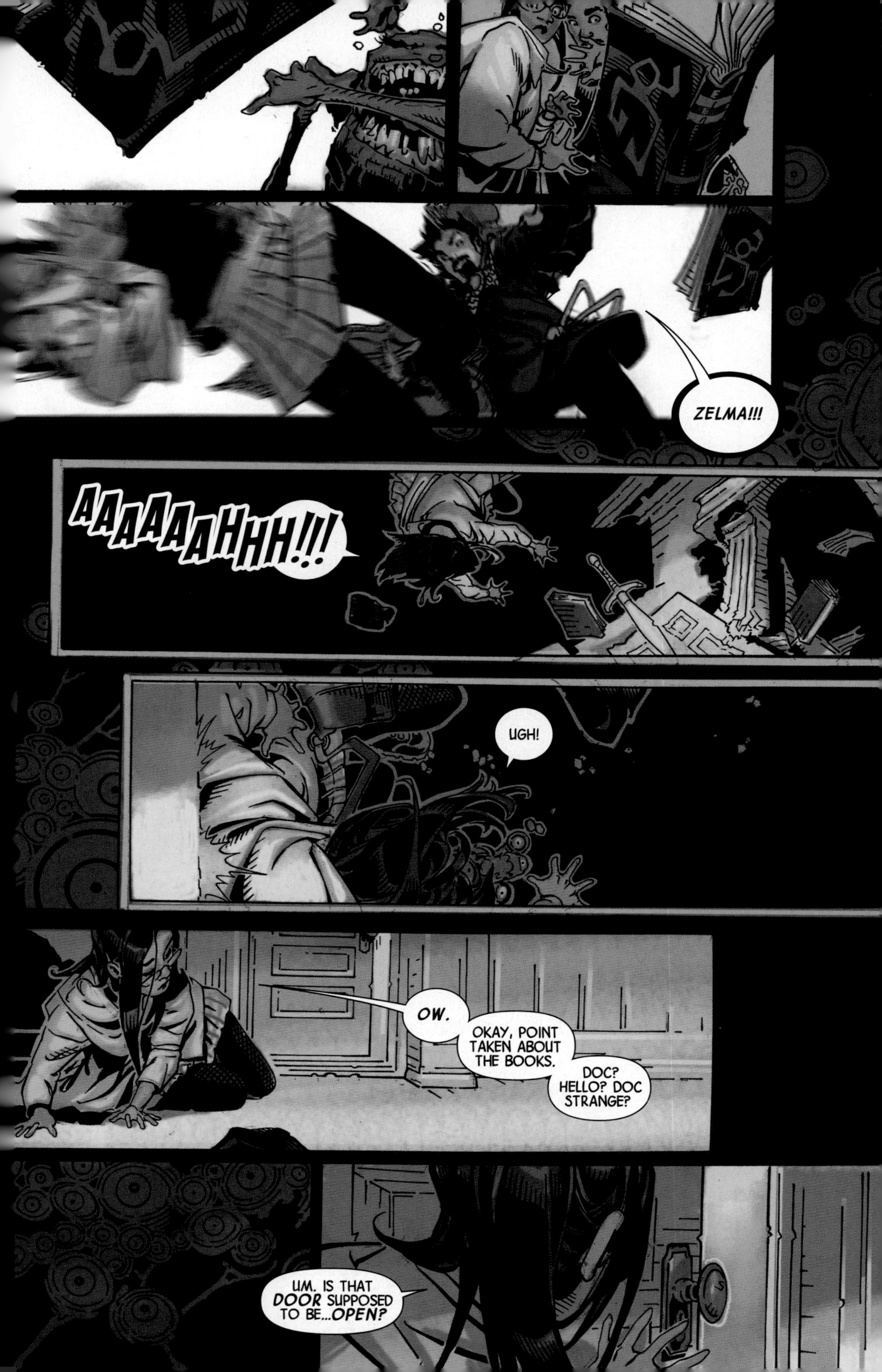
ZELMA!!!
AAAAAAHHH!!!
UGH!
OW.
OKAY, POINT TAKEN ABOUT THE BOOKS.
DOC? HELLO? DOC STRANGE?
UM. IS THAT DOOR SUPPOSED TO BE...OPEN?

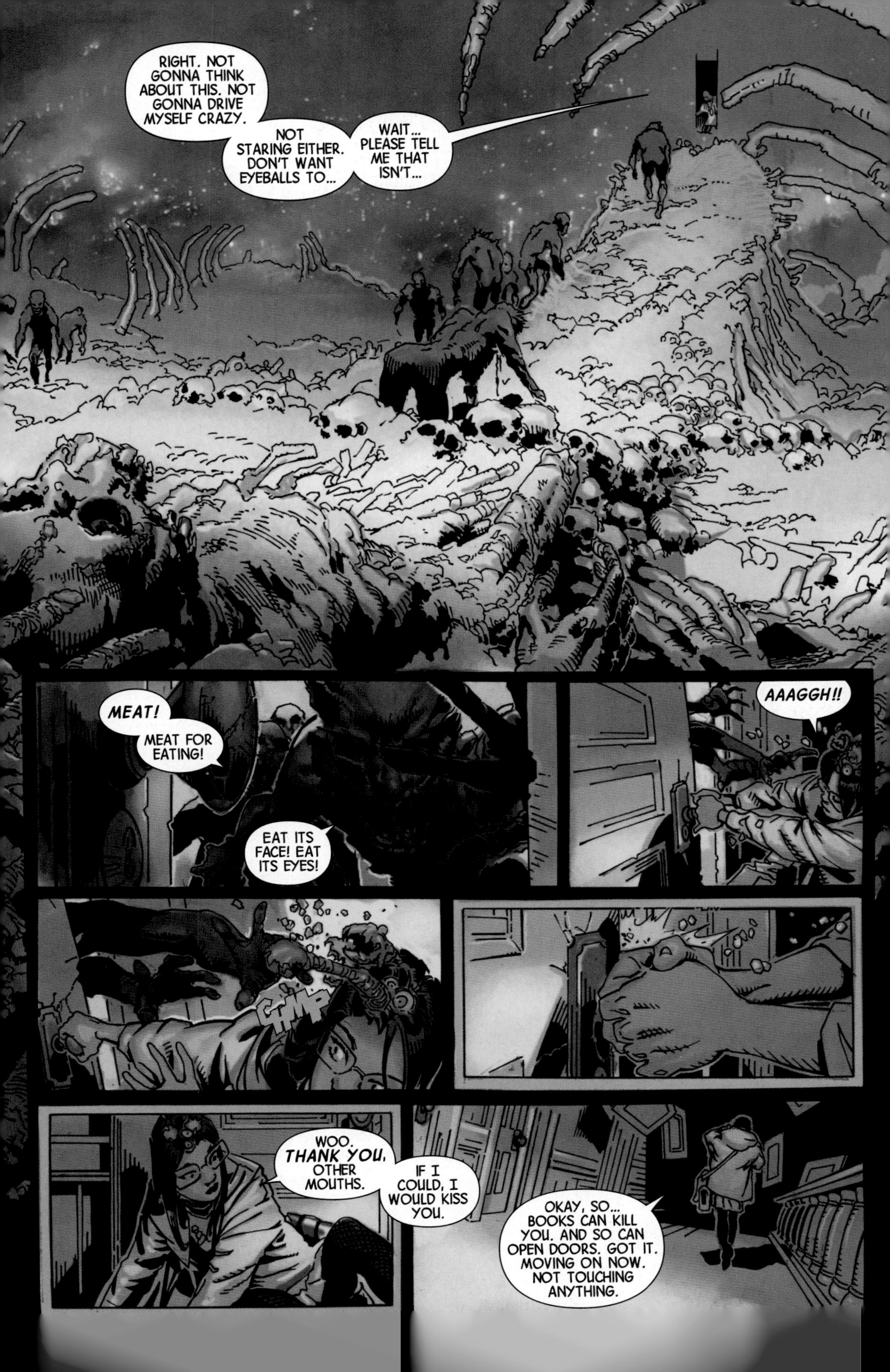
RIGHT. NOT GONNA THINK ABOUT THIS. NOT GONNA DRIVE MYSELF CRAZY.
NOT STARING EITHER. DON'T WANT EYEBALLS TO...
WAIT... PLEASE TELL ME THAT ISN'T...
MEAT!
MEAT FOR EATING!
EAT ITS FACE! EAT ITS EYES!
AAAGGH!!
GMP
WOO. THANK YOU, OTHER MOUTHS.
IF I COULD, I WOULD KISS YOU.
OKAY, SO... BOOKS CAN KILL YOU. AND SO CAN OPEN DOORS. GOT IT. MOVING ON NOW. NOT TOUCHING ANYTHING.

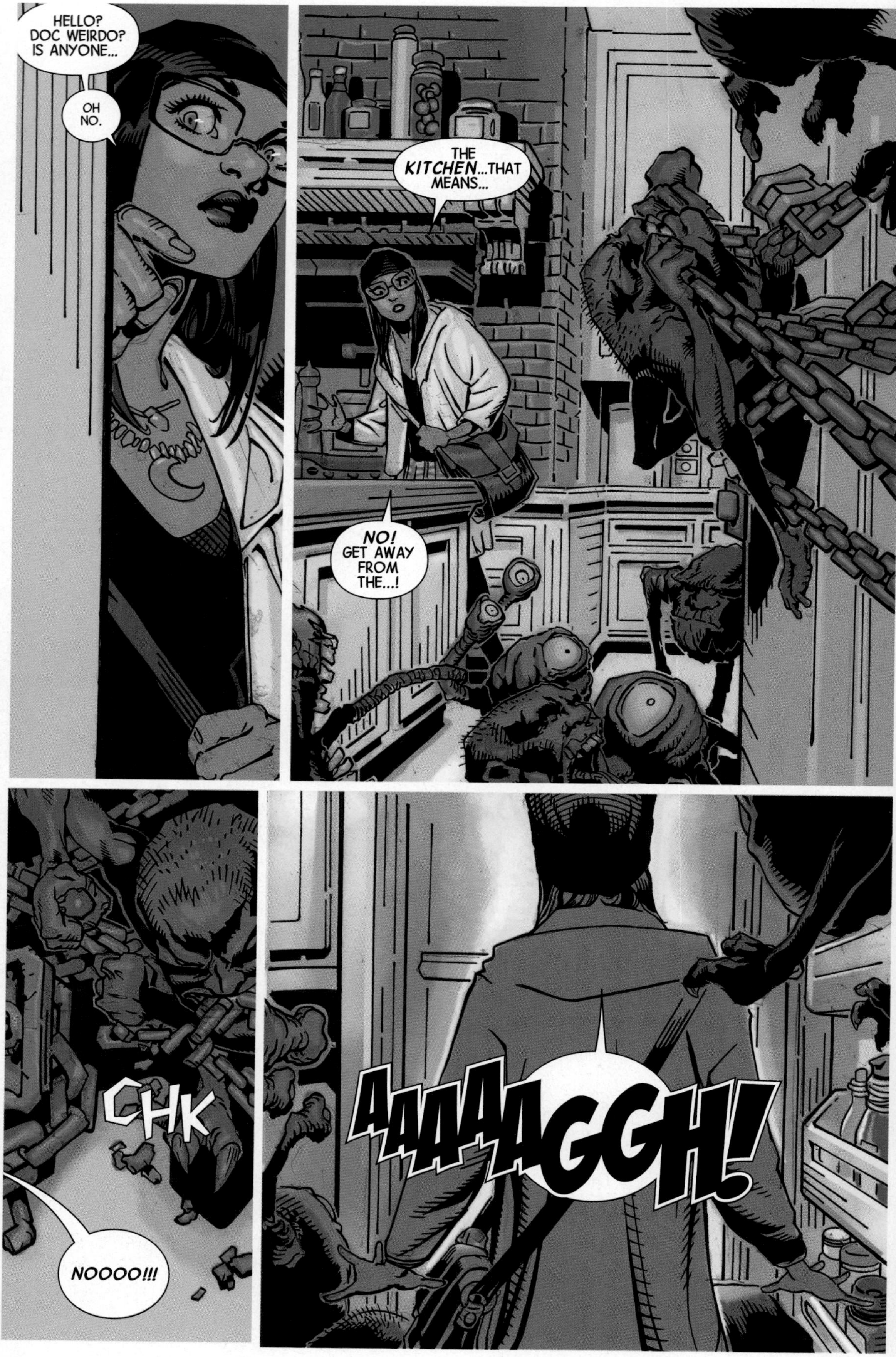
HELLO? DOC WEIRDO? IS ANYONE...
OH NO.
THE KITCHEN...THAT MEANS...
NO! GET AWAY FROM THE...!
CHK
NOOOO!!!
AAAAAAGGH!

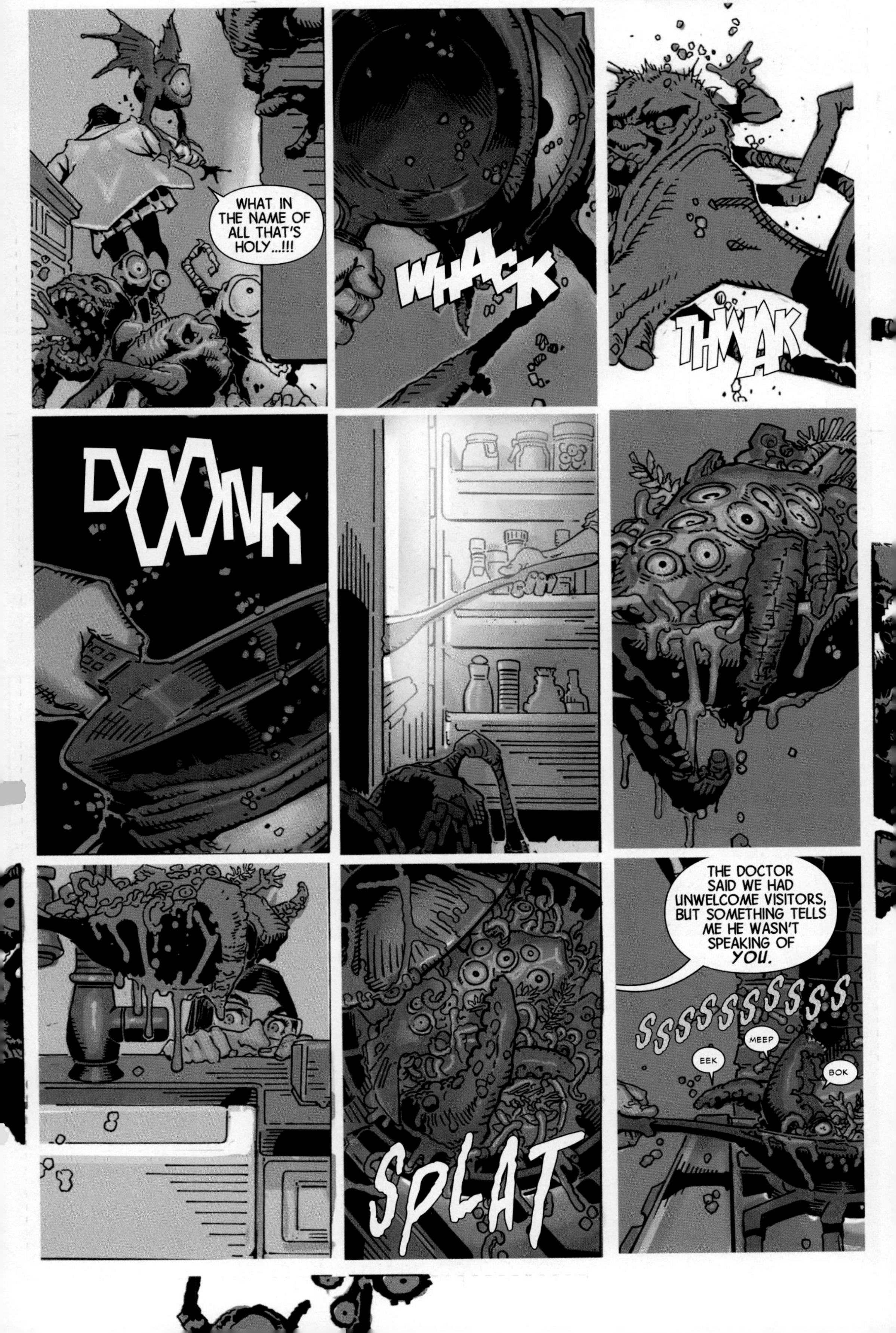

WHAT IN THE NAME OF ALL THAT'S HOLY...!!!
WHACK
THWAK
DOONK
THE DOCTOR SAID WE HAD UNWELCOME VISITORS, BUT SOMETHING TELLS ME HE WASN'T SPEAKING OF YOU.
SPLAT
SSSSSSSSSS
EEK
MEEP
BOK

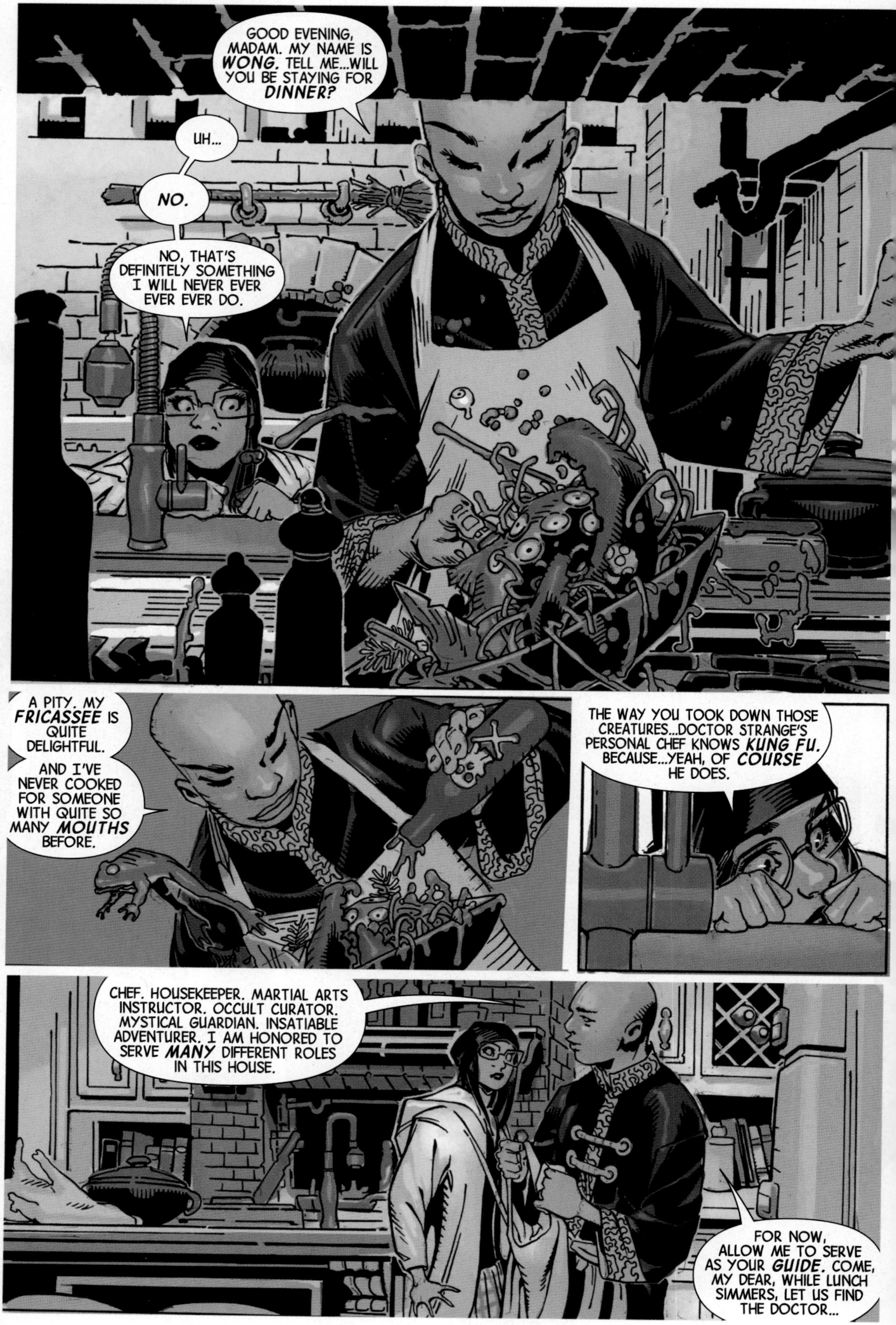
GOOD EVENING, MADAM. MY NAME IS WONG. TELL ME...WILL YOU BE STAYING FOR DINNER?
UH...
NO.
NO, THAT'S DEFINITELY SOMETHING I WILL NEVER EVER EVER EVER DO.
A PITY. MY FRICASSEE IS QUITE DELIGHTFUL.
AND I'VE NEVER COOKED FOR SOMEONE WITH QUITE SO MANY MOUTHS BEFORE.
THE WAY YOU TOOK DOWN THOSE CREATURES...DOCTOR STRANGE'S PERSONAL CHEF KNOWS KUNG FU. BECAUSE...YEAH, OF COURSE HE DOES.
CHEF. HOUSEKEEPER. MARTIAL ARTS INSTRUCTOR. OCCULT CURATOR. MYSTICAL GUARDIAN. INSATIABLE ADVENTURER. I AM HONORED TO SERVE MANY DIFFERENT ROLES IN THIS HOUSE.
FOR NOW, ALLOW ME TO SERVE AS YOUR GUIDE. COME, MY DEAR, WHILE LUNCH SIMMERS, LET US FIND THE DOCTOR...

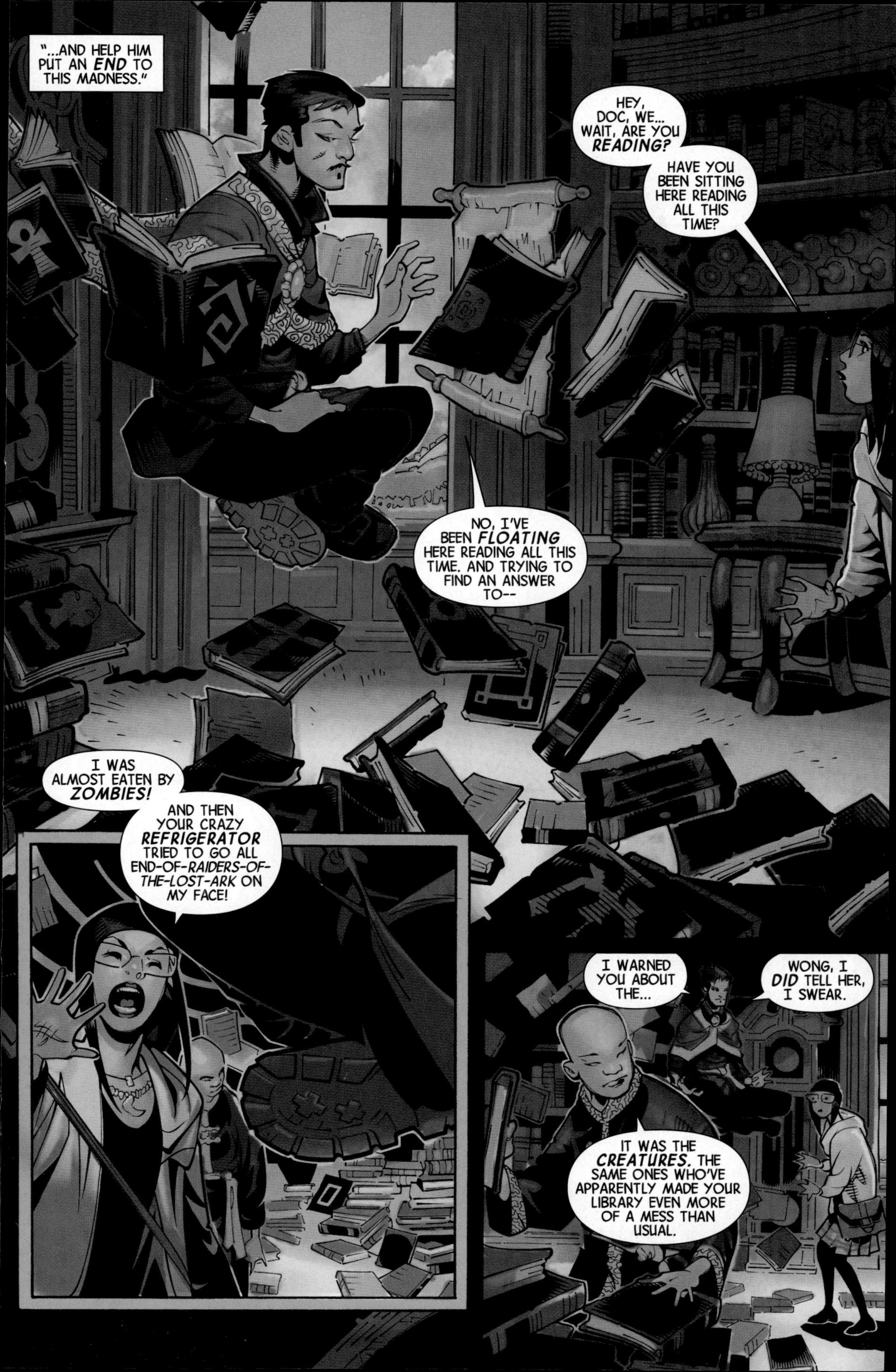
"...AND HELP HIM PUT AN *END* TO THIS MADNESS."
HEY, DOC, WE... WAIT, ARE YOU *READING?*
HAVE YOU BEEN SITTING HERE READING ALL THIS TIME?
NO, I'VE BEEN *FLOATING* HERE READING ALL THIS TIME. AND TRYING TO FIND AN ANSWER TO--
I WAS ALMOST EATEN BY *ZOMBIES!*
AND THEN YOUR CRAZY *REFRIGERATOR* TRIED TO GO ALL END-OF-*RAIDERS-OF-THE-LOST-ARK* ON MY FACE!
I WARNED YOU ABOUT THE...
WONG, I *DID* TELL HER, I SWEAR.
IT WAS THE *CREATURES.* THE SAME ONES WHO'VE APPARENTLY MADE YOUR LIBRARY EVEN MORE OF A MESS THAN USUAL.

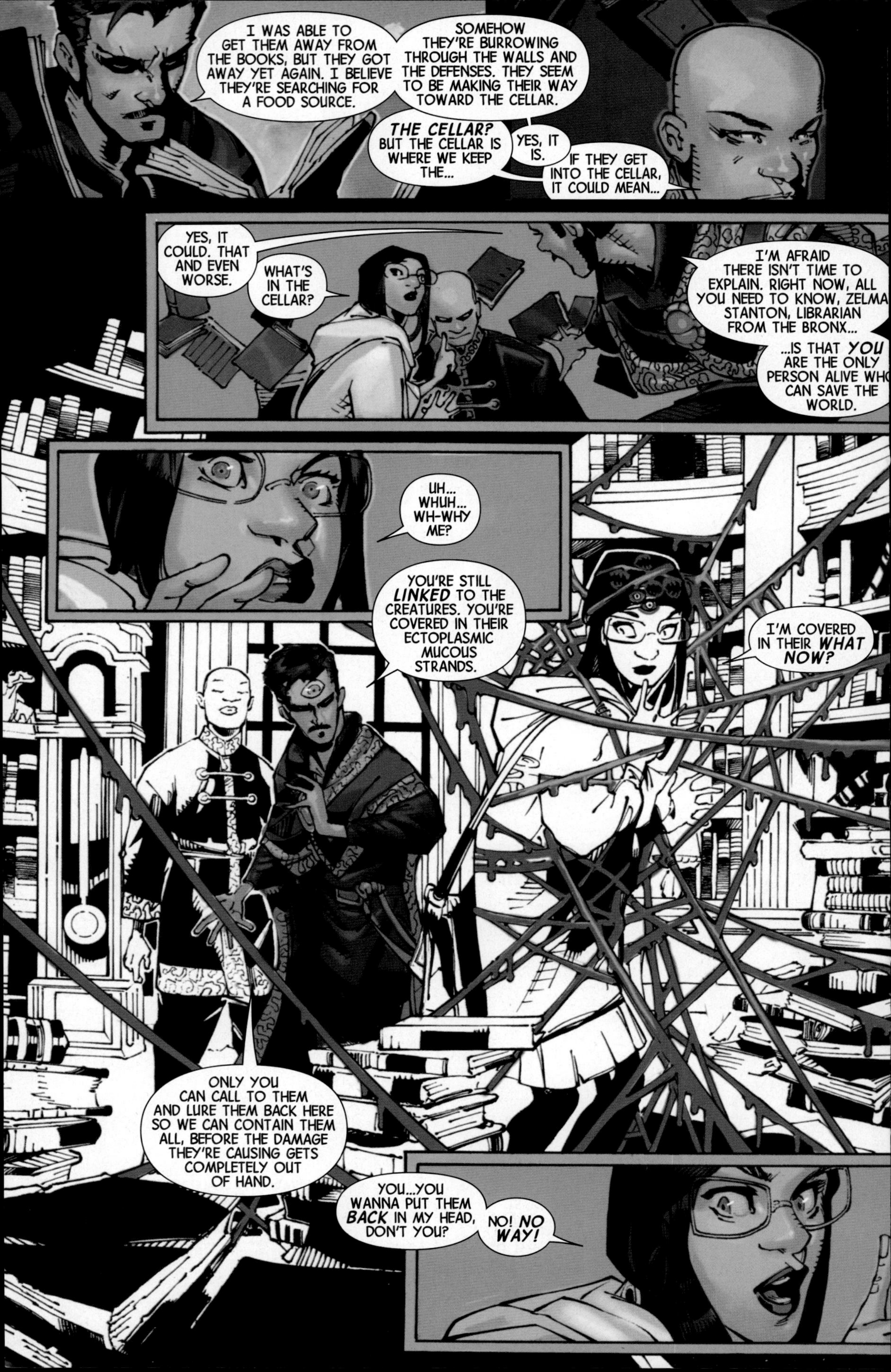
I WAS ABLE TO GET THEM AWAY FROM THE BOOKS, BUT THEY GOT AWAY YET AGAIN. I BELIEVE THEY'RE SEARCHING FOR A FOOD SOURCE.
SOMEHOW THEY'RE BURROWING THROUGH THE WALLS AND THE DEFENSES. THEY SEEM TO BE MAKING THEIR WAY TOWARD THE CELLAR.
THE CELLAR? BUT THE CELLAR IS WHERE WE KEEP THE...
YES, IT IS.
IF THEY GET INTO THE CELLAR, IT COULD MEAN...
YES, IT COULD. THAT AND EVEN WORSE.
WHAT'S IN THE CELLAR?
I'M AFRAID THERE ISN'T TIME TO EXPLAIN. RIGHT NOW, ALL YOU NEED TO KNOW, ZELMA STANTON, LIBRARIAN FROM THE BRONX...
...IS THAT YOU ARE THE ONLY PERSON ALIVE WHO CAN SAVE THE WORLD.
UH... WHUH... WH-WHY ME?
YOU'RE STILL LINKED TO THE CREATURES. YOU'RE COVERED IN THEIR ECTOPLASMIC MUCOUS STRANDS.
I'M COVERED IN THEIR WHAT NOW?
ONLY YOU CAN CALL TO THEM AND LURE THEM BACK HERE SO WE CAN CONTAIN THEM ALL, BEFORE THE DAMAGE THEY'RE CAUSING GETS COMPLETELY OUT OF HAND.
YOU...YOU WANNA PUT THEM BACK IN MY HEAD, DON'T YOU?
NO! NO WAY!

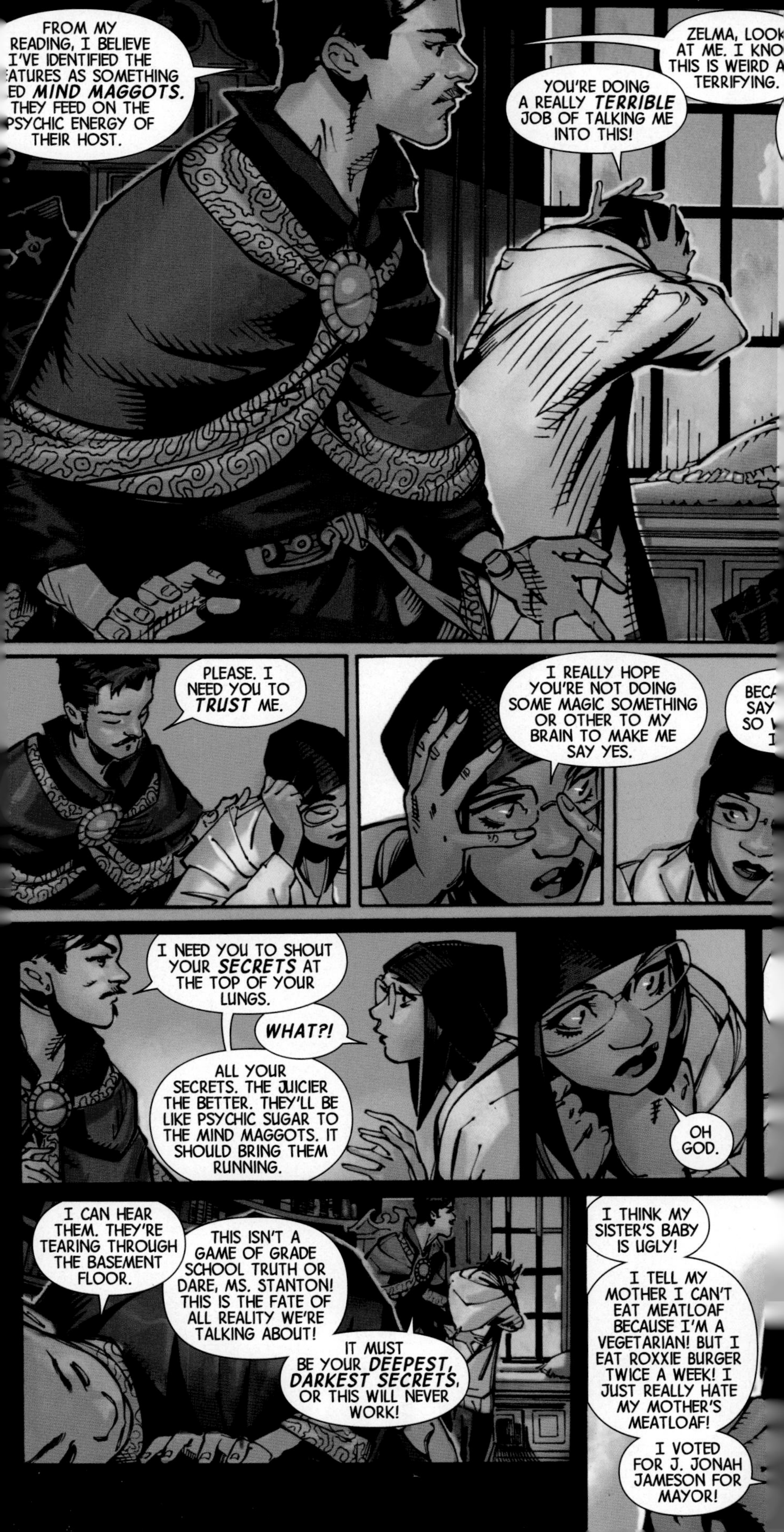

FROM MY READING, I BELIEVE I'VE IDENTIFIED THE
EATURES AS SOMETHING
ED MIND MAGGOTS.
THEY FEED ON THE
PSYCHIC ENERGY OF THEIR HOST.
ZELMA, LOOK AT ME. I KNO THIS IS WEIRD A TERRIFYING.
YOU'RE DOING A REALLY TERRIBLE JOB OF TALKING ME INTO THIS!
PLEASE. I NEED YOU TO TRUST ME.
I REALLY HOPE YOU'RE NOT DOING SOME MAGIC SOMETHING OR OTHER TO MY BRAIN TO MAKE ME SAY YES.
I NEED YOU TO SHOUT YOUR SECRETS AT THE TOP OF YOUR LUNGS.
WHAT?!
ALL YOUR SECRETS. THE JUICIER THE BETTER. THEY'LL BE LIKE PSYCHIC SUGAR TO THE MIND MAGGOTS. IT SHOULD BRING THEM RUNNING.
OH GOD.
I CAN HEAR THEM. THEY'RE TEARING THROUGH THE BASEMENT FLOOR.
THIS ISN'T A GAME OF GRADE SCHOOL TRUTH OR DARE, MS. STANTON! THIS IS THE FATE OF ALL REALITY WE'RE TALKING ABOUT!
IT MUST BE YOUR DEEPEST, DARKEST SECRETS, OR THIS WILL NEVER WORK!
I THINK MY SISTER'S BABY IS UGLY!
I TELL MY MOTHER I CAN'T EAT MEATLOAF BECAUSE I'M A VEGETARIAN! BUT I EAT ROXXIE BURGER TWICE A WEEK! I JUST REALLY HATE MY MOTHER'S MEATLOAF!
I VOTED FOR J. JONAH JAMESON FOR MAYOR!

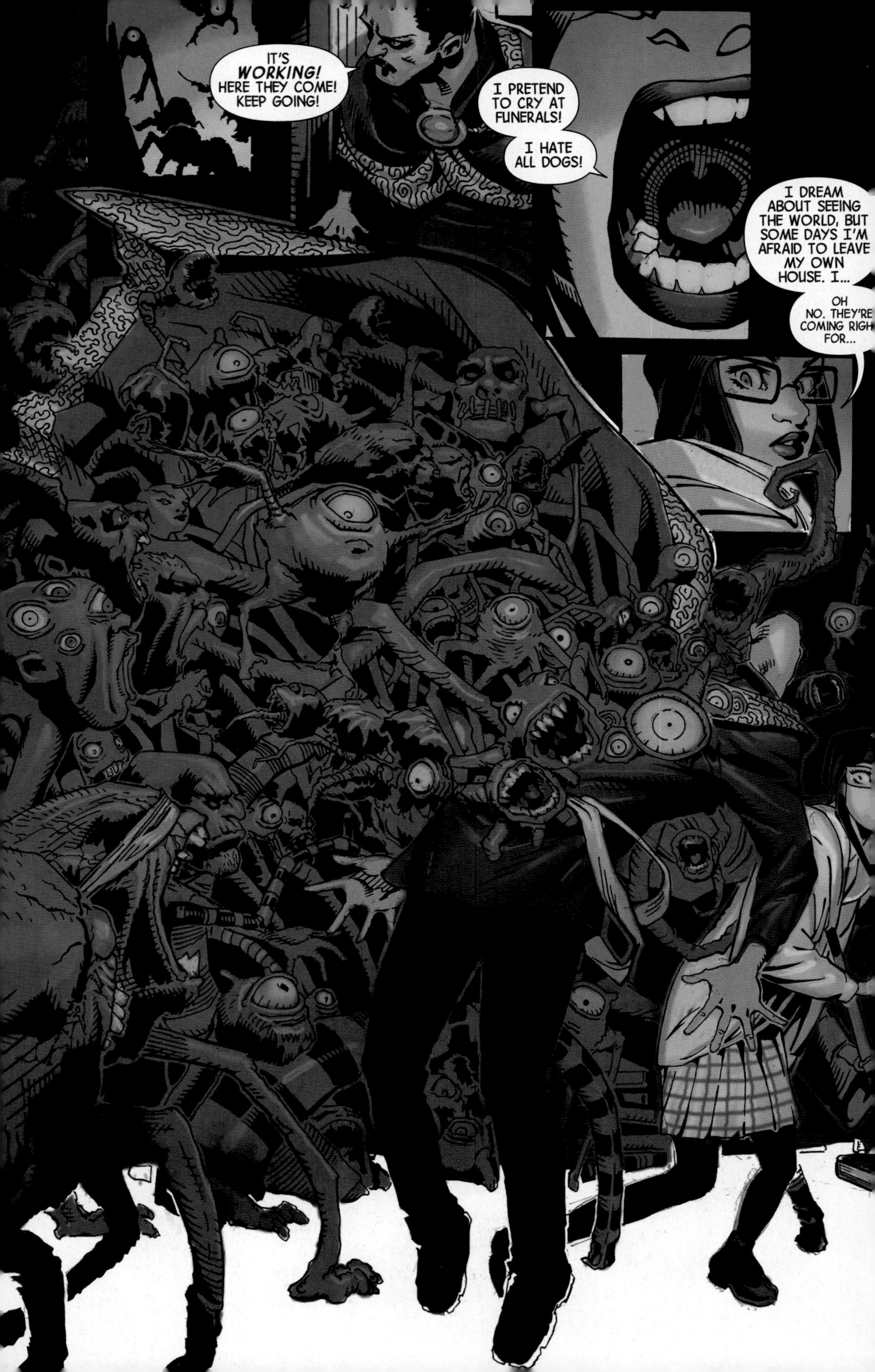
IT'S *WORKING!* HERE THEY COME! KEEP GOING!
I PRETEND TO CRY AT FUNERALS!
I HATE ALL DOGS!
I DREAM ABOUT SEEING THE WORLD, BUT SOME DAYS I'M AFRAID TO LEAVE MY OWN HOUSE. I...
OH NO. THEY'RE COMING RIGH FOR...

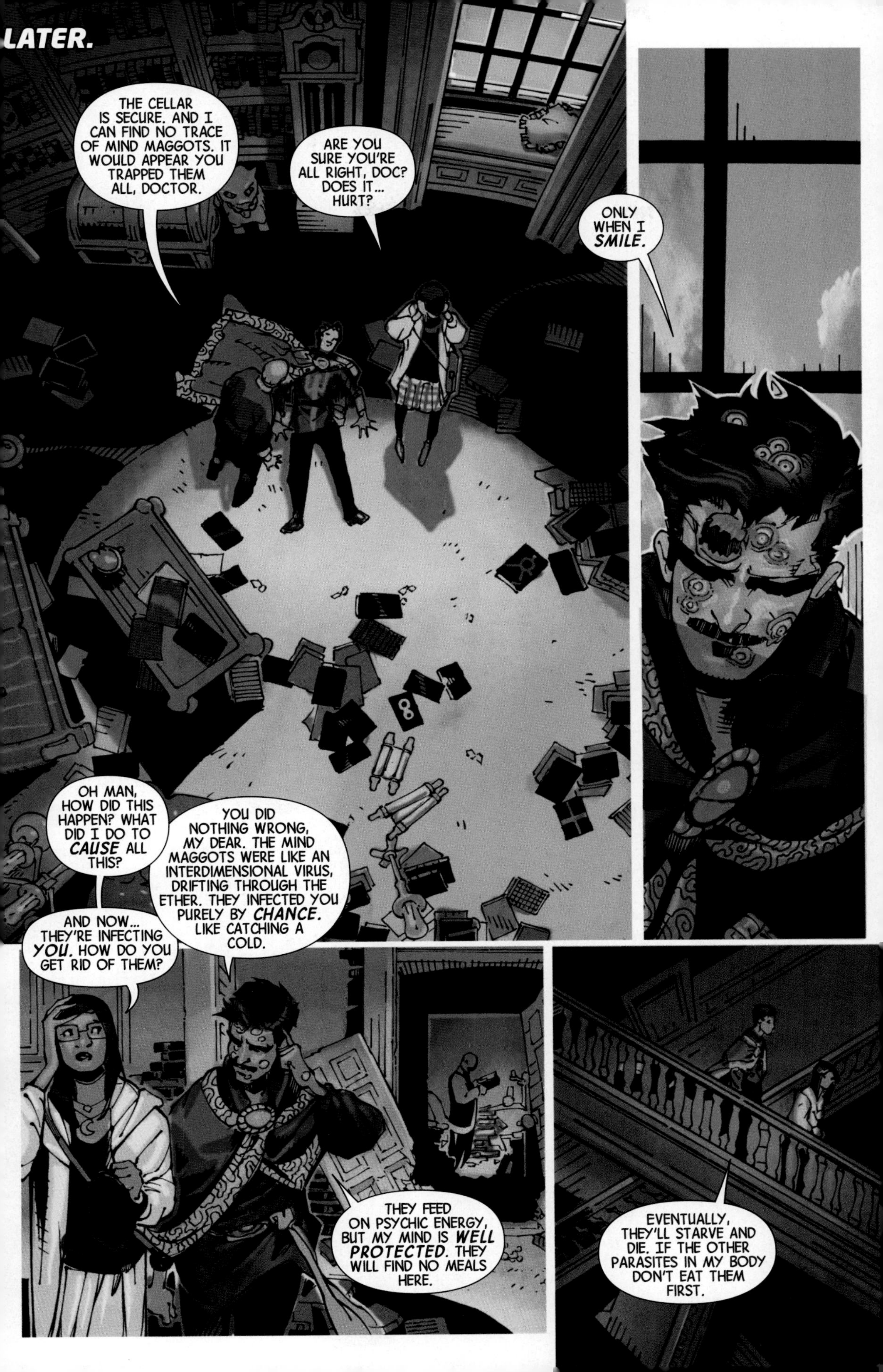
LATER.
THE CELLAR IS SECURE. AND I CAN FIND NO TRACE OF MIND MAGGOTS. IT WOULD APPEAR YOU TRAPPED THEM ALL, DOCTOR.
ARE YOU SURE YOU'RE ALL RIGHT, DOC? DOES IT... HURT?
ONLY WHEN I SMILE.
OH MAN, HOW DID THIS HAPPEN? WHAT DID I DO TO CAUSE ALL THIS?
YOU DID NOTHING WRONG, MY DEAR. THE MIND MAGGOTS WERE LIKE AN INTERDIMENSIONAL VIRUS, DRIFTING THROUGH THE ETHER. THEY INFECTED YOU PURELY BY CHANCE. LIKE CATCHING A COLD.
AND NOW... THEY'RE INFECTING YOU. HOW DO YOU GET RID OF THEM?
THEY FEED ON PSYCHIC ENERGY, BUT MY MIND IS WELL PROTECTED. THEY WILL FIND NO MEALS HERE.
EVENTUALLY, THEY'LL STARVE AND DIE. IF THE OTHER PARASITES IN MY BODY DON'T EAT THEM FIRST.

AND ON *THAT* NOTE...I THINK IT'S TIME I HEAD BACK TO THE BRONX. THANK YOU FOR EVERYTHING, DOC. IT'S BEEN... AN INTERESTING DAY.

INDEED, IT HAS. AND PLEASE, CALL ME *STEPHEN*.

CHMP

OW.

SORRY.

OKAY. WELL. I GUESS I'LL SEE YOU AROUND MAYBE. OR NOT. PROBABLY NOT. BUT ANYWAY...

WOULD YOU LIKE TO COME *SORT MY BOOKS* SOMETIME?

I... WAIT, IT THAT A *EUPHEMISM*?

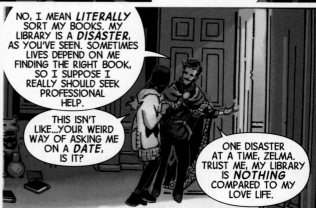

NO, I MEAN *LITERALLY* SORT MY BOOKS. MY LIBRARY IS A *DISASTER*, AS YOU'VE SEEN. SOMETIMES LIVES DEPEND ON ME FINDING THE RIGHT BOOK, SO I SUPPOSE I REALLY SHOULD SEEK PROFESSIONAL HELP.

THIS ISN'T LIKE...YOUR WEIRD WAY OF ASKING ME ON A *DATE*, IS IT?

ONE DISASTER AT A TIME, ZELMA. TRUST ME, MY LIBRARY IS *NOTHING* COMPARED TO MY LOVE LIFE.

THOUGH IF MY LIFE AND HOUSE AND KUNG FU MANSERVANT AND THE MIND-STAGGERING SECRETS OF MY REFRIGERATOR ARE ENTIRELY TOO WEIRD FOR YOU AND YOU WISH *NEVER* TO RETURN...

BELIEVE ME, I'LL UNDERSTAND.

I CAN BE WEIRD FOR ONE DAY A WEEK.

I'M FREE ON SATURDAYS. SEE YA THEN, DOC.

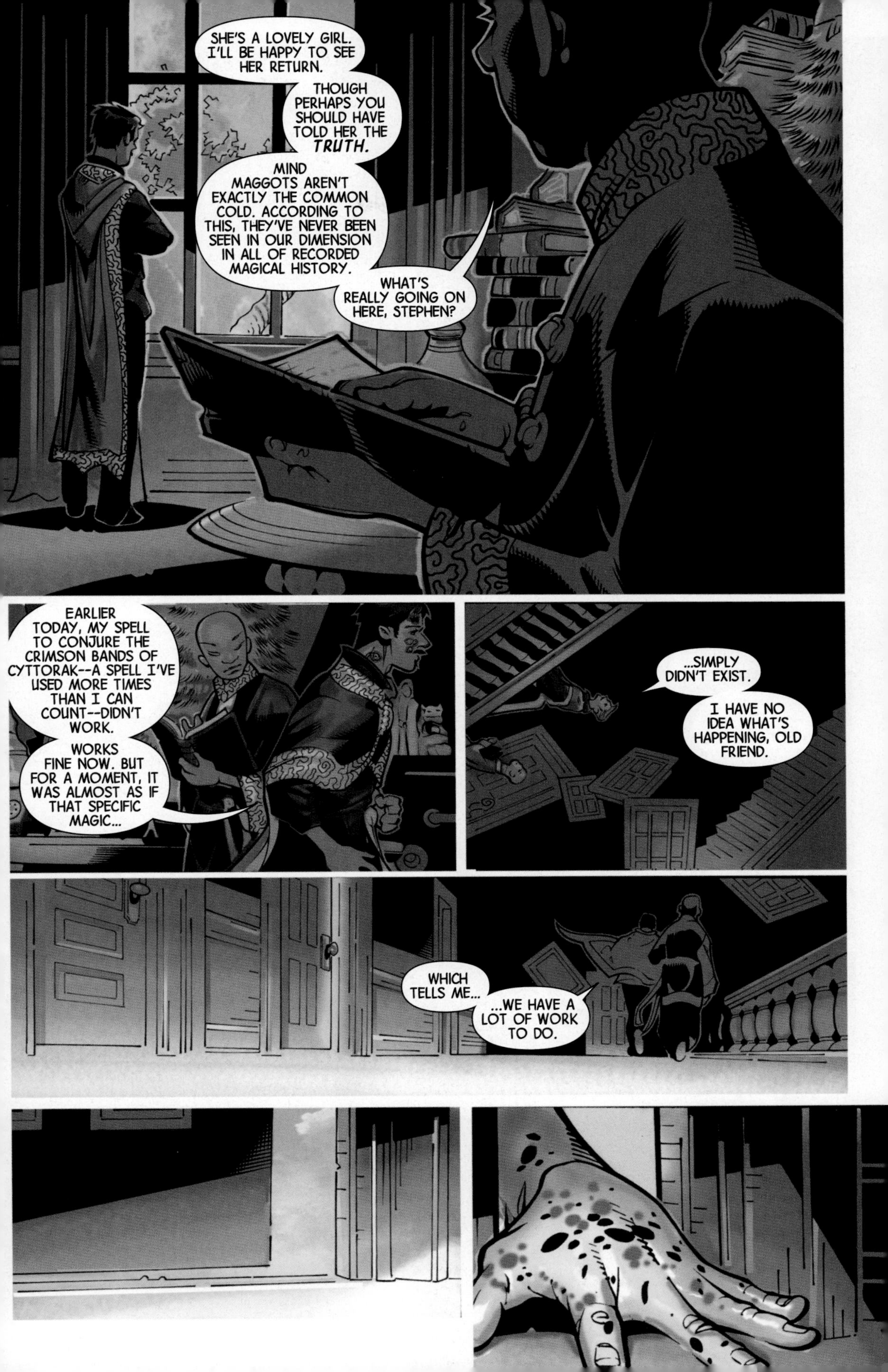
SHE'S A LOVELY GIRL. I'LL BE HAPPY TO SEE HER RETURN.
THOUGH PERHAPS YOU SHOULD HAVE TOLD HER THE TRUTH.
MIND MAGGOTS AREN'T EXACTLY THE COMMON COLD. ACCORDING TO THIS, THEY'VE NEVER BEEN SEEN IN OUR DIMENSION IN ALL OF RECORDED MAGICAL HISTORY.
WHAT'S REALLY GOING ON HERE, STEPHEN?
EARLIER TODAY, MY SPELL TO CONJURE THE CRIMSON BANDS OF CYTTORAK--A SPELL I'VE USED MORE TIMES THAN I CAN COUNT--DIDN'T WORK.
WORKS FINE NOW. BUT FOR A MOMENT, IT WAS ALMOST AS IF THAT SPECIFIC MAGIC...
...SIMPLY DIDN'T EXIST.
I HAVE NO IDEA WHAT'S HAPPENING, OLD FRIEND.
WHICH TELLS ME...
...WE HAVE A LOT OF WORK TO DO.

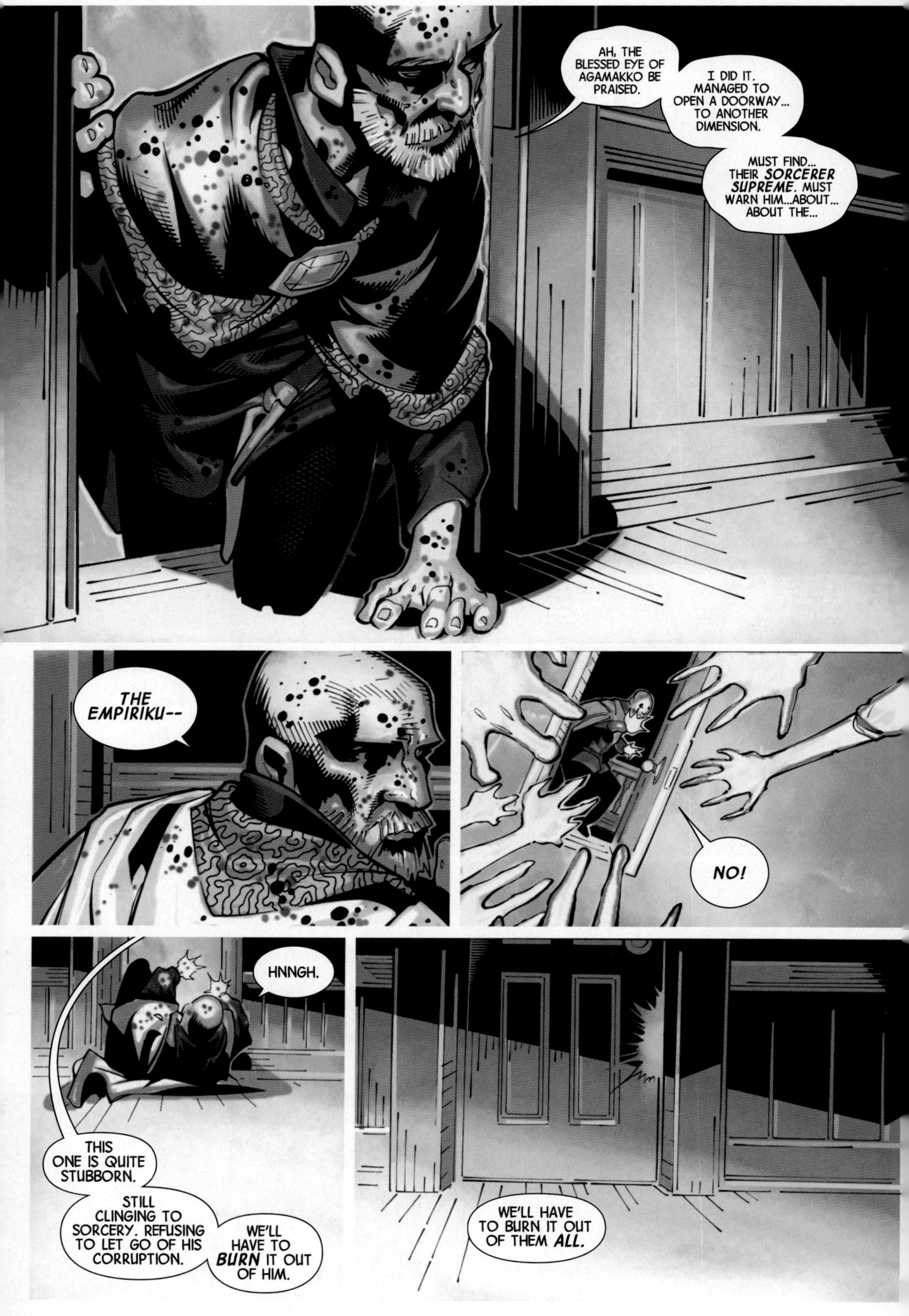
AH, THE BLESSED EYE OF AGAMAKKO BE PRAISED.
I DID IT. MANAGED TO OPEN A DOORWAY... TO ANOTHER DIMENSION.
MUST FIND... THEIR **SORCERER SUPREME**. MUST WARN HIM...ABOUT... ABOUT THE...
**THE EMPIRIKU--**
**NO!**
HNNGH.
THIS ONE IS QUITE STUBBORN.
STILL CLINGING TO SORCERY. REFUSING TO LET GO OF HIS CORRUPTION.
WE'LL HAVE TO **BURN** IT OUT OF HIM.
WE'LL HAVE TO BURN IT OUT OF THEM **ALL.**

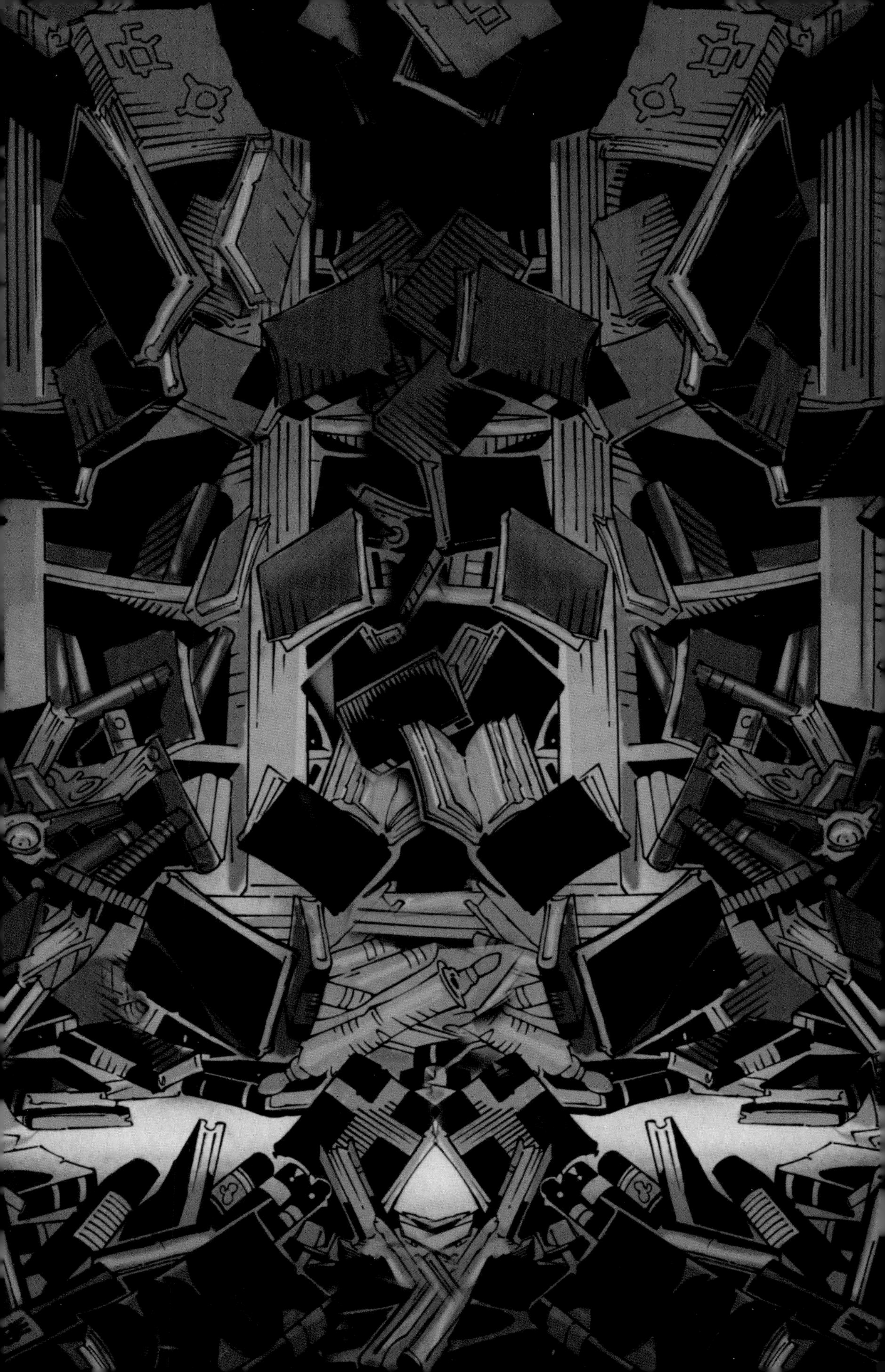

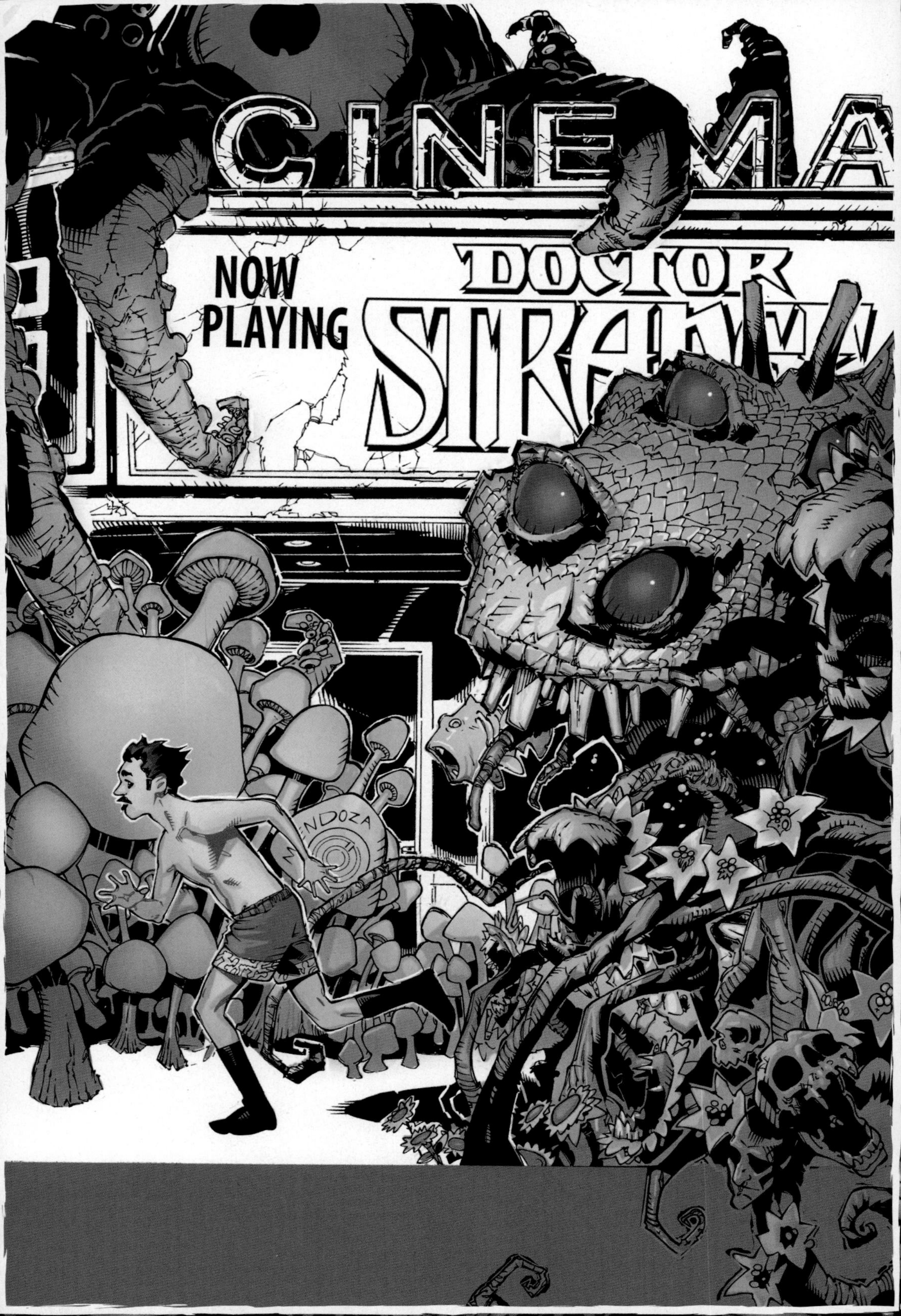
CINEMA
NOW PLAYING
DOCTOR STRANGE
MENDOZA

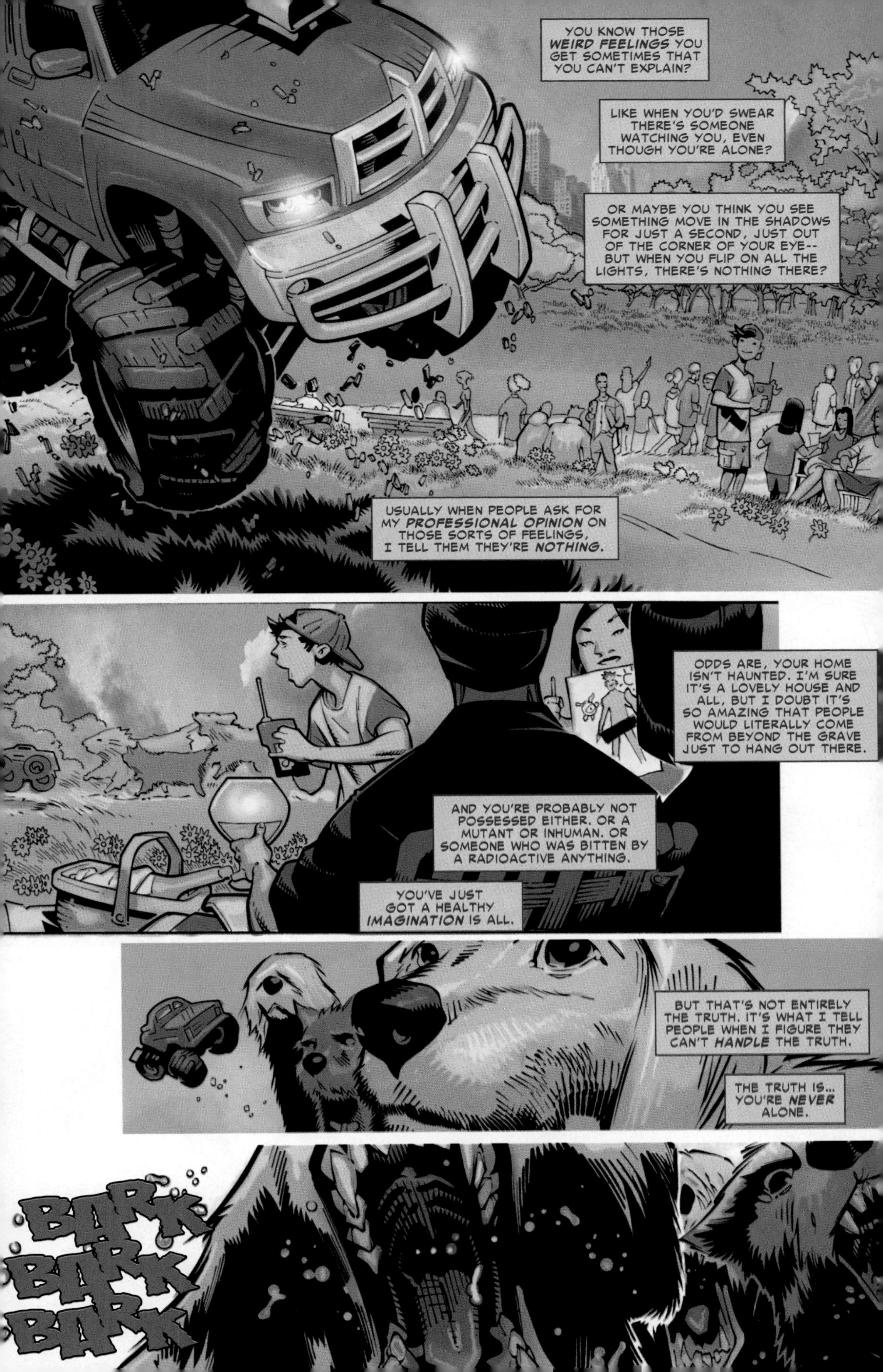
YOU KNOW THOSE WEIRD FEELINGS YOU GET SOMETIMES THAT YOU CAN'T EXPLAIN?
LIKE WHEN YOU'D SWEAR THERE'S SOMEONE WATCHING YOU, EVEN THOUGH YOU'RE ALONE?
OR MAYBE YOU THINK YOU SEE SOMETHING MOVE IN THE SHADOWS FOR JUST A SECOND, JUST OUT OF THE CORNER OF YOUR EYE-- BUT WHEN YOU FLIP ON ALL THE LIGHTS, THERE'S NOTHING THERE?
USUALLY WHEN PEOPLE ASK FOR MY PROFESSIONAL OPINION ON THOSE SORTS OF FEELINGS, I TELL THEM THEY'RE NOTHING.
ODDS ARE, YOUR HOME ISN'T HAUNTED. I'M SURE IT'S A LOVELY HOUSE AND ALL, BUT I DOUBT IT'S SO AMAZING THAT PEOPLE WOULD LITERALLY COME FROM BEYOND THE GRAVE JUST TO HANG OUT THERE.
AND YOU'RE PROBABLY NOT POSSESSED EITHER. OR A MUTANT OR INHUMAN. OR SOMEONE WHO WAS BITTEN BY A RADIOACTIVE ANYTHING.
YOU'VE JUST GOT A HEALTHY IMAGINATION IS ALL.
BUT THAT'S NOT ENTIRELY THE TRUTH. IT'S WHAT I TELL PEOPLE WHEN I FIGURE THEY CAN'T HANDLE THE TRUTH.
THE TRUTH IS... YOU'RE NEVER ALONE.
BARK BARK BARK

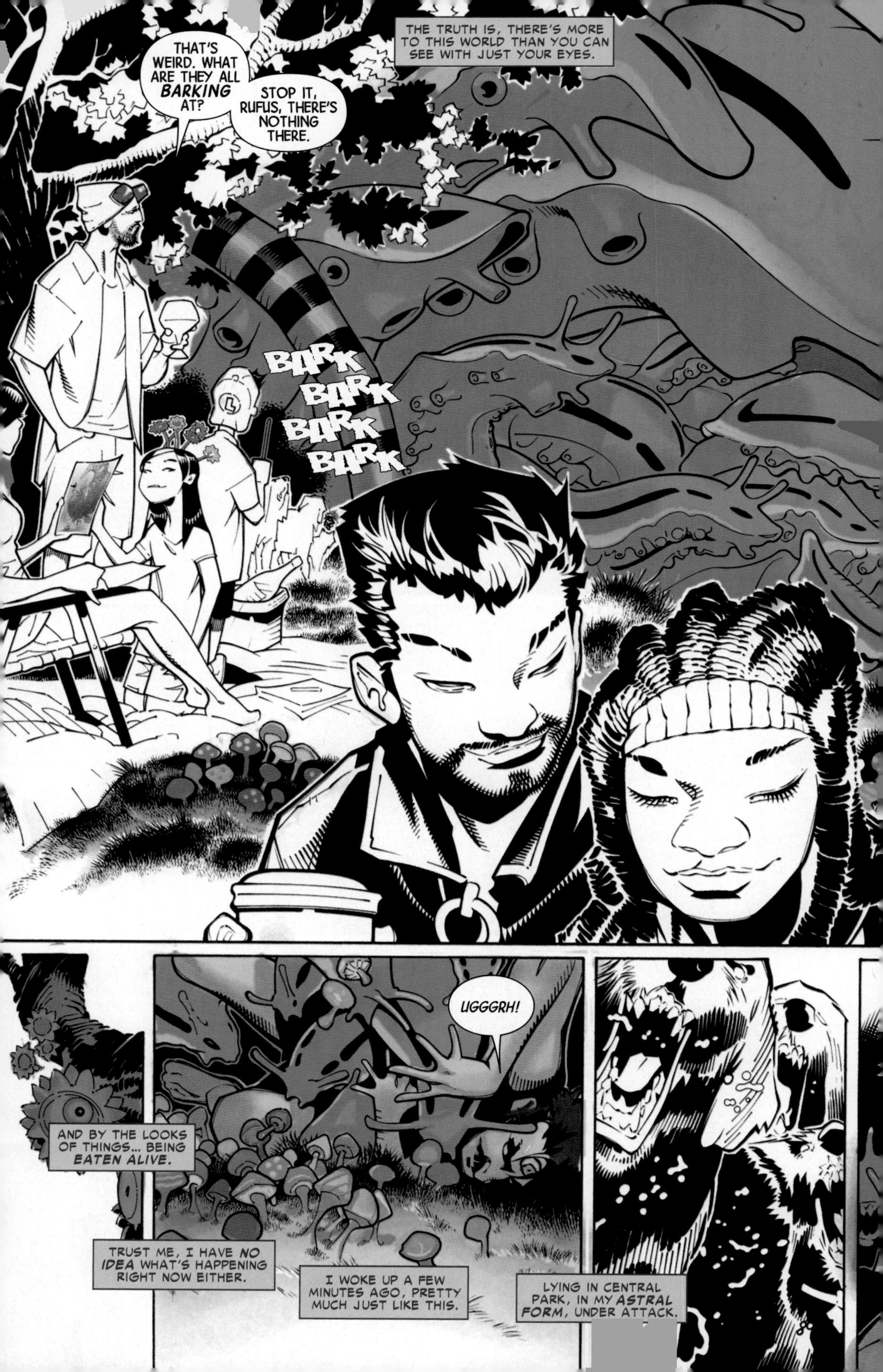
THE TRUTH IS, THERE'S MORE TO THIS WORLD THAN YOU CAN SEE WITH JUST YOUR EYES.
THAT'S WEIRD. WHAT ARE THEY ALL BARKING AT?
STOP IT, RUFUS, THERE'S NOTHING THERE.
BARK BARK BARK BARK
AND BY THE LOOKS OF THINGS... BEING EATEN ALIVE.
UGGGRH!
TRUST ME, I HAVE NO IDEA WHAT'S HAPPENING RIGHT NOW EITHER.
I WOKE UP A FEW MINUTES AGO, PRETTY MUCH JUST LIKE THIS.
LYING IN CENTRAL PARK, IN MY ASTRAL FORM, UNDER ATTACK.

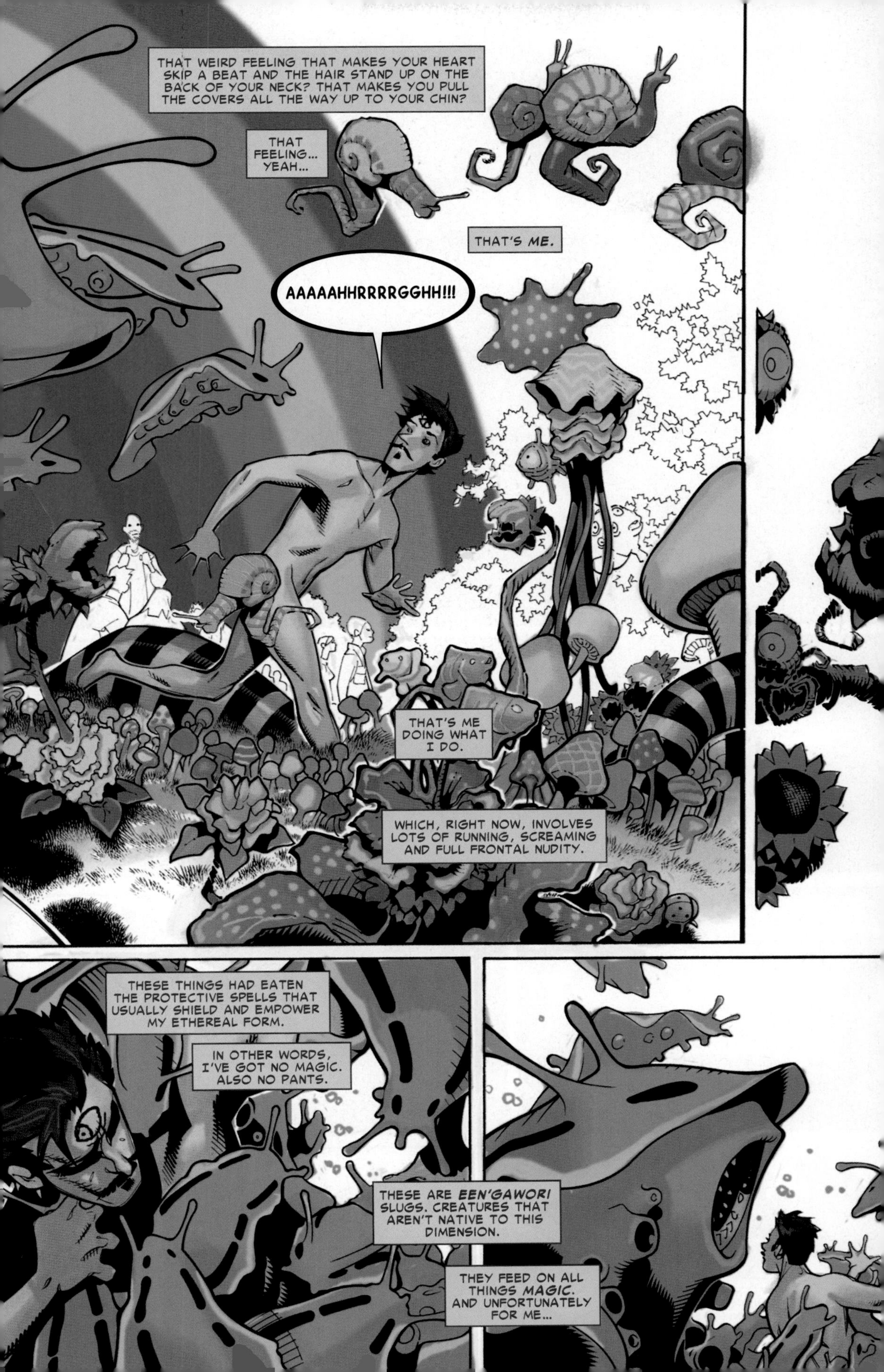
THAT WEIRD FEELING THAT MAKES YOUR HEART SKIP A BEAT AND THE HAIR STAND UP ON THE BACK OF YOUR NECK? THAT MAKES YOU PULL THE COVERS ALL THE WAY UP TO YOUR CHIN?
THAT FEELING... YEAH...
THAT'S *ME.*
AAAAAHHRRRRGGHH!!!
THAT'S ME DOING WHAT I DO.
WHICH, RIGHT NOW, INVOLVES LOTS OF RUNNING, SCREAMING AND FULL FRONTAL NUDITY.
THESE THINGS HAD EATEN THE PROTECTIVE SPELLS THAT USUALLY SHIELD AND EMPOWER MY ETHEREAL FORM.
IN OTHER WORDS, I'VE GOT NO MAGIC. ALSO NO PANTS.
THESE ARE *EEN'GAWORI* SLUGS. CREATURES THAT AREN'T NATIVE TO THIS DIMENSION.
THEY FEED ON ALL THINGS *MAGIC.* AND UNFORTUNATELY FOR ME...

THEY'RE STARVING.

HEY. I KNOW THAT AXE.

BUT SORCERER SUPREME ISN'T ON THE MENU.

NOT TODAY.

RRRGH!

THE AXE OF ANGARRUUMUS.

VERY ANCIENT. VERY POWERFUL.

I FOUND IT IN A WITCH'S CRYPT IN THE CENTER OF THE MOON.

IT HUMS WITH MAGIC.

AS THESE POOR CREATURES SCREAM IN PAIN.

WOOF?

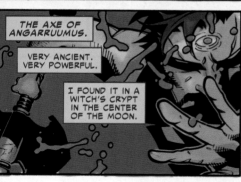

THEY'RE NOT EVIL, THESE SLUGS, THEY'RE NOT MONSTERS.

YIP YIP

THEY'RE JUST HUNGRY ANIMALS TRYING TO FILL THEIR EMPTY BELLIES.

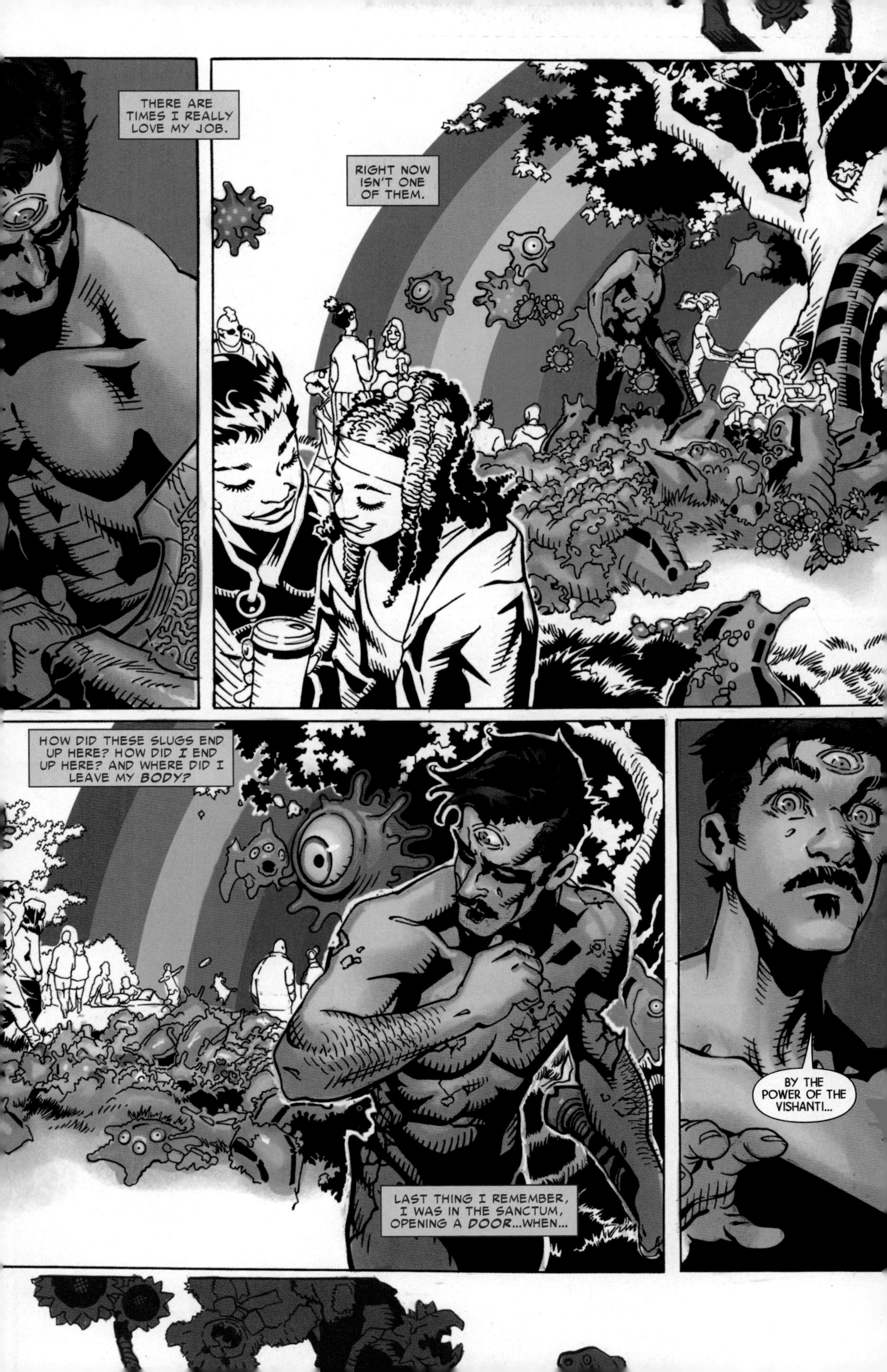

THERE ARE TIMES I REALLY LOVE MY JOB.
RIGHT NOW ISN'T ONE OF THEM.
HOW DID THESE SLUGS END UP HERE? HOW DID *I* END UP HERE? AND WHERE DID I LEAVE MY *BODY?*
LAST THING I REMEMBER, I WAS IN THE SANCTUM, OPENING A *DOOR*...WHEN...
BY THE POWER OF THE VISHANTI...

THEY'VE *INFESTED* THE WHOLE CITY.

NORMALLY A BUSY STREET LIKE THIS WOULD BE *TEEMING* WITH MAGICAL LIFE.

INTERDIMENSIONAL BACTERIA. MYSTICAL ALGAE.

THE SLUGS HAVE SCARED ALMOST ALL OF IT AWAY. OR *EATEN* IT.

HEY! *SOUP'S ON,* SUCK-HEADS!

IF THESE THINGS WANT A MAGICAL NEW YORK MEAL, I SUPPOSE I'LL JUST HAVE TO *GIVE* THEM ONE.

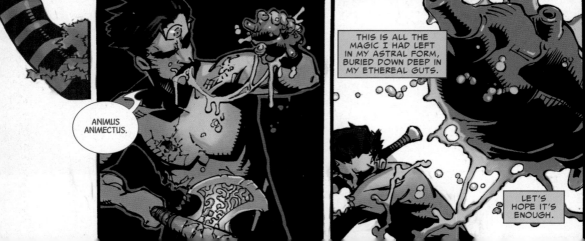

ANIMUS ANIMECTUS.

THIS IS ALL THE MAGIC I HAD LEFT IN MY ASTRAL FORM, BURIED DOWN DEEP IN MY ETHEREAL GUTS.

LET'S HOPE IT'S ENOUGH.

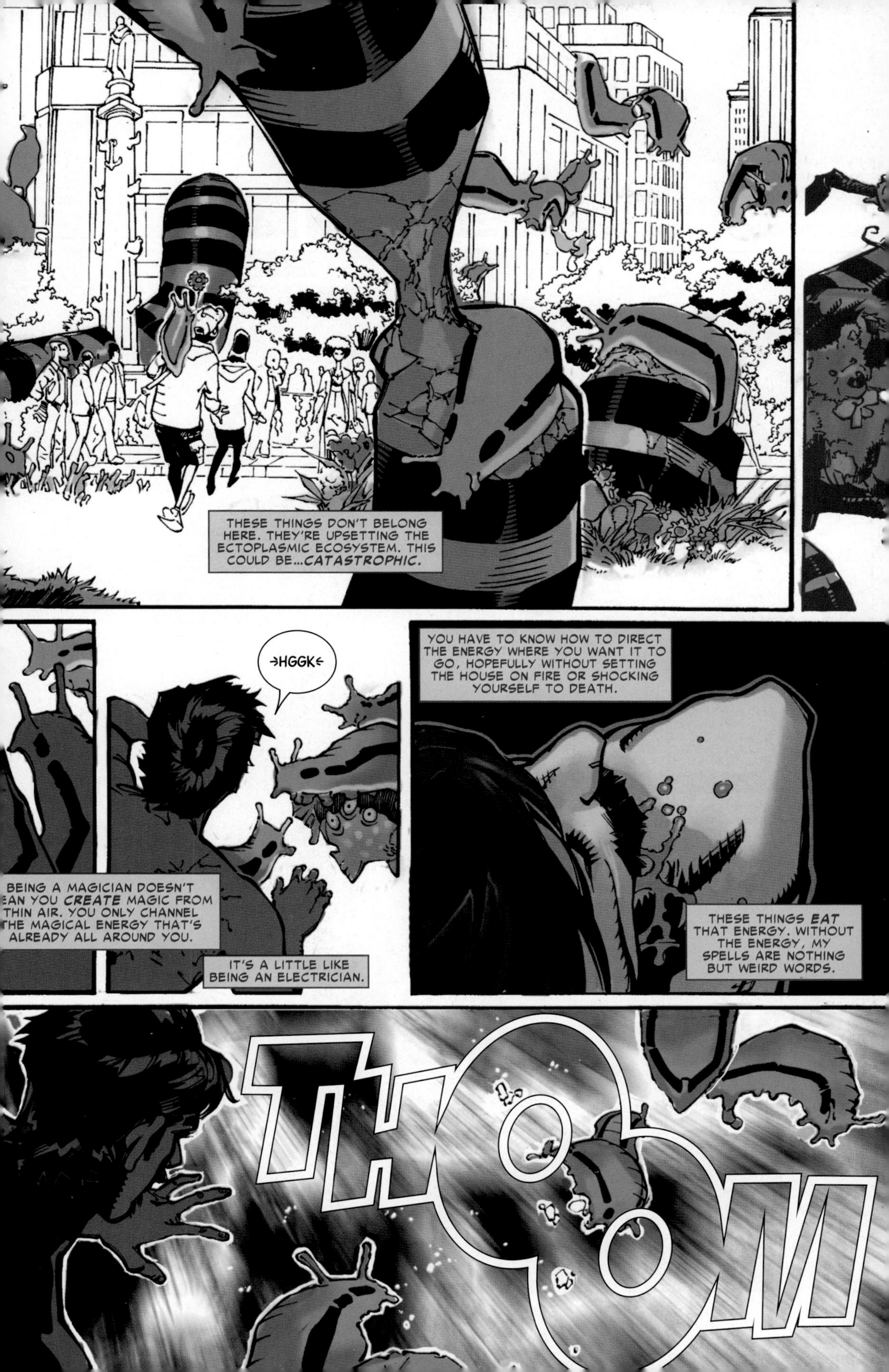
THESE THINGS DON'T BELONG HERE. THEY'RE UPSETTING THE ECTOPLASMIC ECOSYSTEM. THIS COULD BE...CATASTROPHIC.
HGGK
BEING A MAGICIAN DOESN'T EAN YOU CREATE MAGIC FROM THIN AIR. YOU ONLY CHANNEL THE MAGICAL ENERGY THAT'S ALREADY ALL AROUND YOU.
IT'S A LITTLE LIKE BEING AN ELECTRICIAN.
YOU HAVE TO KNOW HOW TO DIRECT THE ENERGY WHERE YOU WANT IT TO GO, HOPEFULLY WITHOUT SETTING THE HOUSE ON FIRE OR SHOCKING YOURSELF TO DEATH.
THESE THINGS EAT THAT ENERGY. WITHOUT THE ENERGY, MY SPELLS ARE NOTHING BUT WEIRD WORDS.
THOOOM

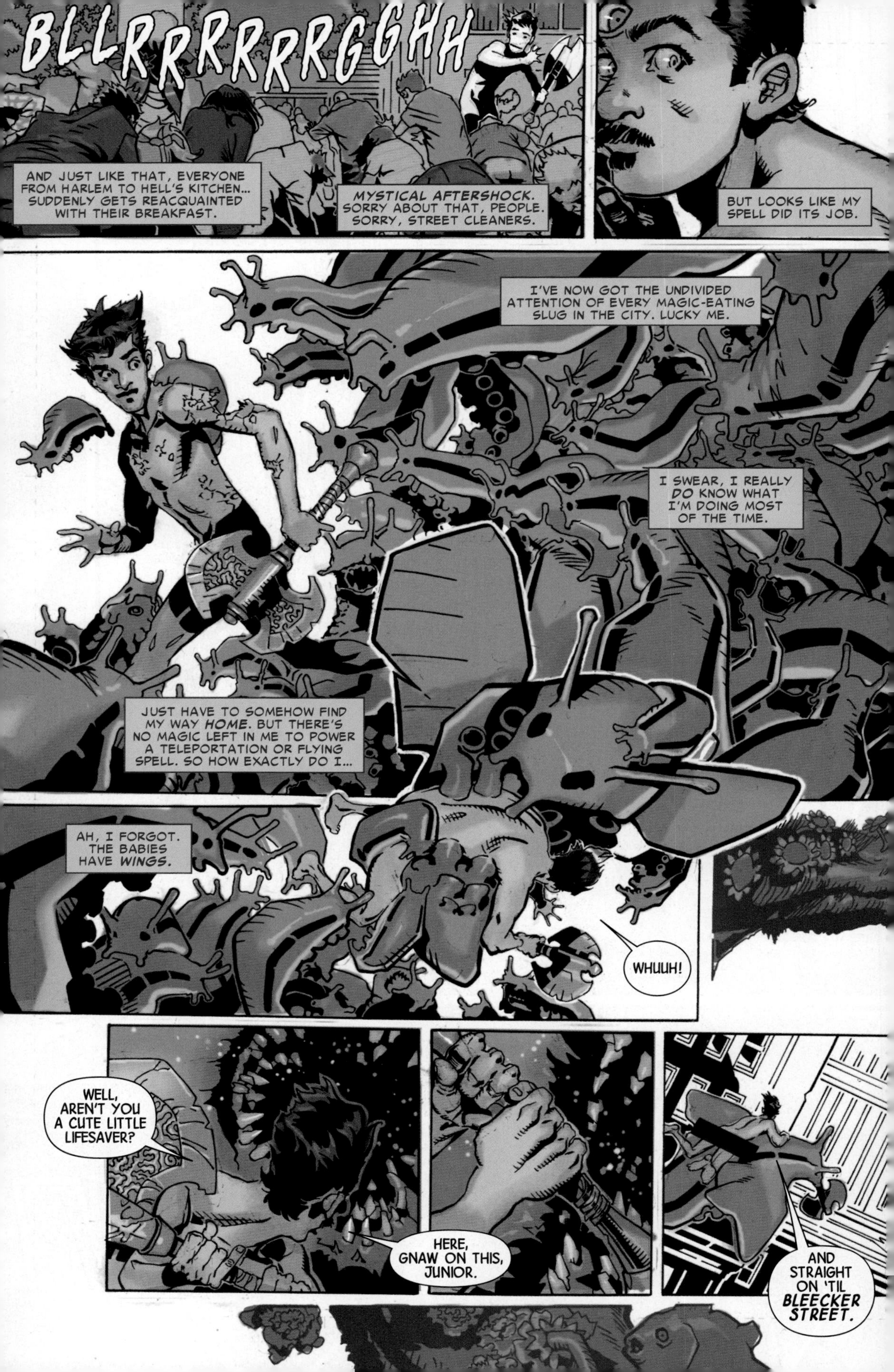
BLLRRRRRRGGHH
AND JUST LIKE THAT, EVERYONE FROM HARLEM TO HELL'S KITCHEN... SUDDENLY GETS REACQUAINTED WITH THEIR BREAKFAST.
MYSTICAL AFTERSHOCK. SORRY ABOUT THAT, PEOPLE. SORRY, STREET CLEANERS.
BUT LOOKS LIKE MY SPELL DID ITS JOB.
I'VE NOW GOT THE UNDIVIDED ATTENTION OF EVERY MAGIC-EATING SLUG IN THE CITY. LUCKY ME.
I SWEAR, I REALLY DO KNOW WHAT I'M DOING MOST OF THE TIME.
JUST HAVE TO SOMEHOW FIND MY WAY HOME. BUT THERE'S NO MAGIC LEFT IN ME TO POWER A TELEPORTATION OR FLYING SPELL. SO HOW EXACTLY DO I...
AH, I FORGOT. THE BABIES HAVE WINGS.
WHUUH!
WELL, AREN'T YOU A CUTE LITTLE LIFESAVER?
HERE, GNAW ON THIS, JUNIOR.
AND STRAIGHT ON 'TIL BLEECKER STREET.

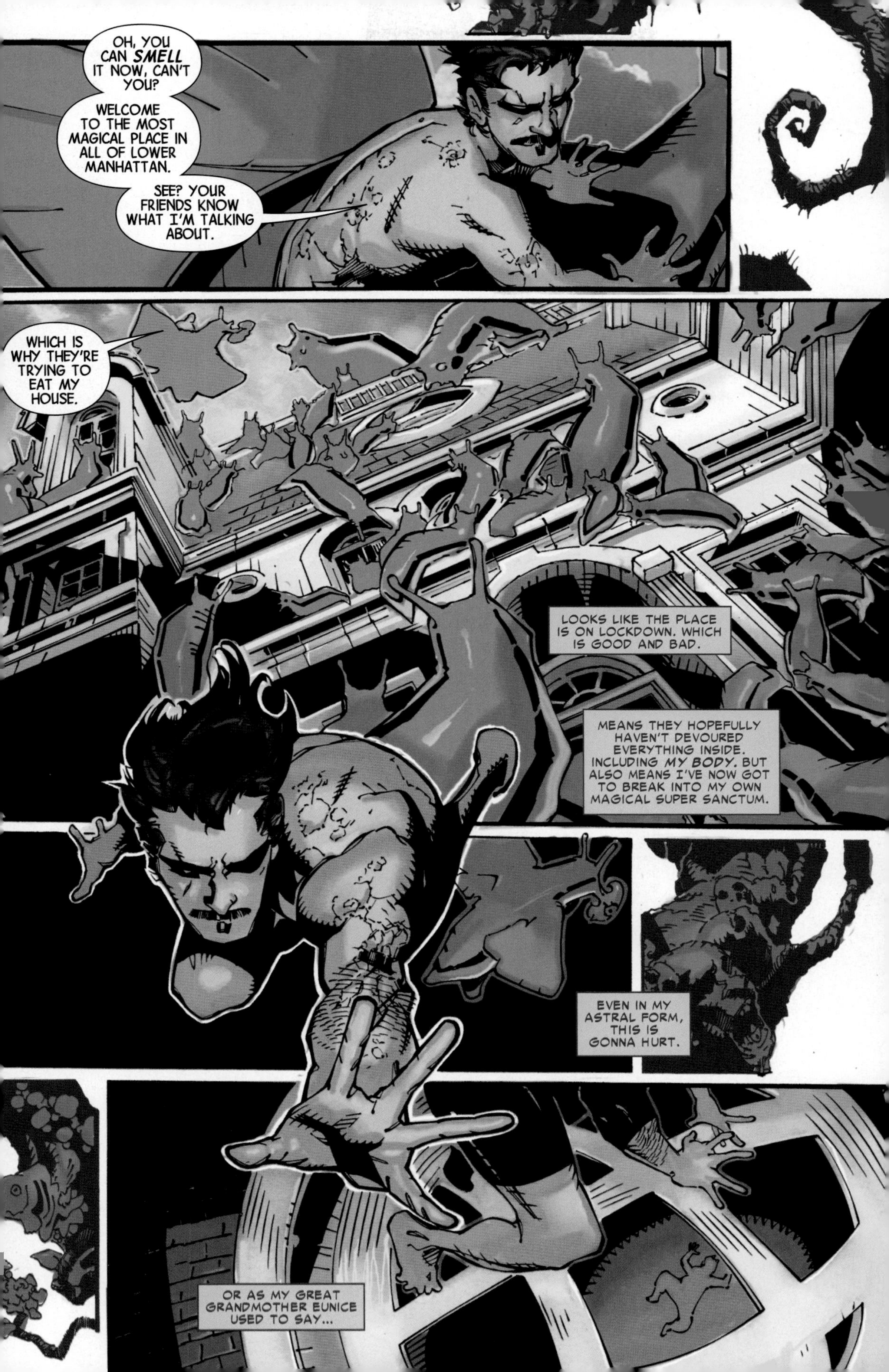
OH, YOU CAN SMELL IT NOW, CAN'T YOU?
WELCOME TO THE MOST MAGICAL PLACE IN ALL OF LOWER MANHATTAN.
SEE? YOUR FRIENDS KNOW WHAT I'M TALKING ABOUT.
WHICH IS WHY THEY'RE TRYING TO EAT MY HOUSE.
LOOKS LIKE THE PLACE IS ON LOCKDOWN. WHICH IS GOOD AND BAD.
MEANS THEY HOPEFULLY HAVEN'T DEVOURED EVERYTHING INSIDE. INCLUDING MY BODY. BUT ALSO MEANS I'VE NOW GOT TO BREAK INTO MY OWN MAGICAL SUPER SANCTUM.
EVEN IN MY ASTRAL FORM, THIS IS GONNA HURT.
OR AS MY GREAT GRANDMOTHER EUNICE USED TO SAY...

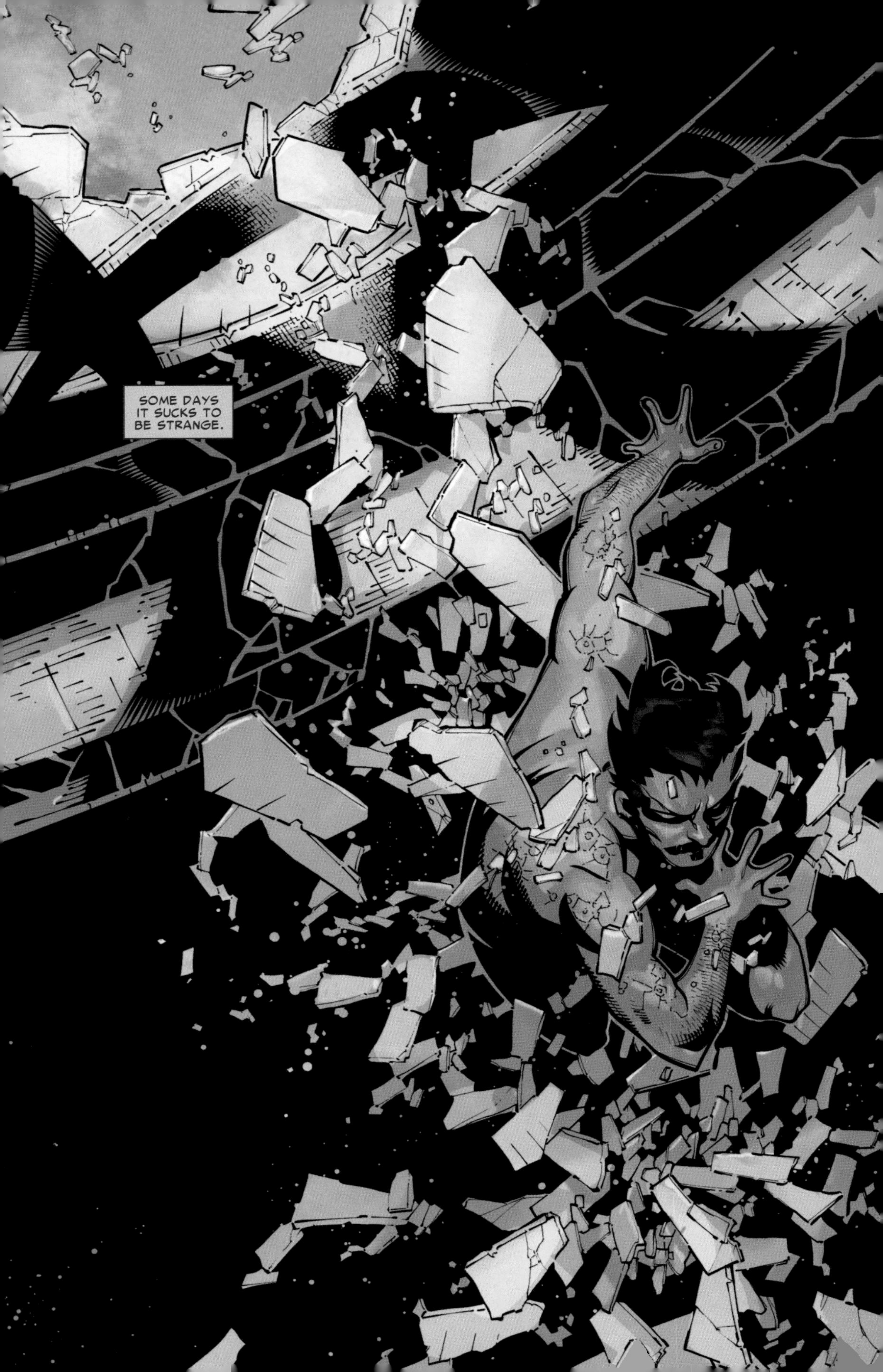
SOME DAYS IT SUCKS TO BE STRANGE.

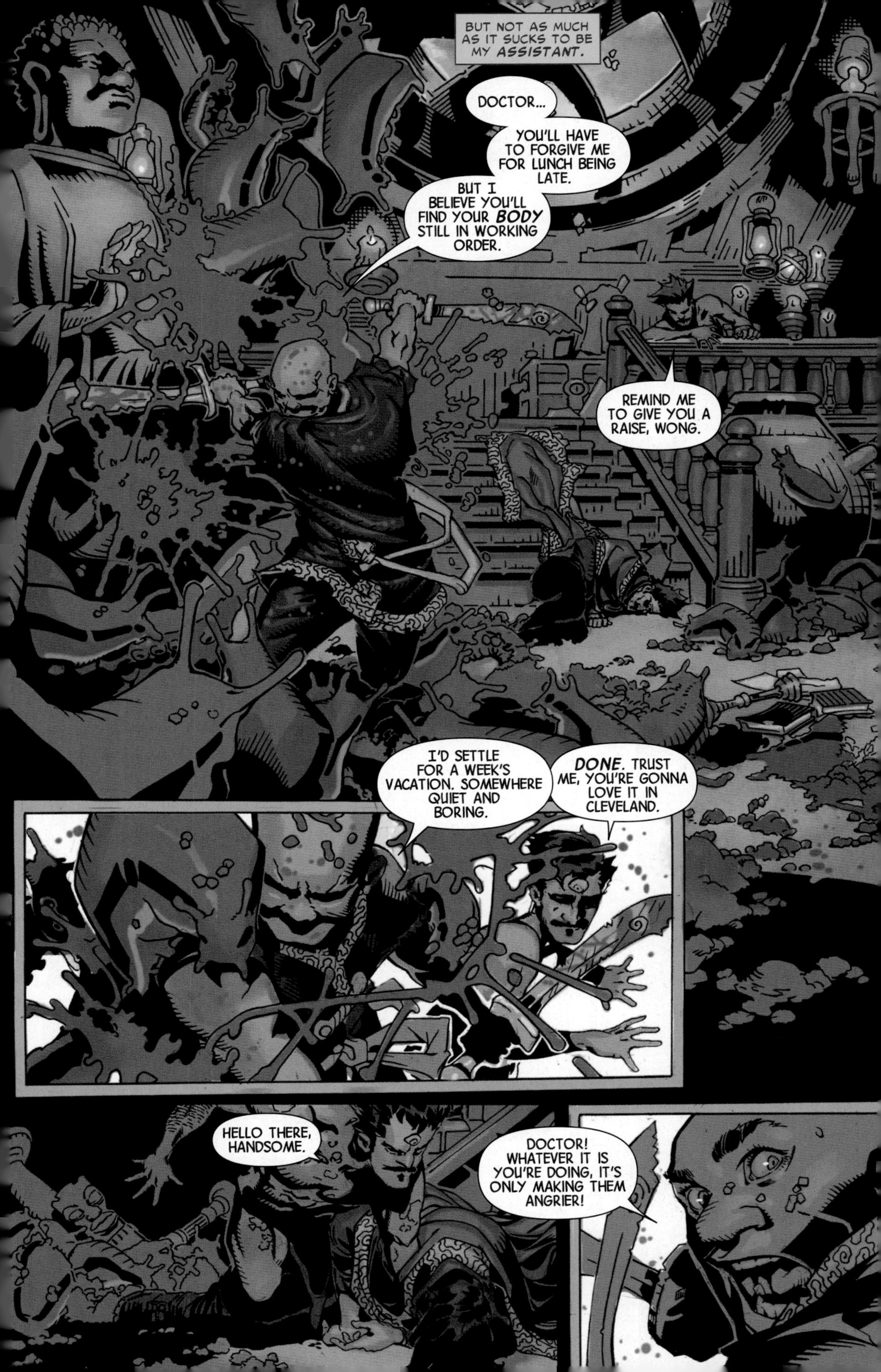
BUT NOT AS MUCH AS IT SUCKS TO BE MY ASSISTANT.
DOCTOR...
YOU'LL HAVE TO FORGIVE ME FOR LUNCH BEING LATE.
BUT I BELIEVE YOU'LL FIND YOUR BODY STILL IN WORKING ORDER.
REMIND ME TO GIVE YOU A RAISE, WONG.
I'D SETTLE FOR A WEEK'S VACATION. SOMEWHERE QUIET AND BORING.
DONE. TRUST ME, YOU'RE GONNA LOVE IT IN CLEVELAND.
HELLO THERE, HANDSOME.
DOCTOR! WHATEVER IT IS YOU'RE DOING, IT'S ONLY MAKING THEM ANGRIER!

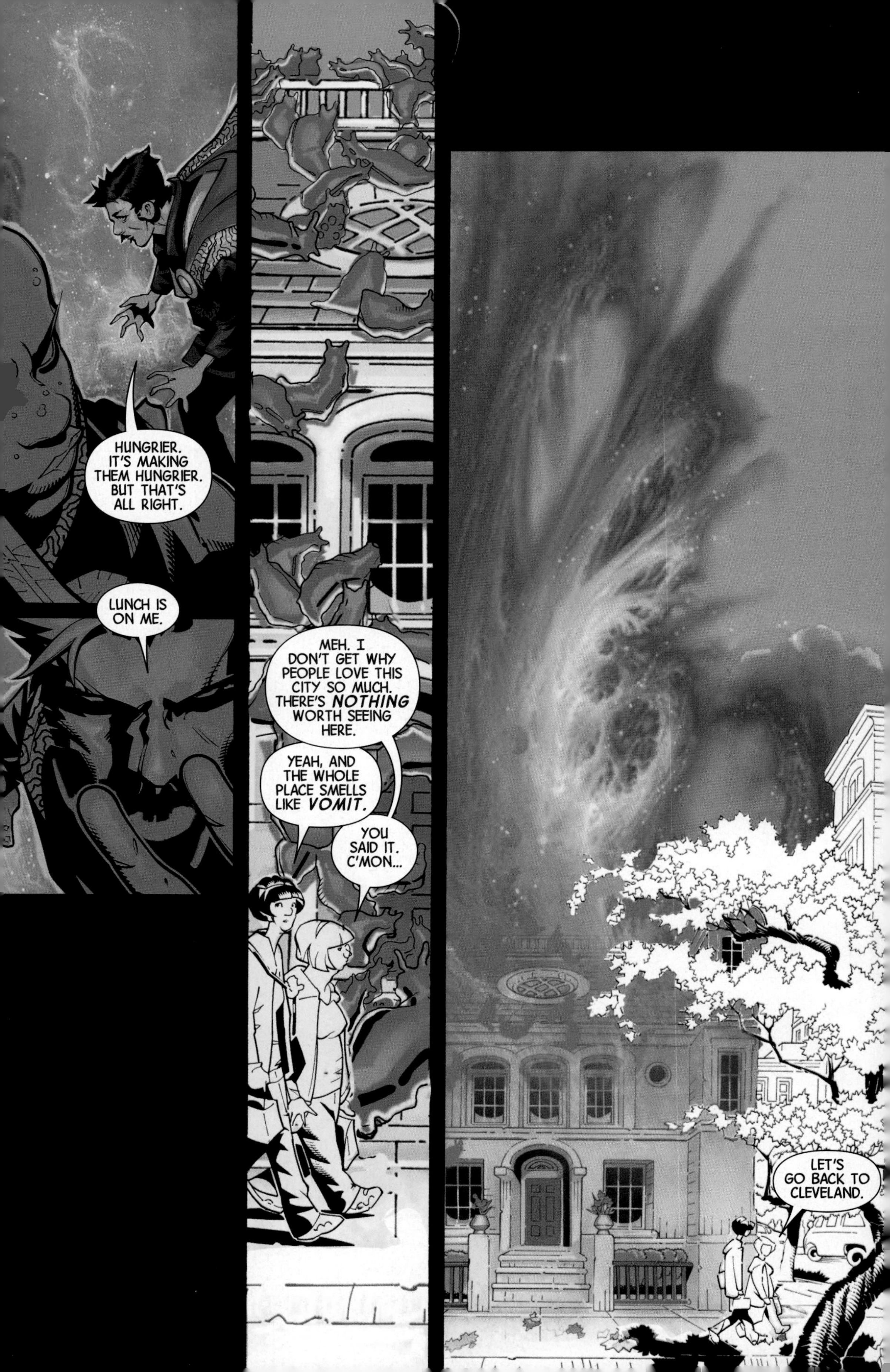
HUNGRIER. IT'S MAKING THEM HUNGRIER. BUT THAT'S ALL RIGHT.
LUNCH IS ON ME.
MEH. I DON'T GET WHY PEOPLE LOVE THIS CITY SO MUCH. THERE'S NOTHING WORTH SEEING HERE.
YEAH, AND THE WHOLE PLACE SMELLS LIKE VOMIT.
YOU SAID IT. C'MON...
LET'S GO BACK TO CLEVELAND.

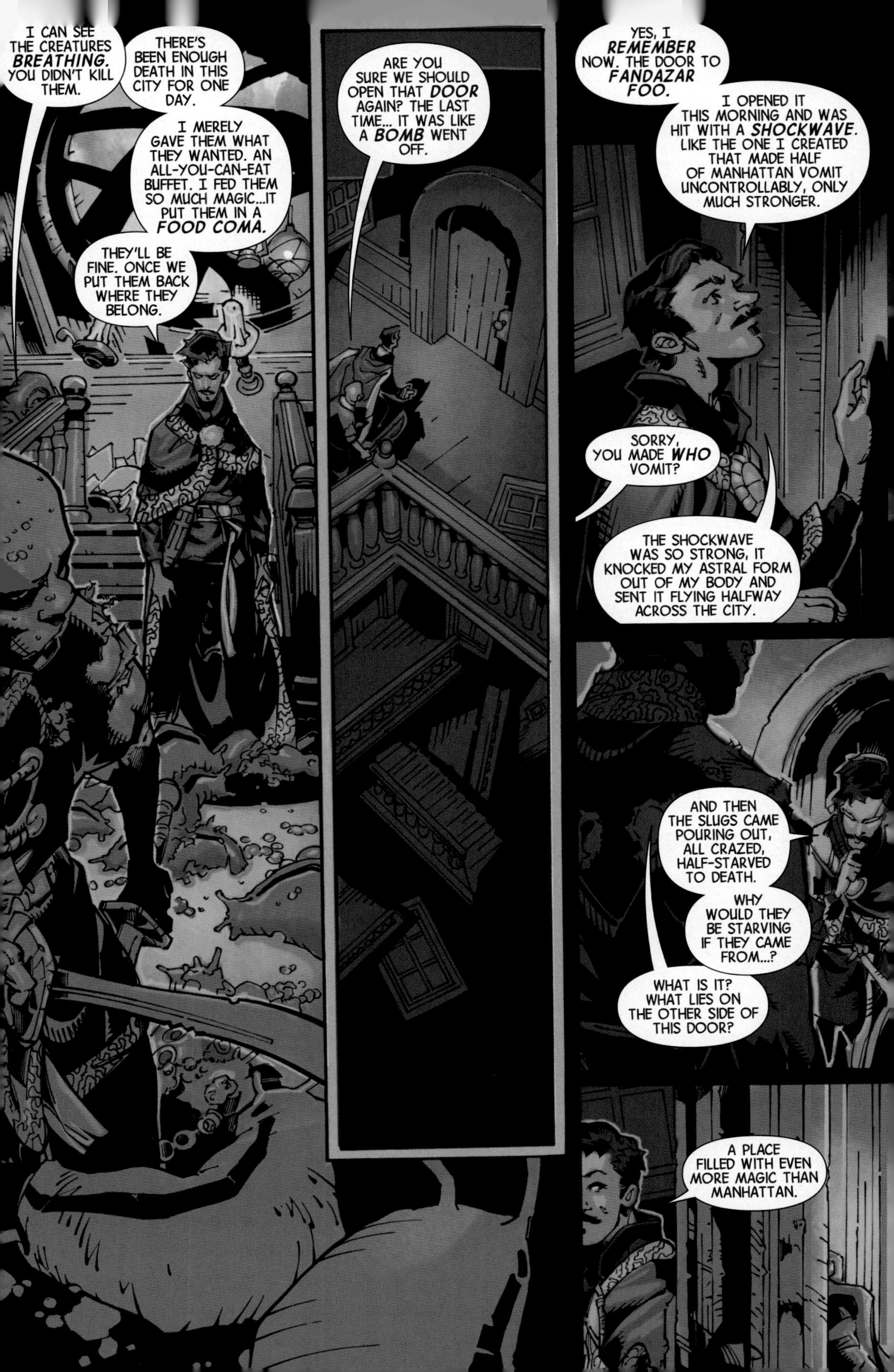
I CAN SEE THE CREATURES BREATHING. YOU DIDN'T KILL THEM.
THERE'S BEEN ENOUGH DEATH IN THIS CITY FOR ONE DAY.
I MERELY GAVE THEM WHAT THEY WANTED. AN ALL-YOU-CAN-EAT BUFFET. I FED THEM SO MUCH MAGIC...IT PUT THEM IN A FOOD COMA.
THEY'LL BE FINE. ONCE WE PUT THEM BACK WHERE THEY BELONG.
ARE YOU SURE WE SHOULD OPEN THAT DOOR AGAIN? THE LAST TIME... IT WAS LIKE A BOMB WENT OFF.
YES, I REMEMBER NOW. THE DOOR TO FANDAZAR FOO.
I OPENED IT THIS MORNING AND WAS HIT WITH A SHOCKWAVE. LIKE THE ONE I CREATED THAT MADE HALF OF MANHATTAN VOMIT UNCONTROLLABLY, ONLY MUCH STRONGER.
SORRY, YOU MADE WHO VOMIT?
THE SHOCKWAVE WAS SO STRONG, IT KNOCKED MY ASTRAL FORM OUT OF MY BODY AND SENT IT FLYING HALFWAY ACROSS THE CITY.
AND THEN THE SLUGS CAME POURING OUT, ALL CRAZED, HALF-STARVED TO DEATH.
WHY WOULD THEY BE STARVING IF THEY CAME FROM...?
WHAT IS IT? WHAT LIES ON THE OTHER SIDE OF THIS DOOR?
A PLACE FILLED WITH EVEN MORE MAGIC THAN MANHATTAN.

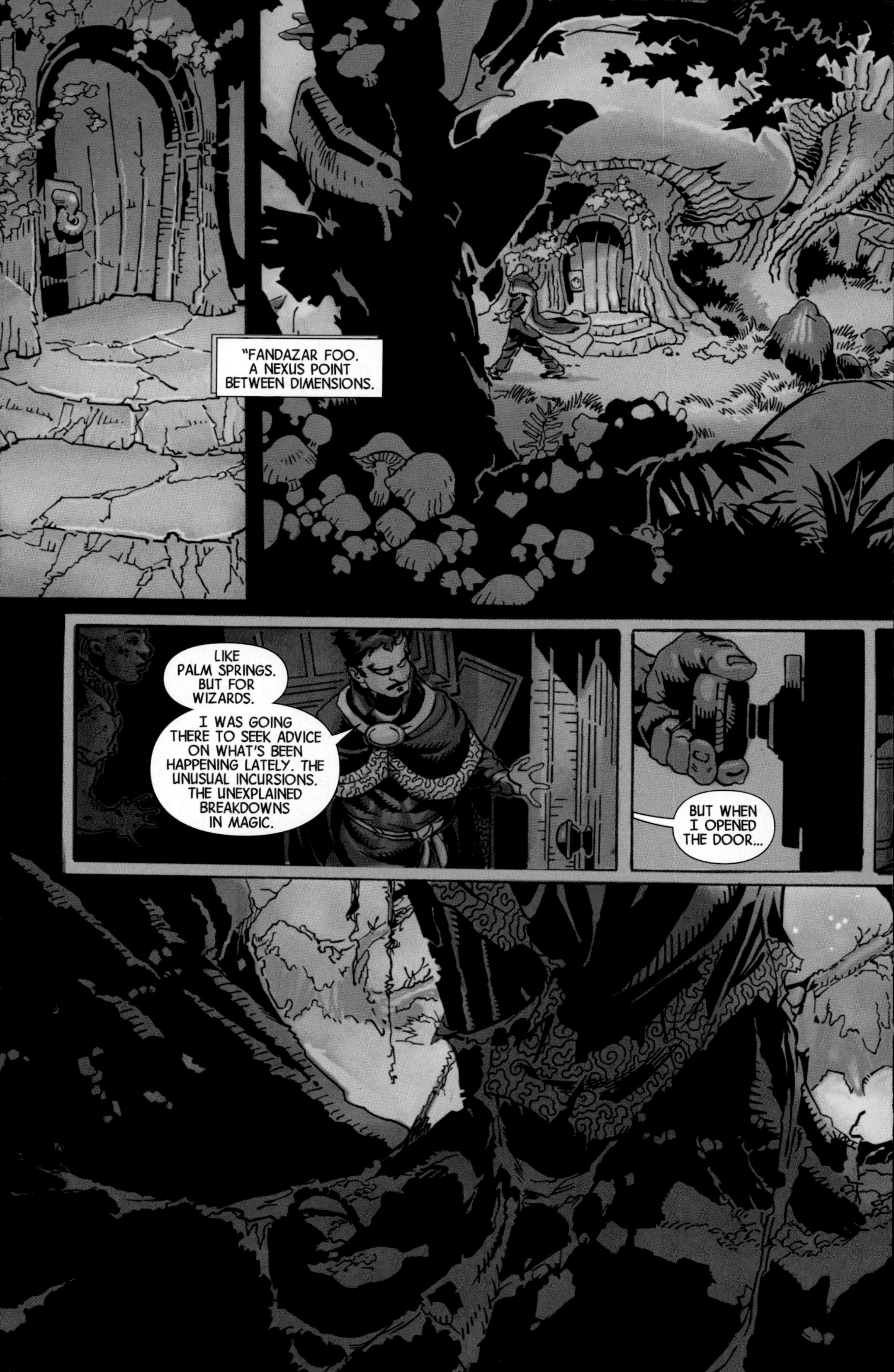
"FANDAZAR FOO. A NEXUS POINT BETWEEN DIMENSIONS.
LIKE PALM SPRINGS. BUT FOR WIZARDS.
I WAS GOING THERE TO SEEK ADVICE ON WHAT'S BEEN HAPPENING LATELY. THE UNUSUAL INCURSIONS. THE UNEXPLAINED BREAKDOWNS IN MAGIC.
BUT WHEN I OPENED THE DOOR...

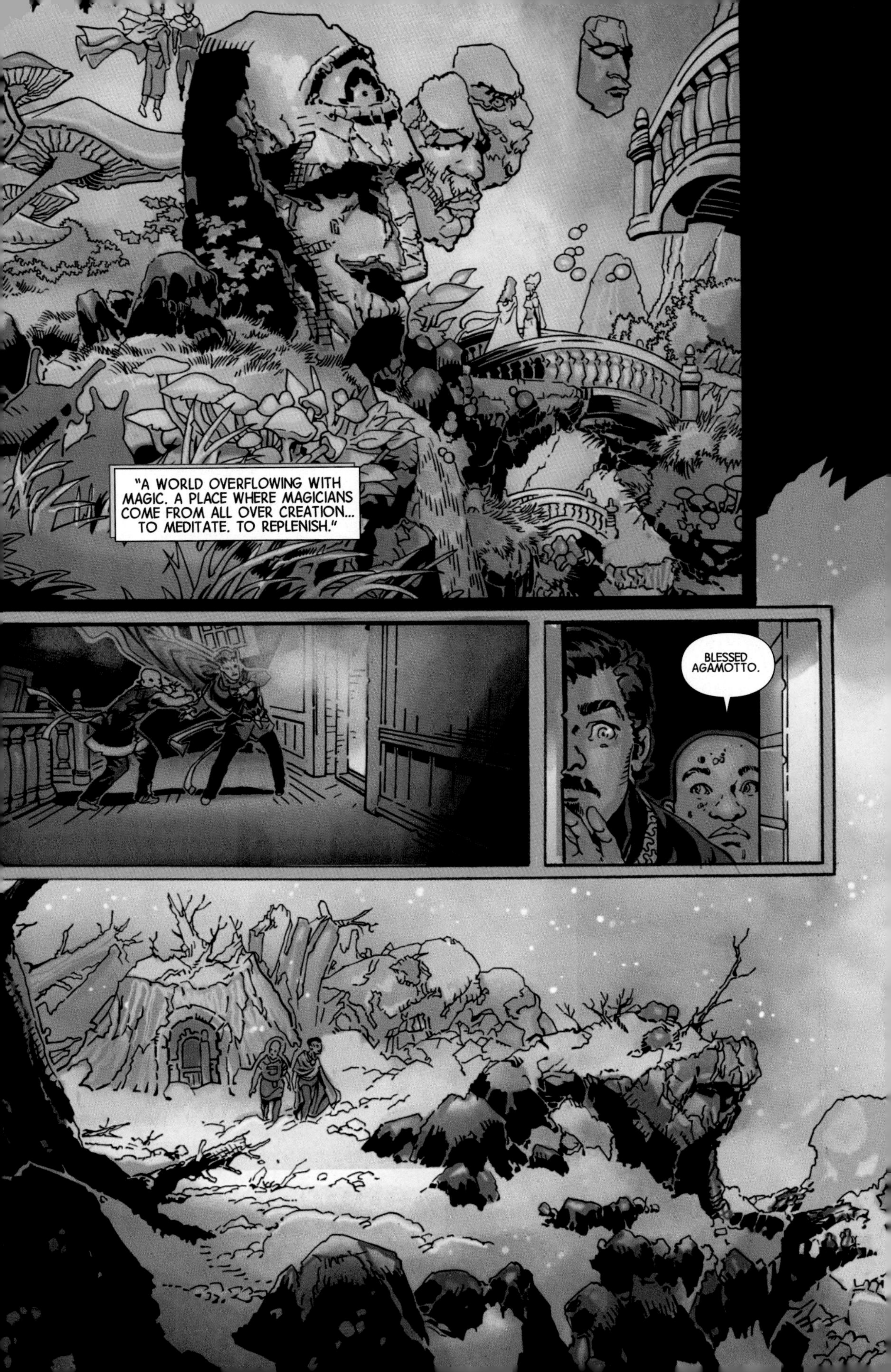
"A WORLD OVERFLOWING WITH MAGIC. A PLACE WHERE MAGICIANS COME FROM ALL OVER CREATION... TO MEDITATE. TO REPLENISH."
BLESSED AGAMOTTO.

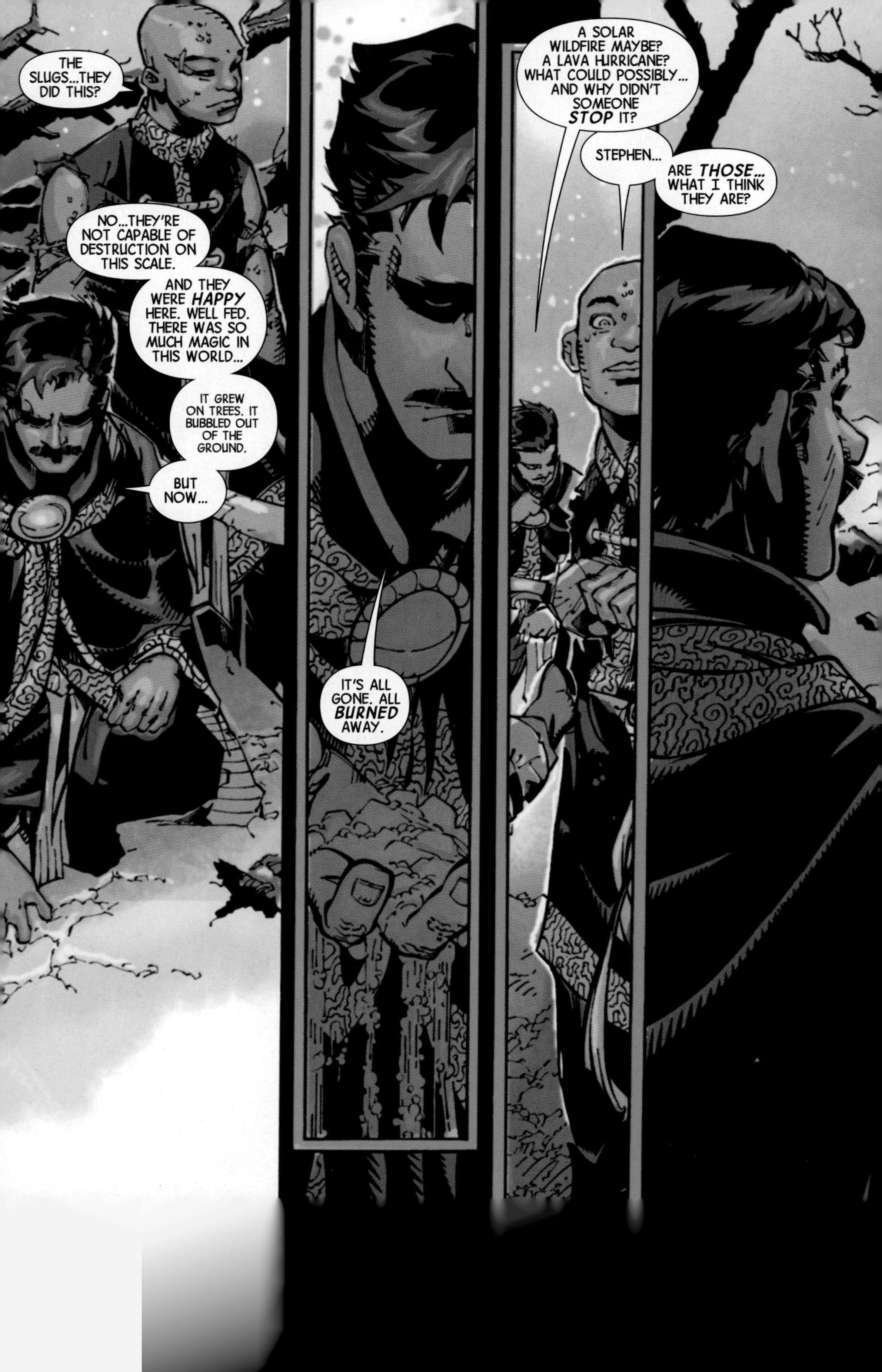
THE SLUGS...THEY DID THIS?
NO...THEY'RE NOT CAPABLE OF DESTRUCTION ON THIS SCALE.
AND THEY WERE HAPPY HERE. WELL FED. THERE WAS SO MUCH MAGIC IN THIS WORLD...
IT GREW ON TREES. IT BUBBLED OUT OF THE GROUND.
BUT NOW...
IT'S ALL GONE. ALL BURNED AWAY.
A SOLAR WILDFIRE MAYBE? A LAVA HURRICANE? WHAT COULD POSSIBLY... AND WHY DIDN'T SOMEONE STOP IT?
STEPHEN...
ARE THOSE... WHAT I THINK THEY ARE?

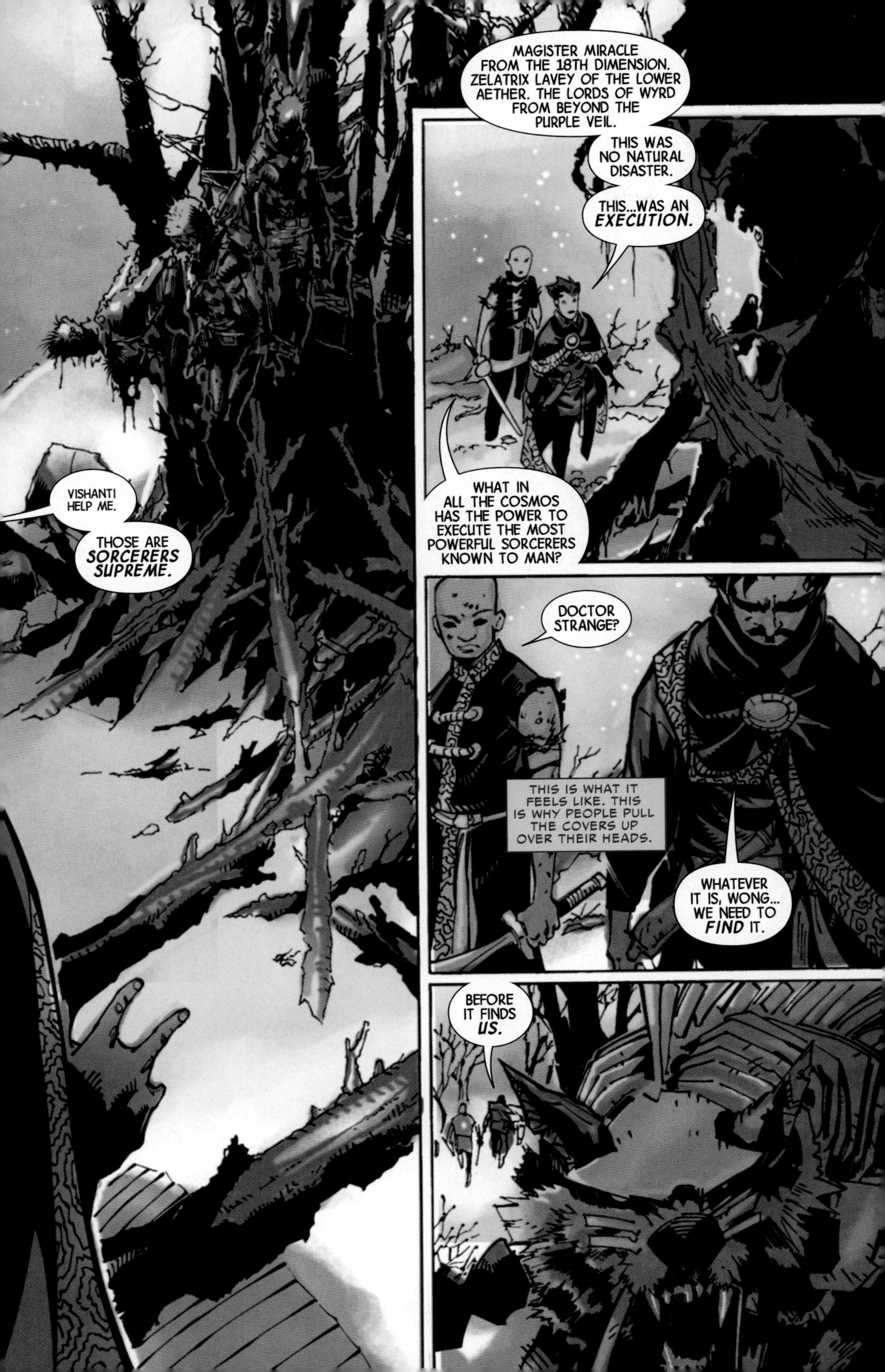
MAGISTER MIRACLE FROM THE 18TH DIMENSION. ZELATRIX LAVEY OF THE LOWER AETHER. THE LORDS OF WYRD FROM BEYOND THE PURPLE VEIL.
THIS WAS NO NATURAL DISASTER.
THIS...WAS AN EXECUTION.
VISHANTI HELP ME.
THOSE ARE SORCERERS SUPREME.
WHAT IN ALL THE COSMOS HAS THE POWER TO EXECUTE THE MOST POWERFUL SORCERERS KNOWN TO MAN?
DOCTOR STRANGE?
THIS IS WHAT IT FEELS LIKE. THIS IS WHY PEOPLE PULL THE COVERS UP OVER THEIR HEADS.
WHATEVER IT IS, WONG... WE NEED TO FIND IT.
BEFORE IT FINDS US.

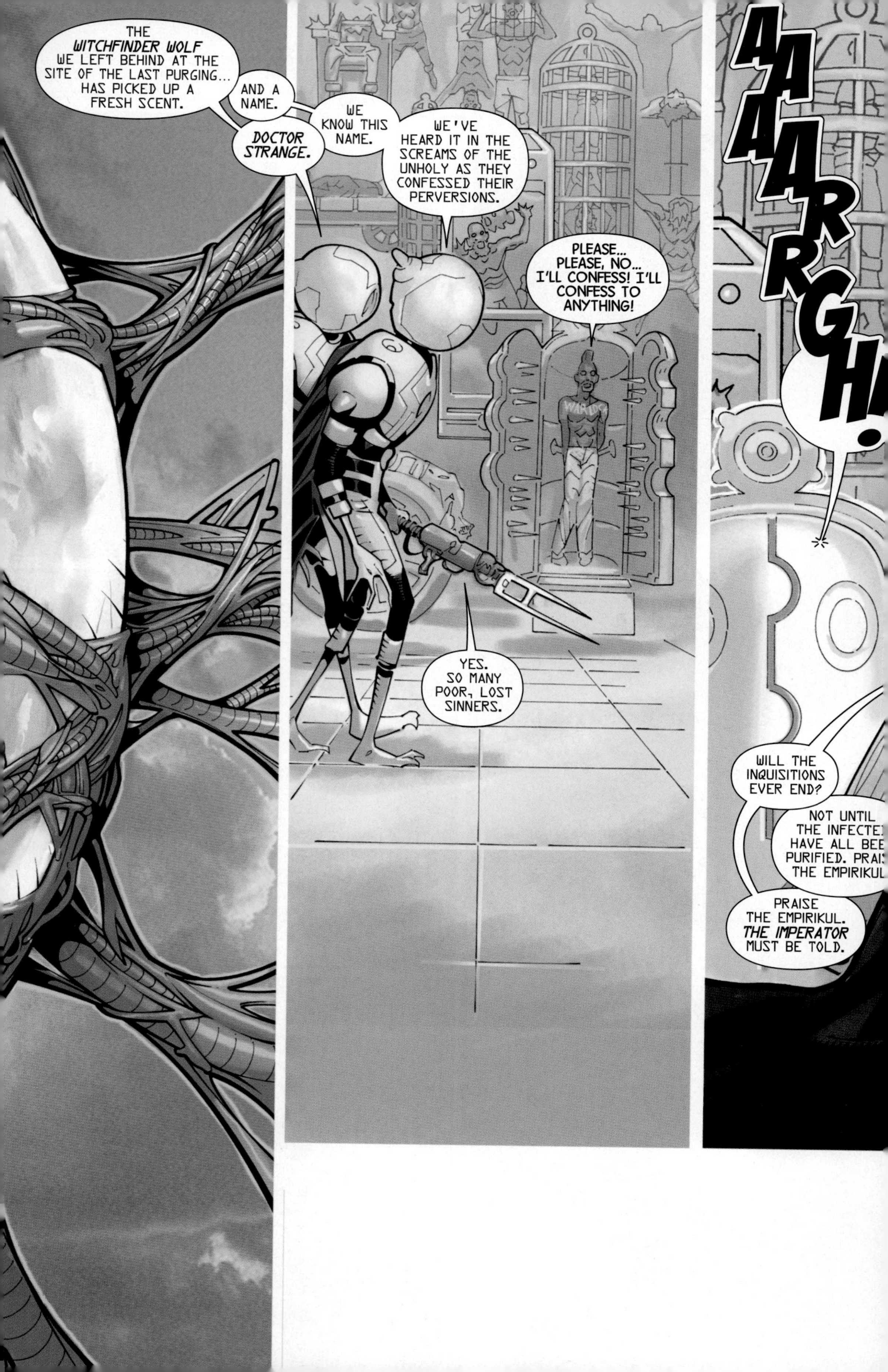
THE *WITCHFINDER WOLF* WE LEFT BEHIND AT THE SITE OF THE LAST PURGING... HAS PICKED UP A FRESH SCENT.
AND A NAME.
*DOCTOR STRANGE.*
WE KNOW THIS NAME.
WE'VE HEARD IT IN THE SCREAMS OF THE UNHOLY AS THEY CONFESSED THEIR PERVERSIONS.
PLEASE... PLEASE, NO... I'LL CONFESS! I'LL CONFESS TO ANYTHING!
YES. SO MANY POOR, LOST SINNERS.
AAAARRGH!
WILL THE INQUISITIONS EVER END?
NOT UNTIL THE INFECTED HAVE ALL BEE PURIFIED. PRAIS THE EMPIRIKUL
PRAISE THE EMPIRIKUL. *THE IMPERATOR* MUST BE TOLD.

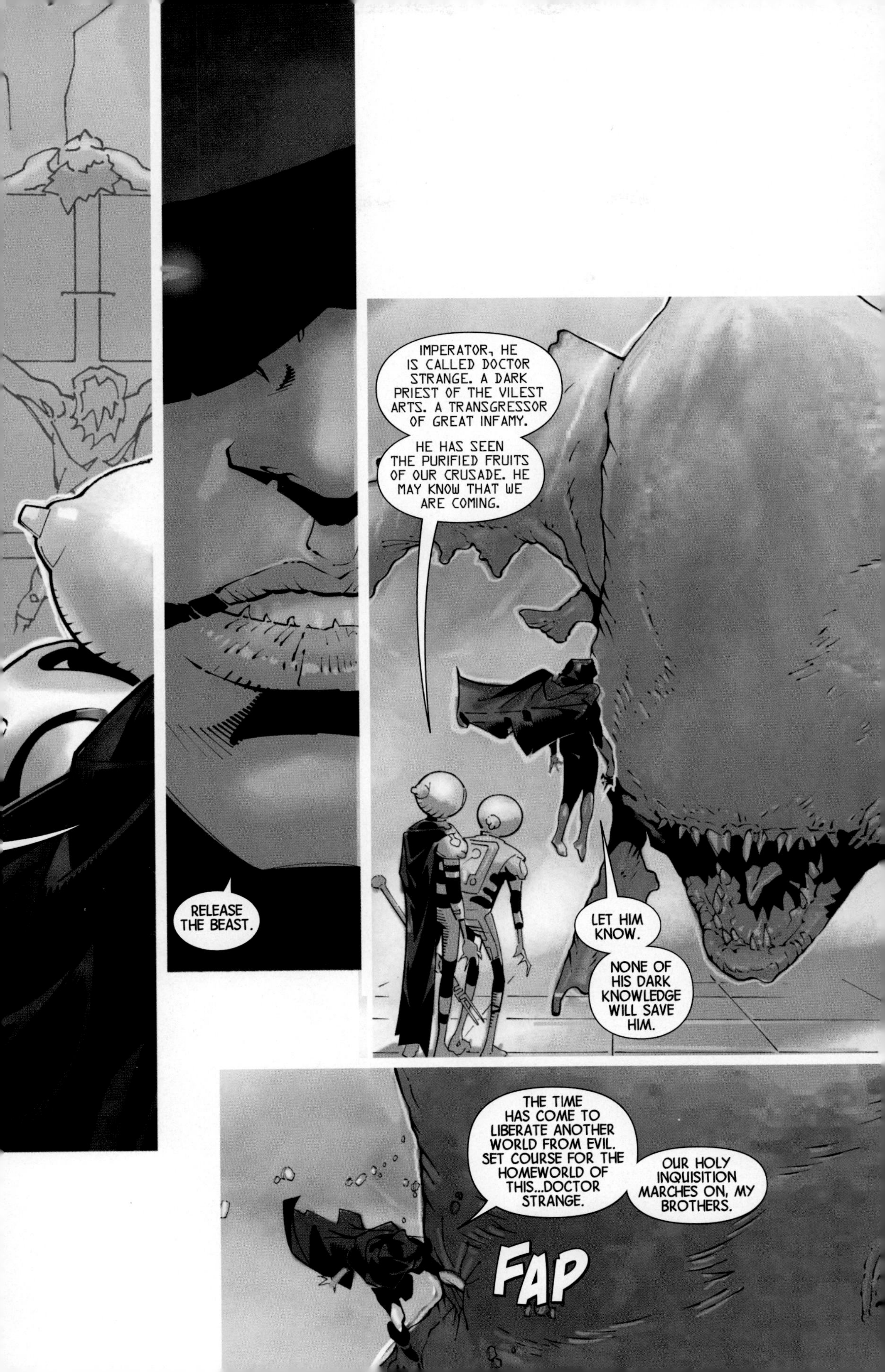

RELEASE THE BEAST.
IMPERATOR, HE IS CALLED DOCTOR STRANGE. A DARK PRIEST OF THE VILEST ARTS. A TRANSGRESSOR OF GREAT INFAMY.
HE HAS SEEN THE PURIFIED FRUITS OF OUR CRUSADE. HE MAY KNOW THAT WE ARE COMING.
LET HIM KNOW.
NONE OF HIS DARK KNOWLEDGE WILL SAVE HIM.
THE TIME HAS COME TO LIBERATE ANOTHER WORLD FROM EVIL. SET COURSE FOR THE HOMEWORLD OF THIS...DOCTOR STRANGE.
OUR HOLY INQUISITION MARCHES ON, MY BROTHERS.
FAP

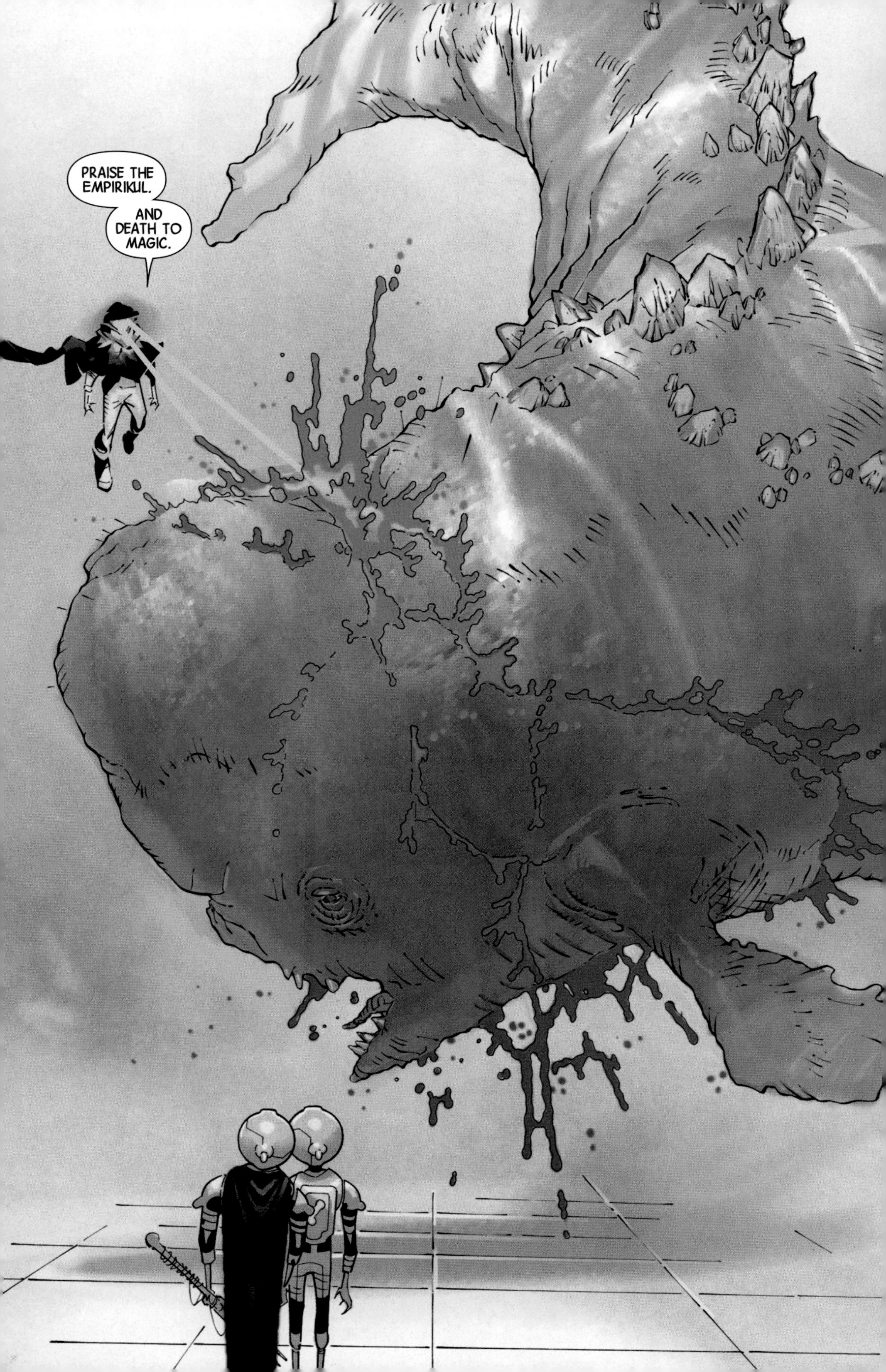
PRAISE THE EMPIRIKUL.
AND DEATH TO MAGIC.

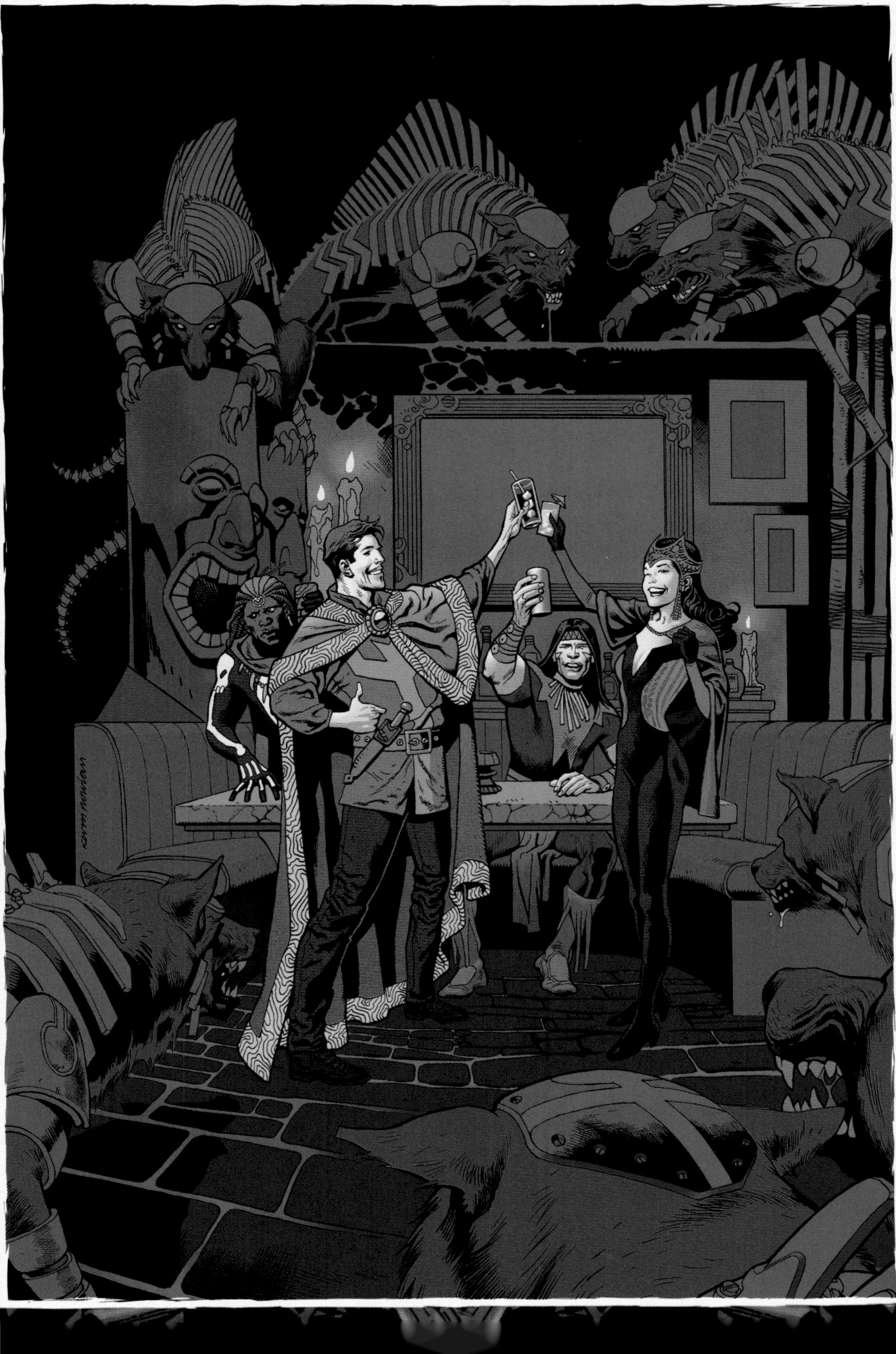

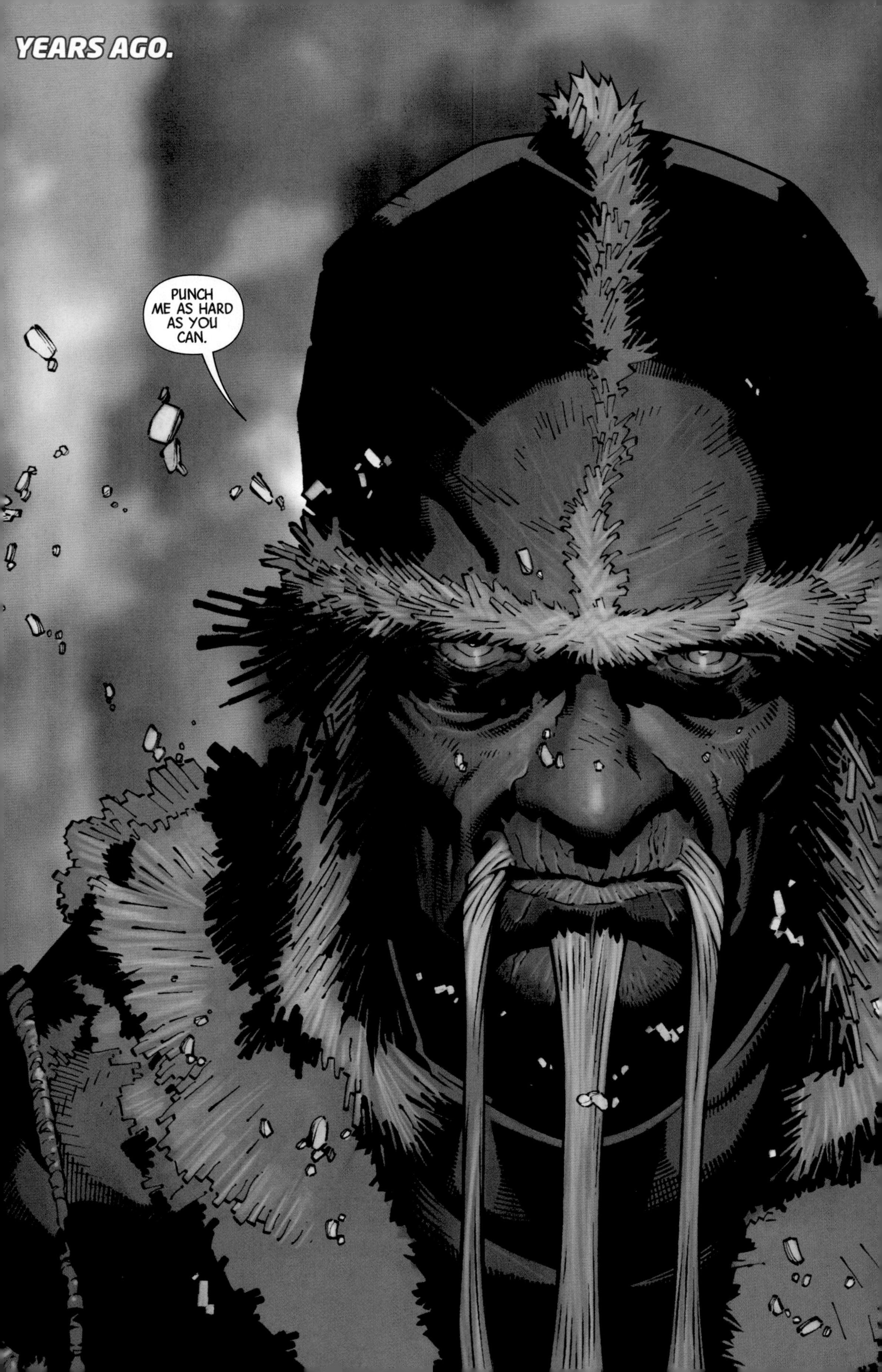
YEARS AGO.
PUNCH ME AS HARD AS YOU CAN.

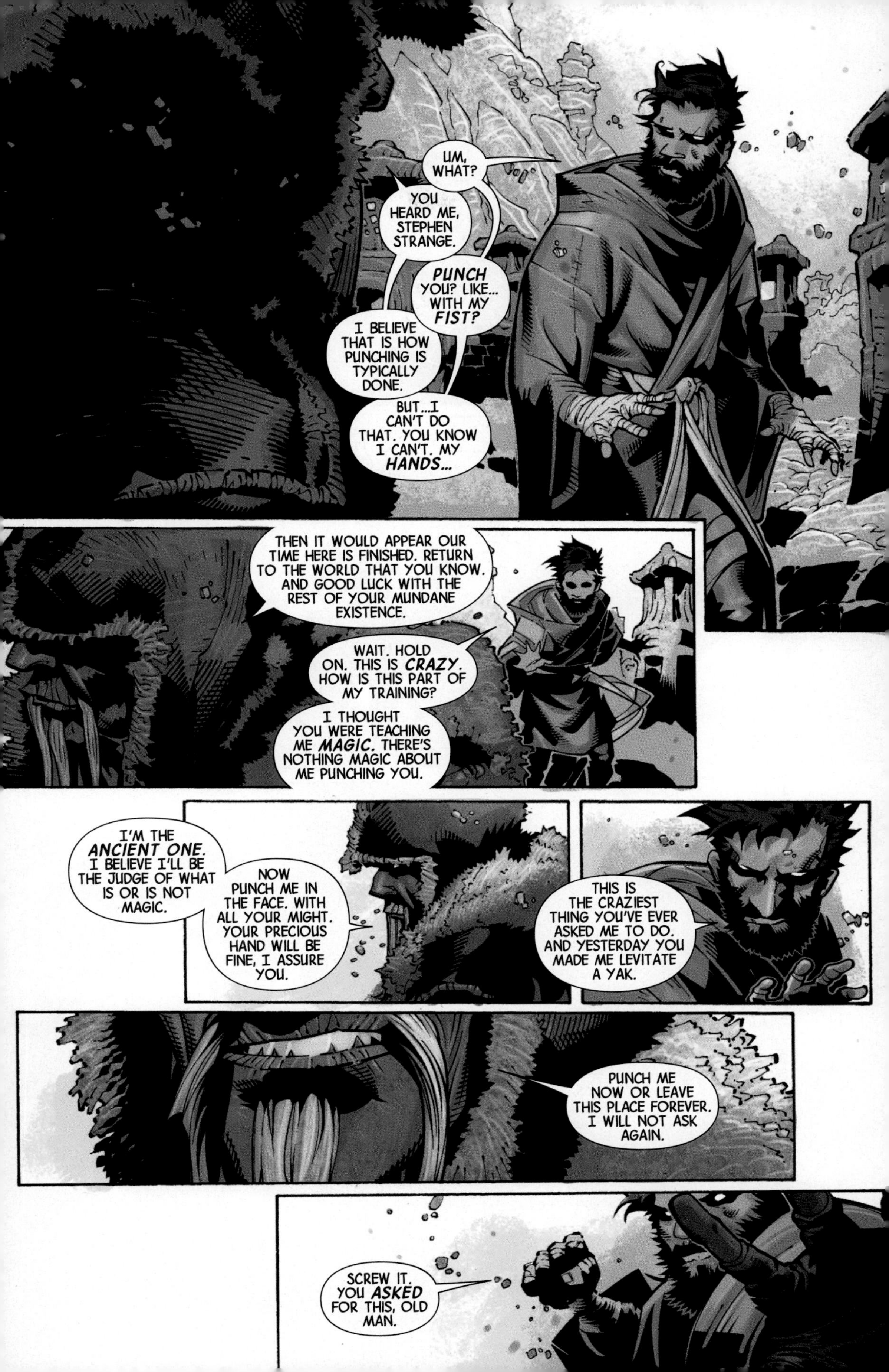
UM, WHAT?
YOU HEARD ME, STEPHEN STRANGE.
PUNCH YOU? LIKE... WITH MY FIST?
I BELIEVE THAT IS HOW PUNCHING IS TYPICALLY DONE.
BUT...I CAN'T DO THAT. YOU KNOW I CAN'T. MY HANDS...
THEN IT WOULD APPEAR OUR TIME HERE IS FINISHED. RETURN TO THE WORLD THAT YOU KNOW. AND GOOD LUCK WITH THE REST OF YOUR MUNDANE EXISTENCE.
WAIT. HOLD ON. THIS IS CRAZY. HOW IS THIS PART OF MY TRAINING?
I THOUGHT YOU WERE TEACHING ME MAGIC. THERE'S NOTHING MAGIC ABOUT ME PUNCHING YOU.
I'M THE ANCIENT ONE. I BELIEVE I'LL BE THE JUDGE OF WHAT IS OR IS NOT MAGIC.
NOW PUNCH ME IN THE FACE. WITH ALL YOUR MIGHT. YOUR PRECIOUS HAND WILL BE FINE, I ASSURE YOU.
THIS IS THE CRAZIEST THING YOU'VE EVER ASKED ME TO DO. AND YESTERDAY YOU MADE ME LEVITATE A YAK.
PUNCH ME NOW OR LEAVE THIS PLACE FOREVER. I WILL NOT ASK AGAIN.
SCREW IT. YOU ASKED FOR THIS, OLD MAN.

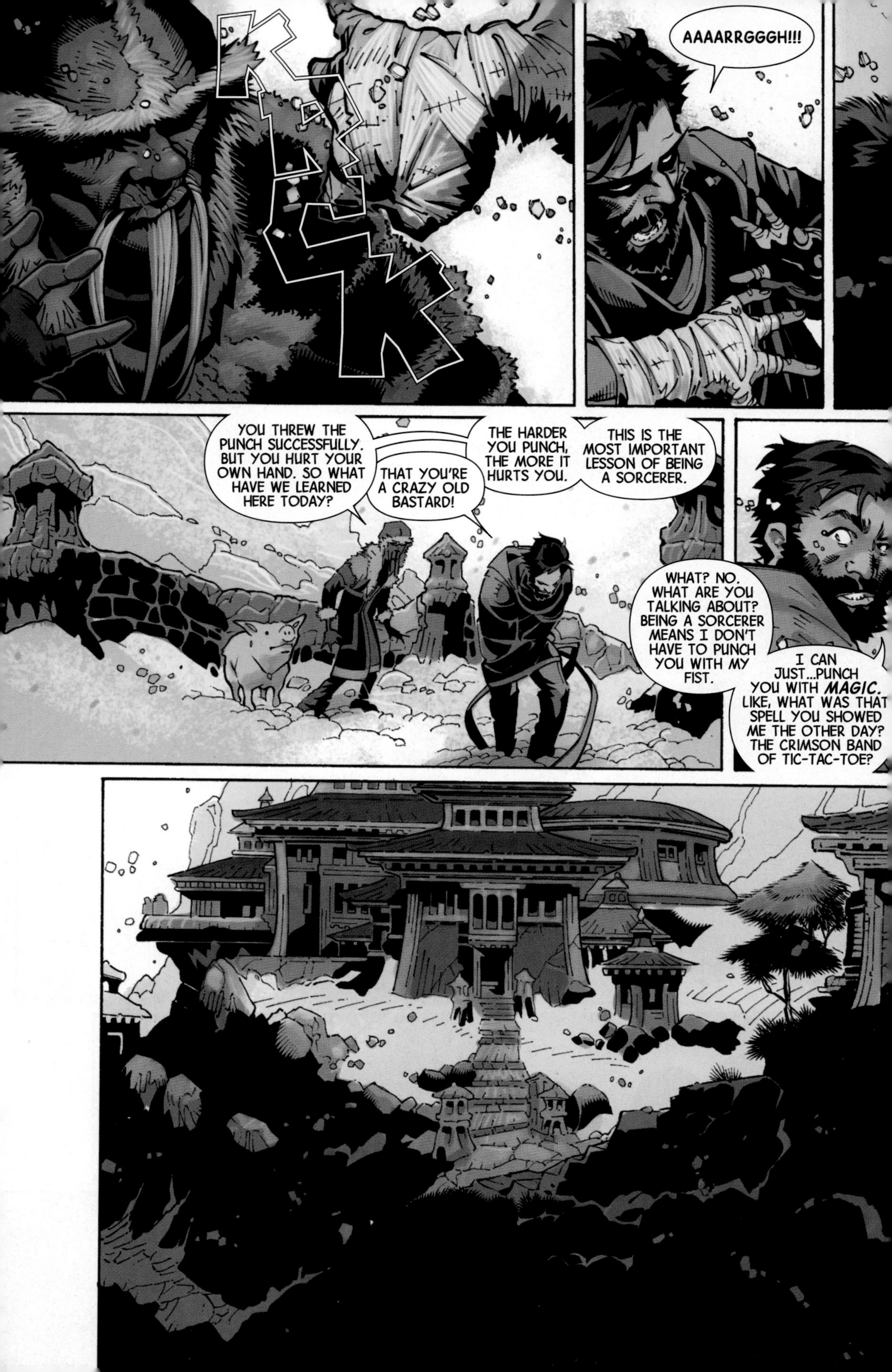
KRAK
AAAARRGGGH!!!
YOU THREW THE PUNCH SUCCESSFULLY. BUT YOU HURT YOUR OWN HAND. SO WHAT HAVE WE LEARNED HERE TODAY?
THAT YOU'RE A CRAZY OLD BASTARD!
THE HARDER YOU PUNCH, THE MORE IT HURTS YOU.
THIS IS THE MOST IMPORTANT LESSON OF BEING A SORCERER.
WHAT? NO. WHAT ARE YOU TALKING ABOUT? BEING A SORCERER MEANS I DON'T HAVE TO PUNCH YOU WITH MY FIST.
I CAN JUST...PUNCH YOU WITH MAGIC. LIKE, WHAT WAS THAT SPELL YOU SHOWED ME THE OTHER DAY? THE CRIMSON BAND OF TIC-TAC-TOE?

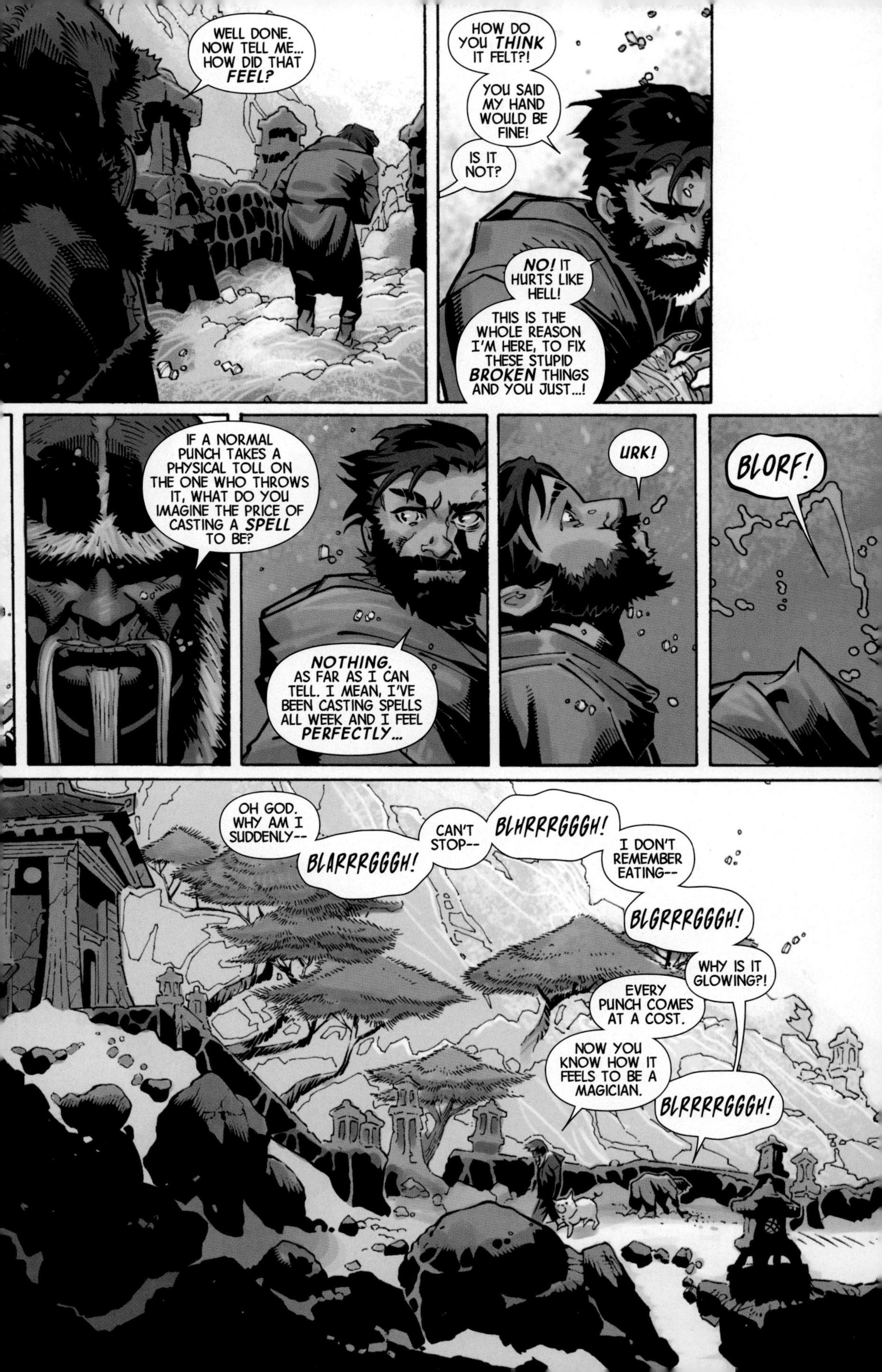

WELL DONE. NOW TELL ME... HOW DID THAT *FEEL?*
HOW DO YOU *THINK* IT FELT?!
YOU SAID MY HAND WOULD BE FINE!
IS IT NOT?
*NO!* IT HURTS LIKE HELL!
THIS IS THE WHOLE REASON I'M HERE, TO FIX THESE STUPID *BROKEN* THINGS AND YOU JUST...!
IF A NORMAL PUNCH TAKES A PHYSICAL TOLL ON THE ONE WHO THROWS IT, WHAT DO YOU IMAGINE THE PRICE OF CASTING A *SPELL* TO BE?
*NOTHING.* AS FAR AS I CAN TELL. I MEAN, I'VE BEEN CASTING SPELLS ALL WEEK AND I FEEL *PERFECTLY...*
URK!
BLORF!
OH GOD. WHY AM I SUDDENLY--
BLARRRGGGH!
CAN'T STOP--
BLHRRRGGGH!
I DON'T REMEMBER EATING--
BLGRRRGGGH!
WHY IS IT GLOWING?!
EVERY PUNCH COMES AT A COST.
NOW YOU KNOW HOW IT FEELS TO BE A MAGICIAN.
BLRRRRGGGH!

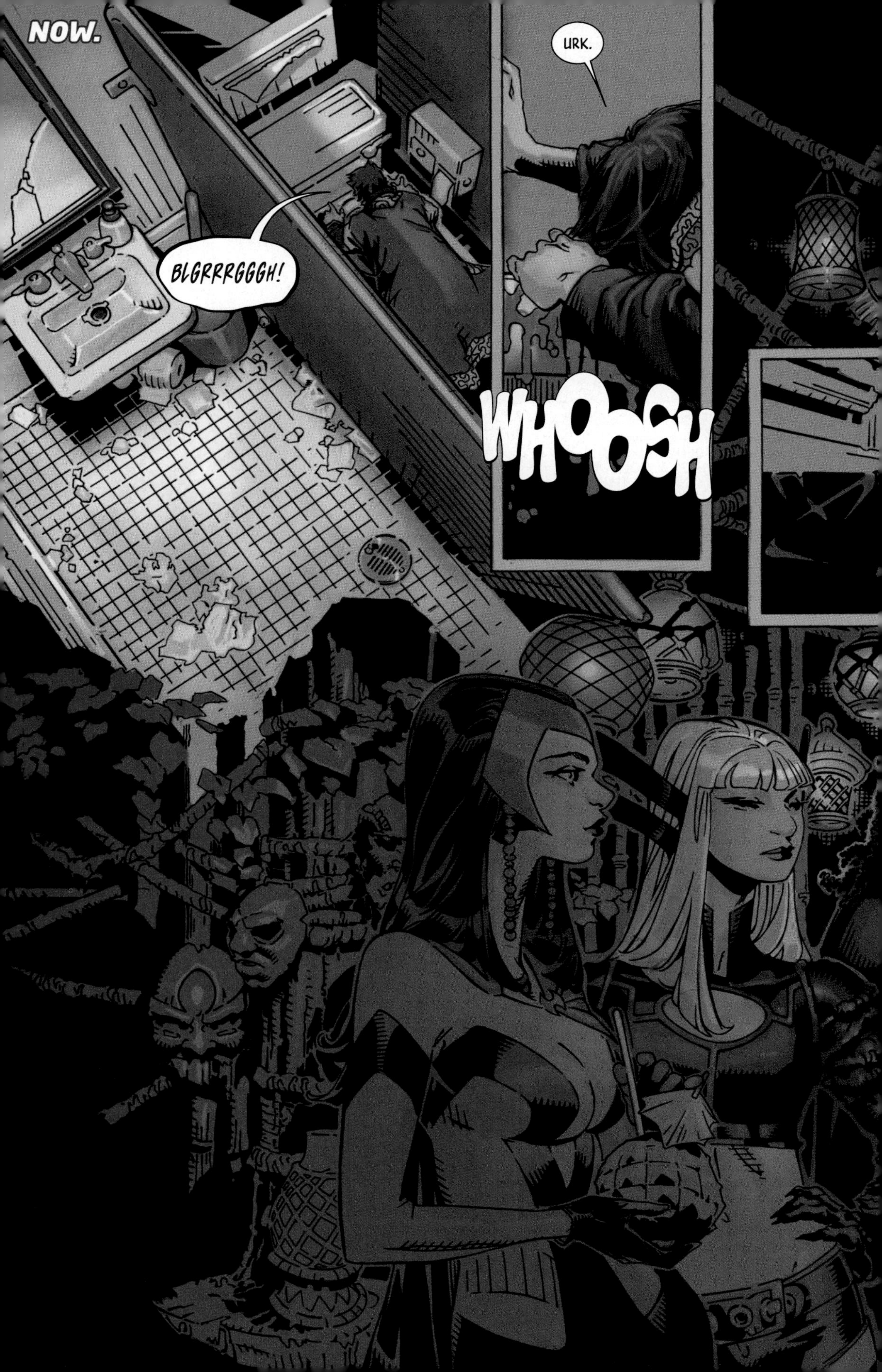
NOW.
BLGRRRGGGH!
URK.
WHOOSH

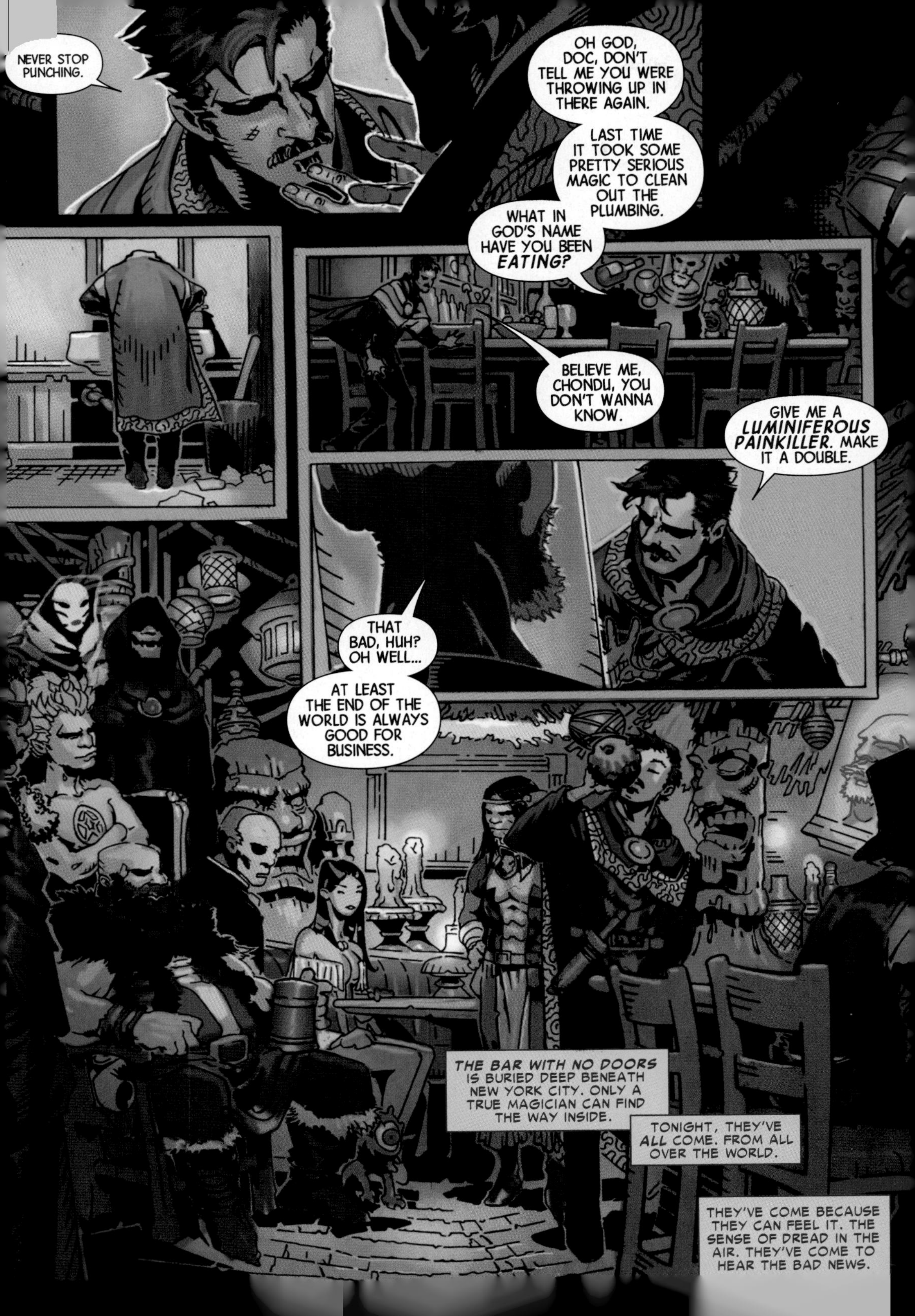

NEVER STOP PUNCHING.
OH GOD, DOC, DON'T TELL ME YOU WERE THROWING UP IN THERE AGAIN.
LAST TIME IT TOOK SOME PRETTY SERIOUS MAGIC TO CLEAN OUT THE PLUMBING.
WHAT IN GOD'S NAME HAVE YOU BEEN *EATING?*
BELIEVE ME, CHONDU, YOU DON'T WANNA KNOW.
GIVE ME A ***LUMINIFEROUS PAINKILLER.*** MAKE IT A DOUBLE.
THAT BAD, HUH? OH WELL...
AT LEAST THE END OF THE WORLD IS ALWAYS GOOD FOR BUSINESS.
*THE BAR WITH NO DOORS* IS BURIED DEEP BENEATH NEW YORK CITY. ONLY A TRUE MAGICIAN CAN FIND THE WAY INSIDE.
TONIGHT, THEY'VE *ALL* COME. FROM ALL OVER THE WORLD.
THEY'VE COME BECAUSE THEY CAN FEEL IT. THE SENSE OF DREAD IN THE AIR. THEY'VE COME TO HEAR THE BAD NEWS.

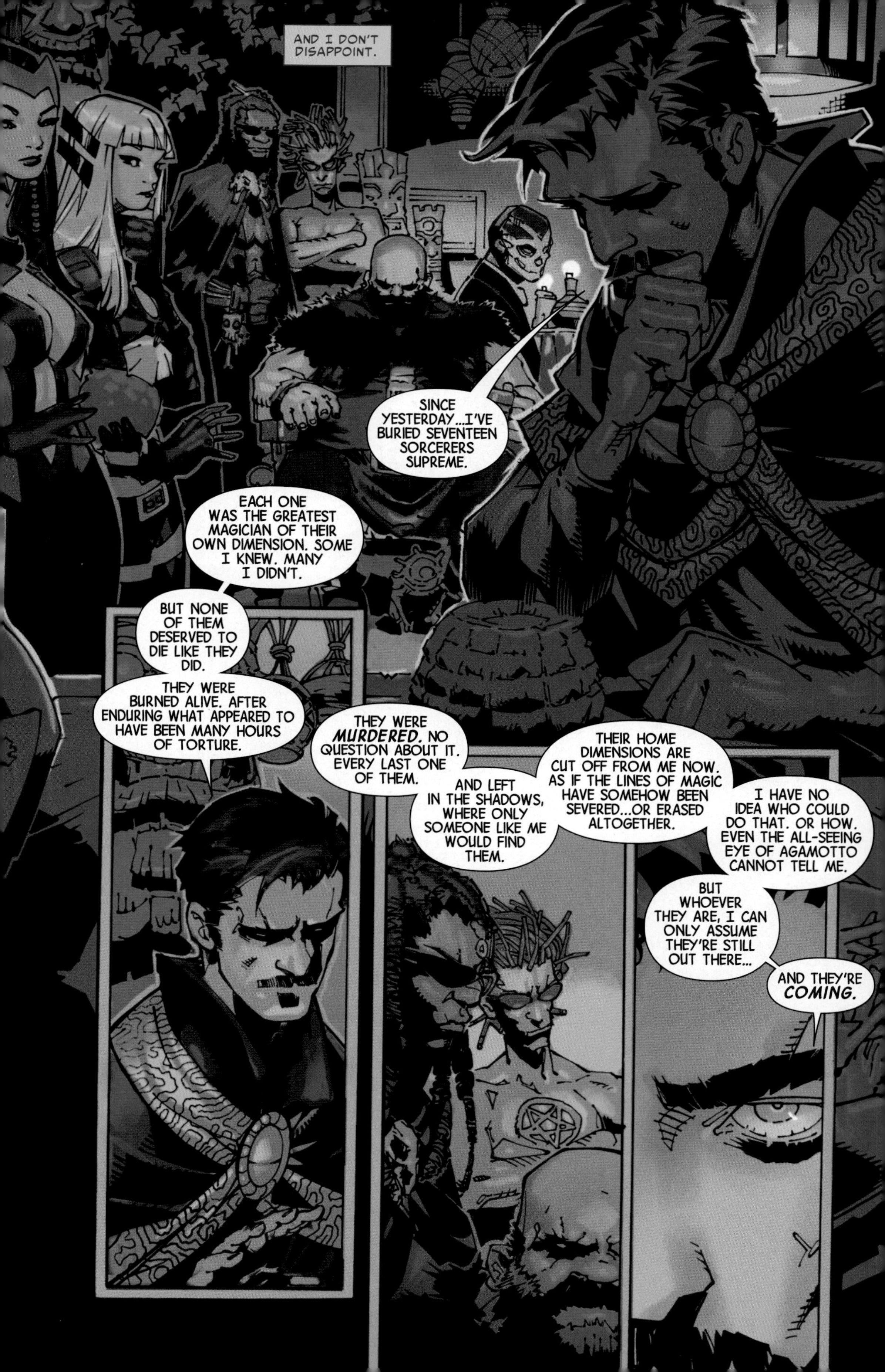
AND I DON'T DISAPPOINT.
SINCE YESTERDAY...I'VE BURIED SEVENTEEN SORCERERS SUPREME.
EACH ONE WAS THE GREATEST MAGICIAN OF THEIR OWN DIMENSION. SOME I KNEW. MANY I DIDN'T.
BUT NONE OF THEM DESERVED TO DIE LIKE THEY DID.
THEY WERE BURNED ALIVE. AFTER ENDURING WHAT APPEARED TO HAVE BEEN MANY HOURS OF TORTURE.
THEY WERE MURDERED. NO QUESTION ABOUT IT. EVERY LAST ONE OF THEM.
AND LEFT IN THE SHADOWS, WHERE ONLY SOMEONE LIKE ME WOULD FIND THEM.
THEIR HOME DIMENSIONS ARE CUT OFF FROM ME NOW. AS IF THE LINES OF MAGIC HAVE SOMEHOW BEEN SEVERED...OR ERASED ALTOGETHER.
I HAVE NO IDEA WHO COULD DO THAT. OR HOW. EVEN THE ALL-SEEING EYE OF AGAMOTTO CANNOT TELL ME.
BUT WHOEVER THEY ARE, I CAN ONLY ASSUME THEY'RE STILL OUT THERE...
AND THEY'RE COMING.

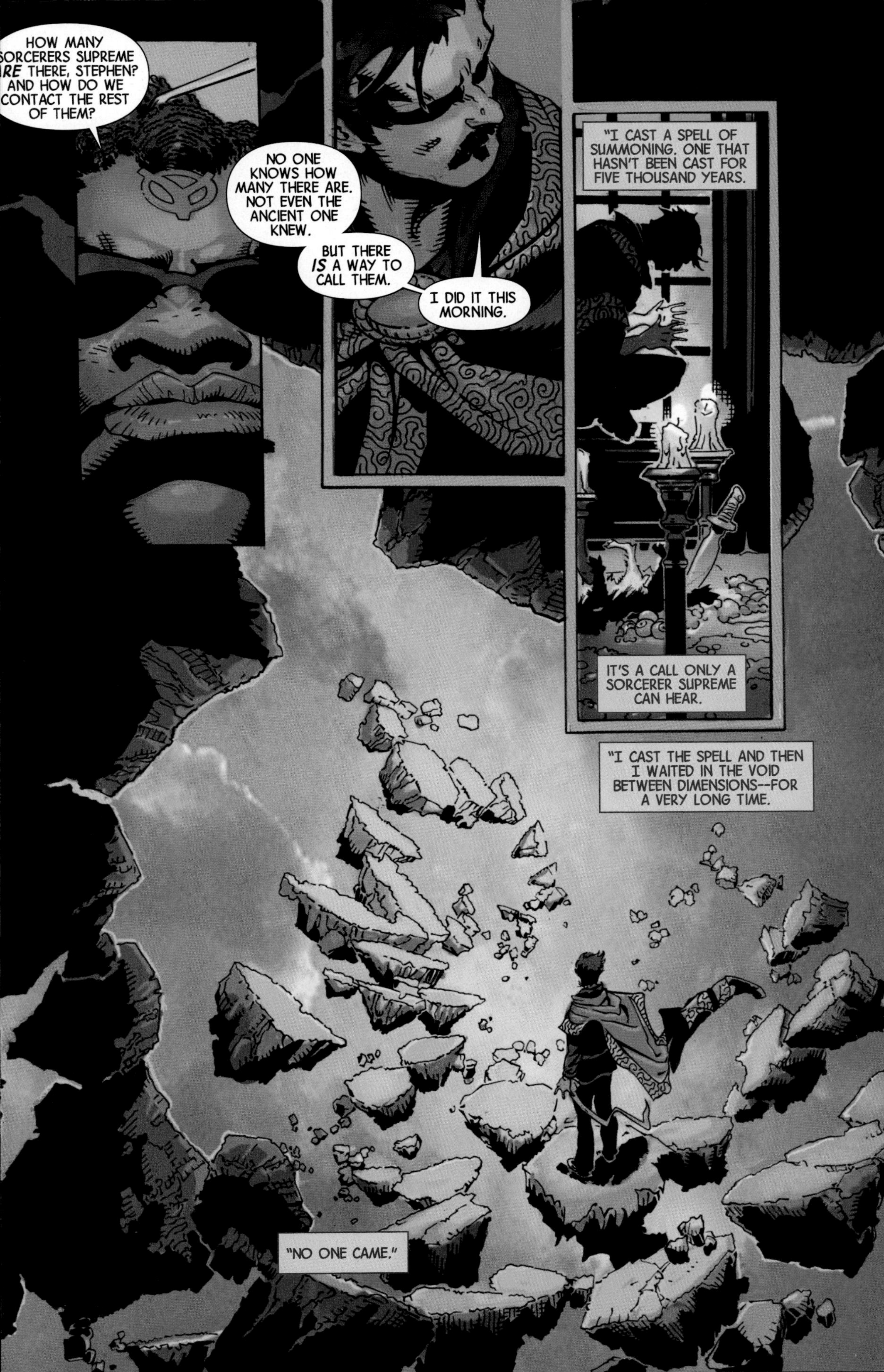
HOW MANY SORCERERS SUPREME ARE THERE, STEPHEN? AND HOW DO WE CONTACT THE REST OF THEM?
NO ONE KNOWS HOW MANY THERE ARE. NOT EVEN THE ANCIENT ONE KNEW.
BUT THERE IS A WAY TO CALL THEM.
I DID IT THIS MORNING.
"I CAST A SPELL OF SUMMONING. ONE THAT HASN'T BEEN CAST FOR FIVE THOUSAND YEARS.
IT'S A CALL ONLY A SORCERER SUPREME CAN HEAR.
"I CAST THE SPELL AND THEN I WAITED IN THE VOID BETWEEN DIMENSIONS--FOR A VERY LONG TIME.
"NO ONE CAME."

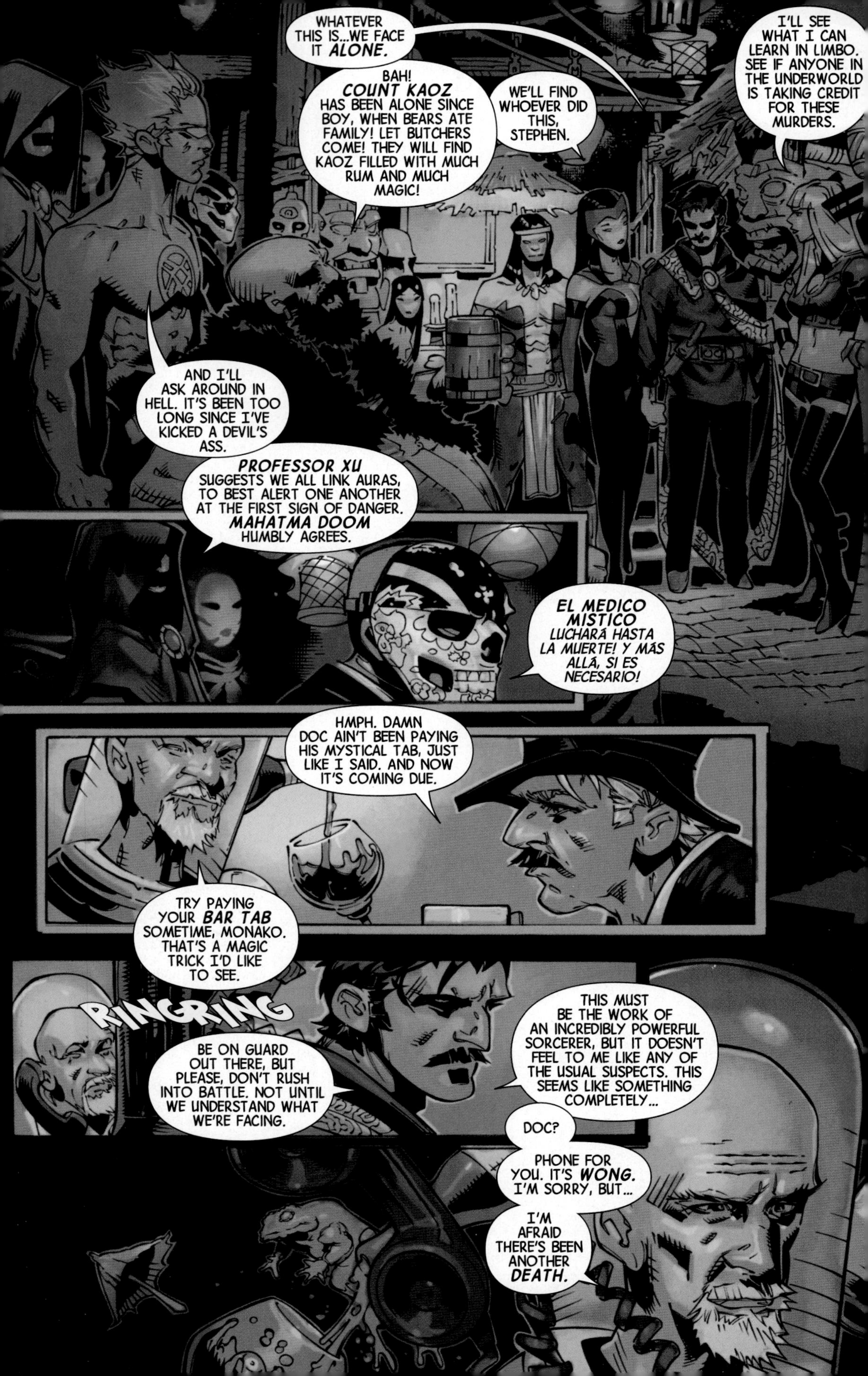
WHATEVER THIS IS...WE FACE IT ALONE.
BAH! COUNT KAOZ HAS BEEN ALONE SINCE BOY, WHEN BEARS ATE FAMILY! LET BUTCHERS COME! THEY WILL FIND KAOZ FILLED WITH MUCH RUM AND MUCH MAGIC!
WE'LL FIND WHOEVER DID THIS, STEPHEN.
I'LL SEE WHAT I CAN LEARN IN LIMBO. SEE IF ANYONE IN THE UNDERWORLD IS TAKING CREDIT FOR THESE MURDERS.
AND I'LL ASK AROUND IN HELL. IT'S BEEN TOO LONG SINCE I'VE KICKED A DEVIL'S ASS.
PROFESSOR XU SUGGESTS WE ALL LINK AURAS, TO BEST ALERT ONE ANOTHER AT THE FIRST SIGN OF DANGER. MAHATMA DOOM HUMBLY AGREES.
EL MEDICO MISTICO LUCHARÁ HASTA LA MUERTE! Y MÁS ALLÁ, SI ES NECESARIO!
HMPH. DAMN DOC AIN'T BEEN PAYING HIS MYSTICAL TAB, JUST LIKE I SAID. AND NOW IT'S COMING DUE.
TRY PAYING YOUR BAR TAB SOMETIME, MONAKO. THAT'S A MAGIC TRICK I'D LIKE TO SEE.
RINGRING
BE ON GUARD OUT THERE, BUT PLEASE, DON'T RUSH INTO BATTLE. NOT UNTIL WE UNDERSTAND WHAT WE'RE FACING.
THIS MUST BE THE WORK OF AN INCREDIBLY POWERFUL SORCERER, BUT IT DOESN'T FEEL TO ME LIKE ANY OF THE USUAL SUSPECTS. THIS SEEMS LIKE SOMETHING COMPLETELY...
DOC?
PHONE FOR YOU. IT'S WONG. I'M SORRY, BUT...
I'M AFRAID THERE'S BEEN ANOTHER DEATH.

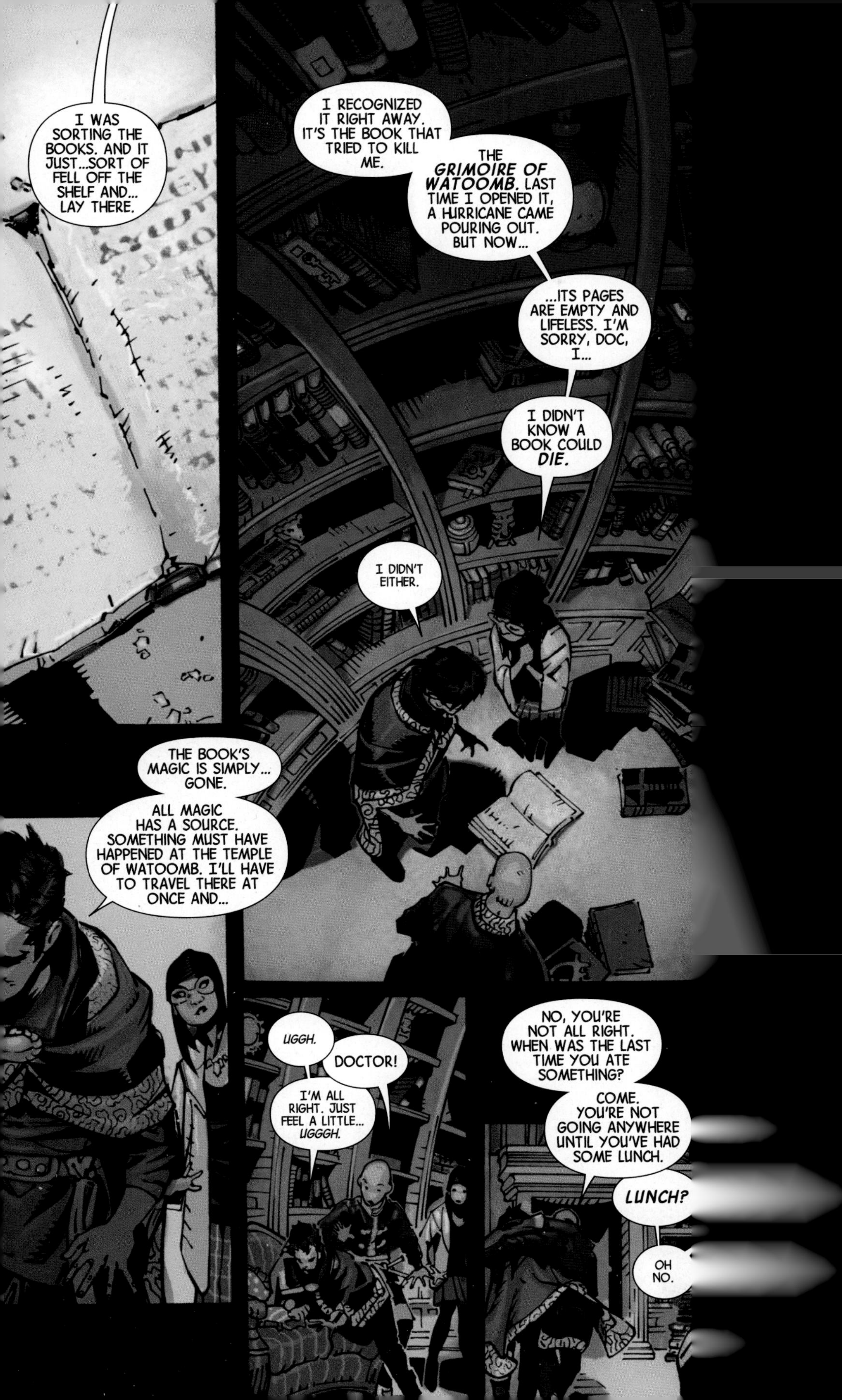
I WAS SORTING THE BOOKS. AND IT JUST...SORT OF FELL OFF THE SHELF AND... LAY THERE.
I RECOGNIZED IT RIGHT AWAY. IT'S THE BOOK THAT TRIED TO KILL ME.
THE GRIMOIRE OF WATOOMB. LAST TIME I OPENED IT, A HURRICANE CAME POURING OUT. BUT NOW...
...ITS PAGES ARE EMPTY AND LIFELESS. I'M SORRY, DOC, I...
I DIDN'T KNOW A BOOK COULD DIE.
I DIDN'T EITHER.
THE BOOK'S MAGIC IS SIMPLY... GONE.
ALL MAGIC HAS A SOURCE. SOMETHING MUST HAVE HAPPENED AT THE TEMPLE OF WATOOMB. I'LL HAVE TO TRAVEL THERE AT ONCE AND...
UGGH.
DOCTOR!
I'M ALL RIGHT. JUST FEEL A LITTLE... UGGGH.
NO, YOU'RE NOT ALL RIGHT. WHEN WAS THE LAST TIME YOU ATE SOMETHING?
COME. YOU'RE NOT GOING ANYWHERE UNTIL YOU'VE HAD SOME LUNCH.
LUNCH?
OH NO.

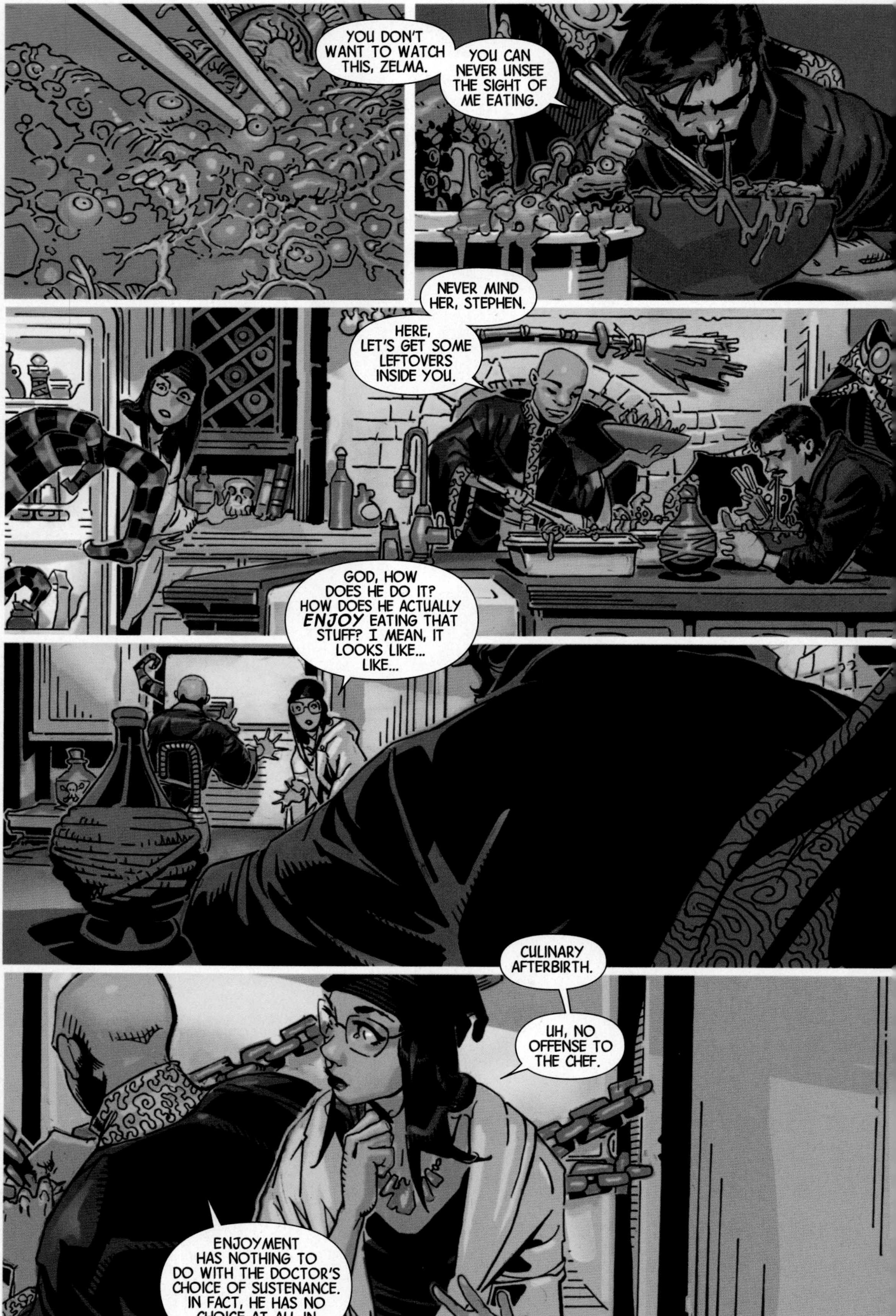
YOU DON'T WANT TO WATCH THIS, ZELMA.
YOU CAN NEVER UNSEE THE SIGHT OF ME EATING.
NEVER MIND HER, STEPHEN.
HERE, LET'S GET SOME LEFTOVERS INSIDE YOU.
GOD, HOW DOES HE DO IT? HOW DOES HE ACTUALLY ENJOY EATING THAT STUFF? I MEAN, IT LOOKS LIKE... LIKE...
CULINARY AFTERBIRTH.
UH, NO OFFENSE TO THE CHEF.
ENJOYMENT HAS NOTHING TO DO WITH THE DOCTOR'S CHOICE OF SUSTENANCE. IN FACT, HE HAS NO CHOICE AT ALL IN THE MATTER.

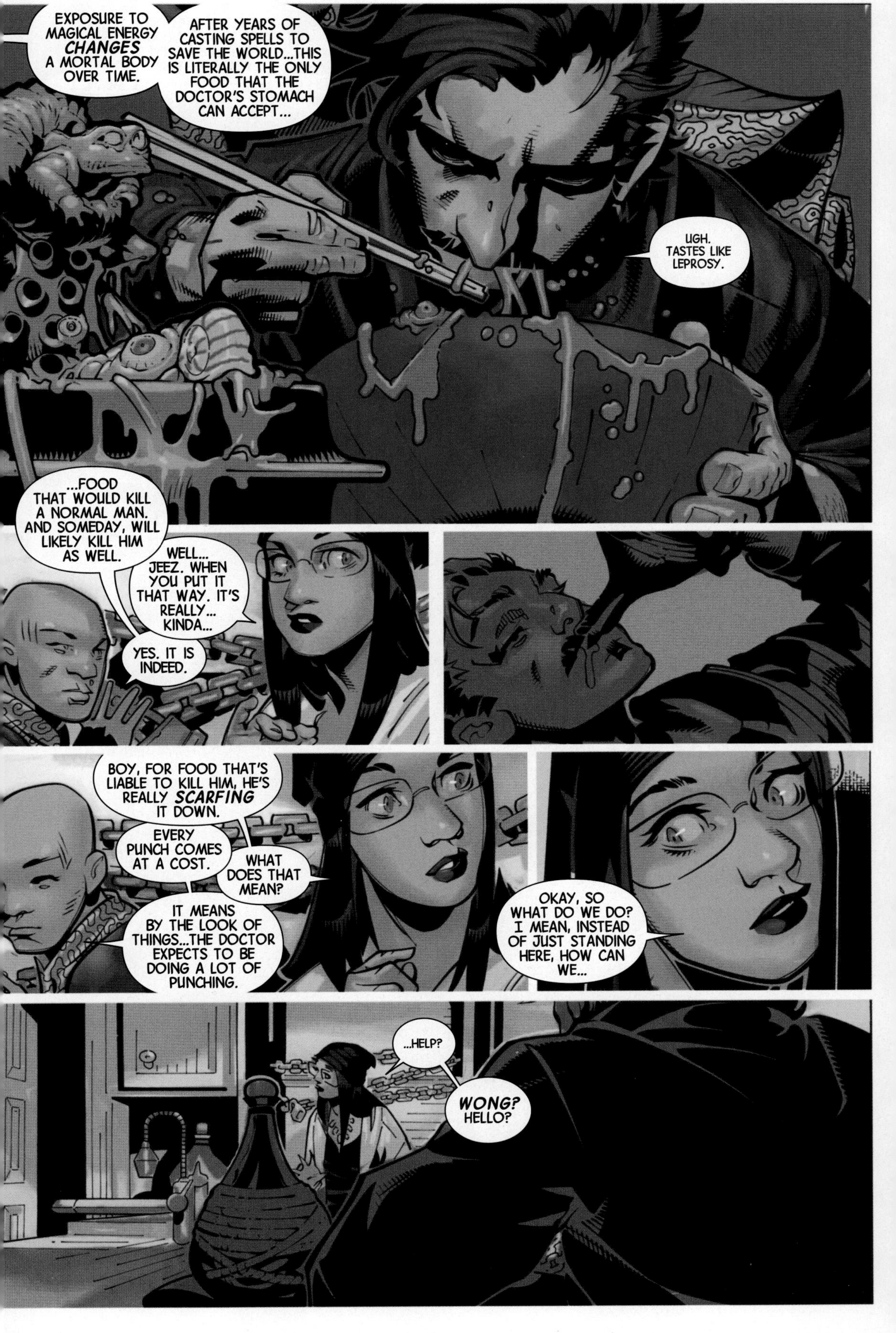
EXPOSURE TO MAGICAL ENERGY *CHANGES* A MORTAL BODY OVER TIME.
AFTER YEARS OF CASTING SPELLS TO SAVE THE WORLD...THIS IS LITERALLY THE ONLY FOOD THAT THE DOCTOR'S STOMACH CAN ACCEPT...
UGH. TASTES LIKE LEPROSY.
...FOOD THAT WOULD KILL A NORMAL MAN. AND SOMEDAY, WILL LIKELY KILL HIM AS WELL.
WELL... JEEZ. WHEN YOU PUT IT THAT WAY. IT'S REALLY... KINDA...
YES. IT IS INDEED.
BOY, FOR FOOD THAT'S LIABLE TO KILL HIM, HE'S REALLY *SCARFING* IT DOWN.
EVERY PUNCH COMES AT A COST.
WHAT DOES THAT MEAN?
IT MEANS BY THE LOOK OF THINGS...THE DOCTOR EXPECTS TO BE DOING A LOT OF PUNCHING.
OKAY, SO WHAT DO WE DO? I MEAN, INSTEAD OF JUST STANDING HERE, HOW CAN WE...
...HELP?
*WONG?* HELLO?

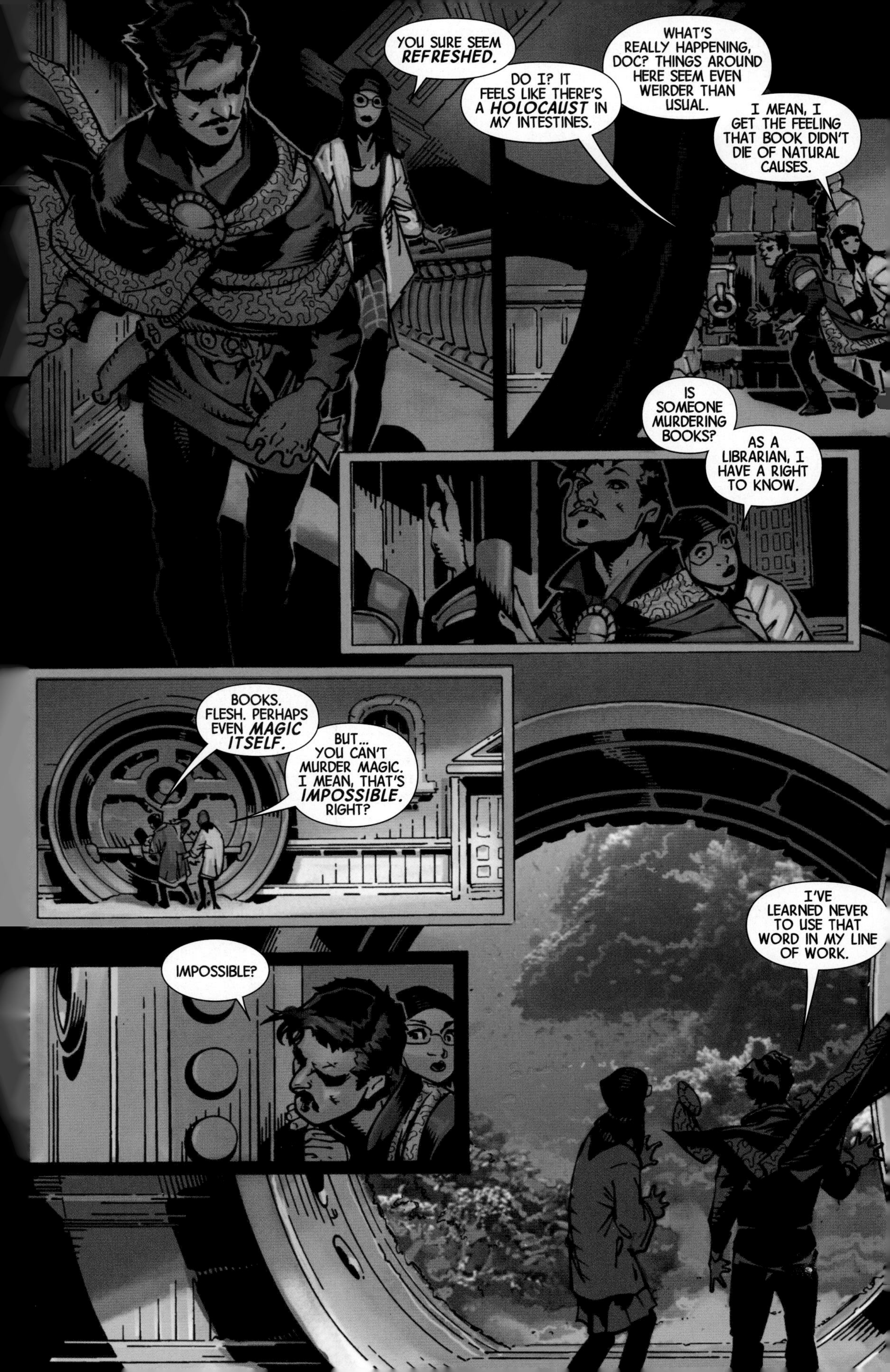
YOU SURE SEEM REFRESHED.
DO I? IT FEELS LIKE THERE'S A HOLOCAUST IN MY INTESTINES.
WHAT'S REALLY HAPPENING, DOC? THINGS AROUND HERE SEEM EVEN WEIRDER THAN USUAL.
I MEAN, I GET THE FEELING THAT BOOK DIDN'T DIE OF NATURAL CAUSES.
IS SOMEONE MURDERING BOOKS?
AS A LIBRARIAN, I HAVE A RIGHT TO KNOW.
BOOKS. FLESH. PERHAPS EVEN MAGIC ITSELF.
BUT... YOU CAN'T MURDER MAGIC. I MEAN, THAT'S IMPOSSIBLE. RIGHT?
IMPOSSIBLE?
I'VE LEARNED NEVER TO USE THAT WORD IN MY LINE OF WORK.

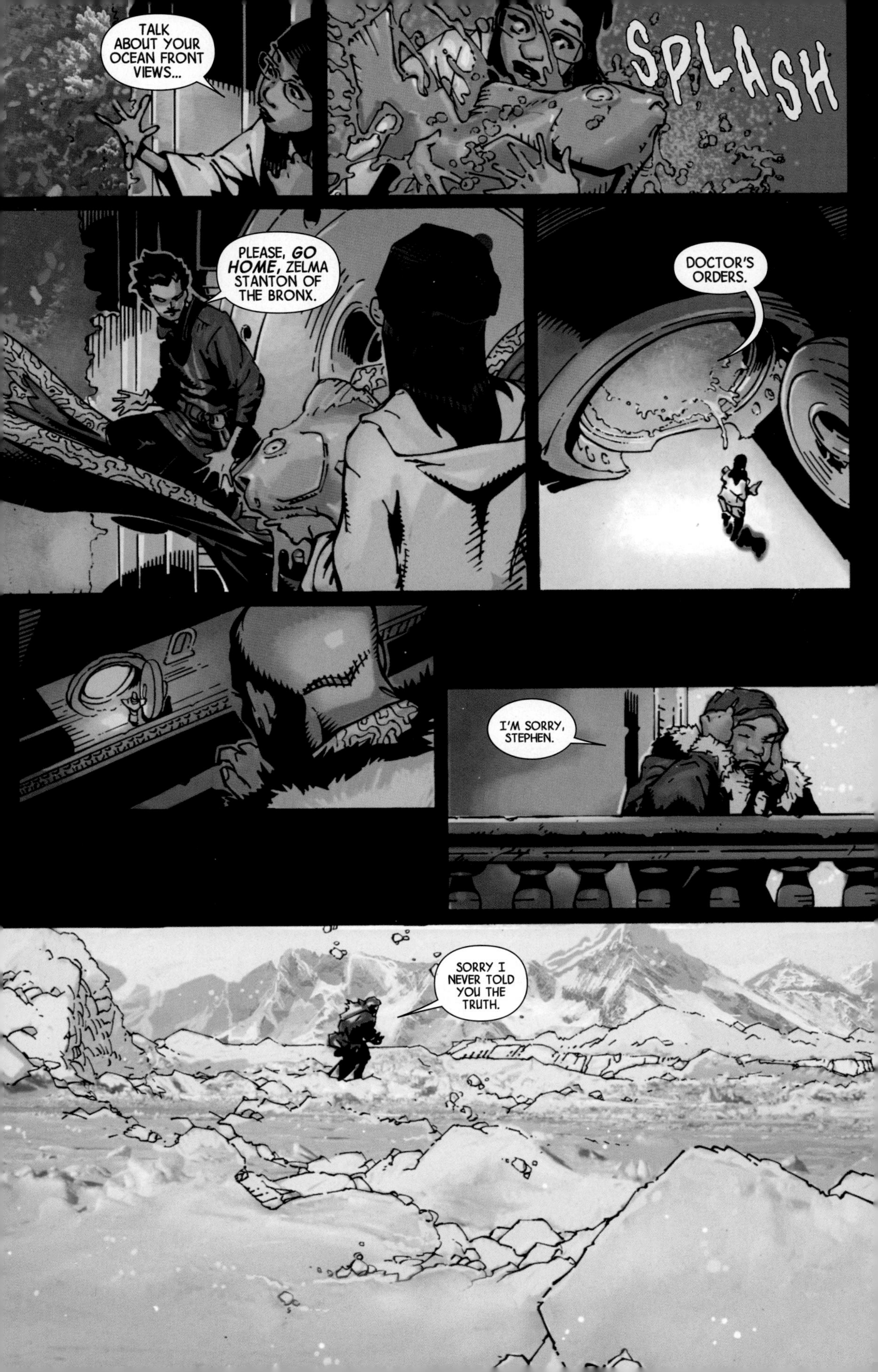
TALK ABOUT YOUR OCEAN FRONT VIEWS...
SPLASH
PLEASE, GO HOME, ZELMA STANTON OF THE BRONX.
DOCTOR'S ORDERS.
I'M SORRY, STEPHEN.
SORRY I NEVER TOLD YOU THE TRUTH.

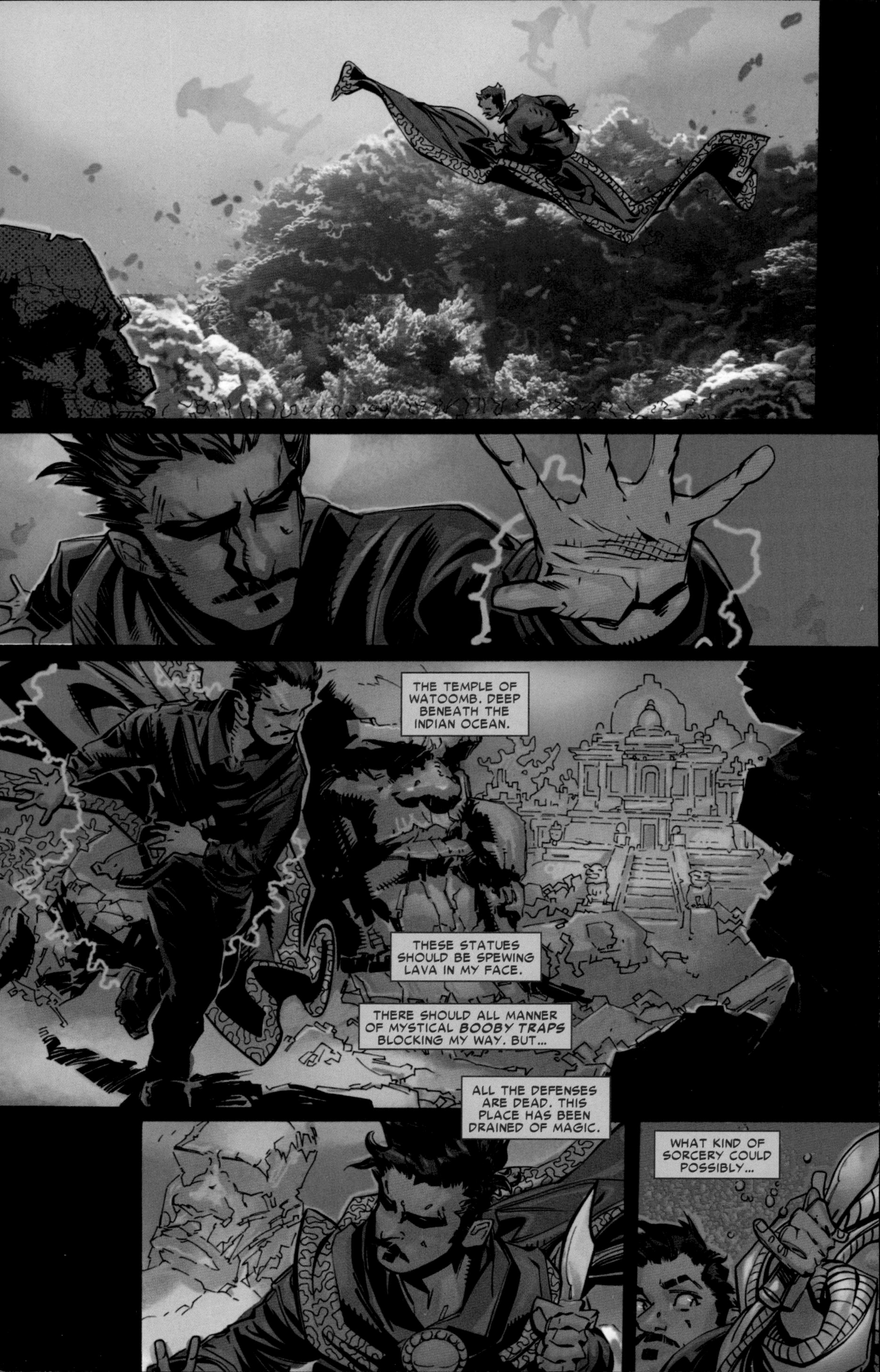
THE TEMPLE OF WATOOMB. DEEP BENEATH THE INDIAN OCEAN.
THESE STATUES SHOULD BE SPEWING LAVA IN MY FACE.
THERE SHOULD ALL MANNER OF MYSTICAL BOOBY TRAPS BLOCKING MY WAY. BUT...
ALL THE DEFENSES ARE DEAD. THIS PLACE HAS BEEN DRAINED OF MAGIC.
WHAT KIND OF SORCERY COULD POSSIBLY...

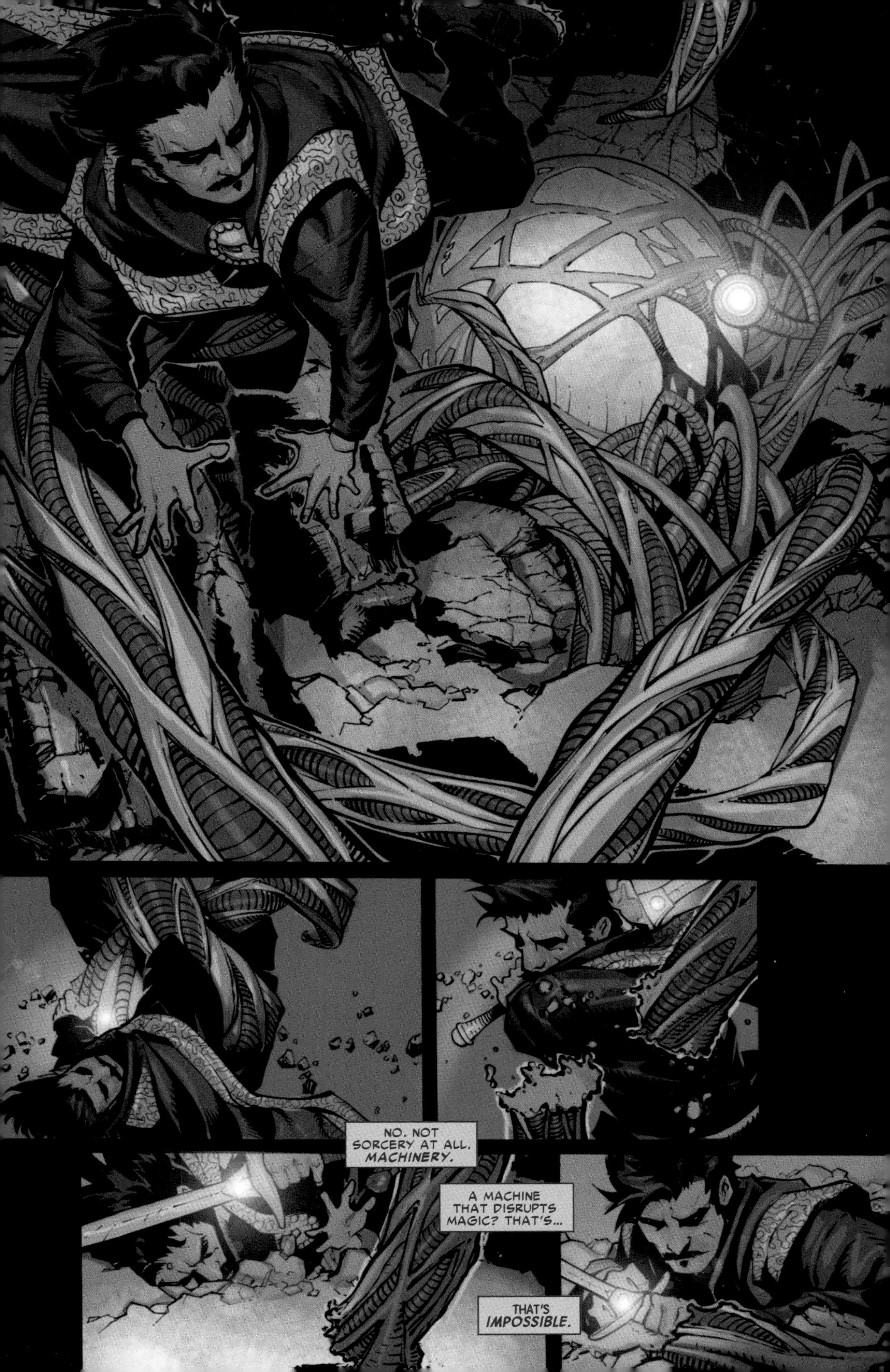
NO. NOT SORCERY AT ALL. MACHINERY.
A MACHINE THAT DISRUPTS MAGIC? THAT'S...
THAT'S IMPOSSIBLE.

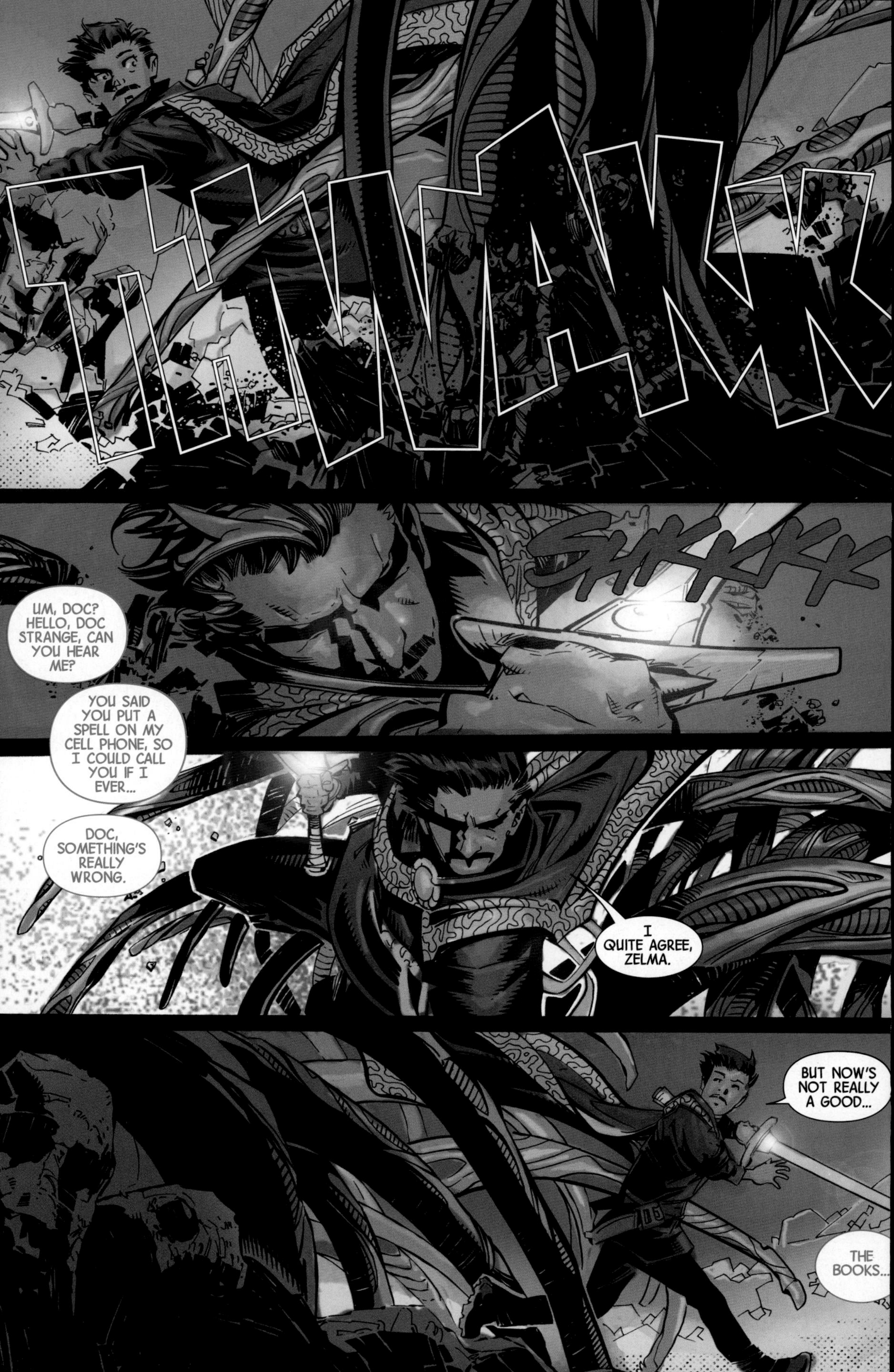
THWAKK
SHKKK
UM, DOC? HELLO, DOC STRANGE, CAN YOU HEAR ME?
YOU SAID YOU PUT A SPELL ON MY CELL PHONE, SO I COULD CALL YOU IF I EVER...
DOC, SOMETHING'S REALLY WRONG.
I QUITE AGREE, ZELMA.
BUT NOW'S NOT REALLY A GOOD...
THE BOOKS...

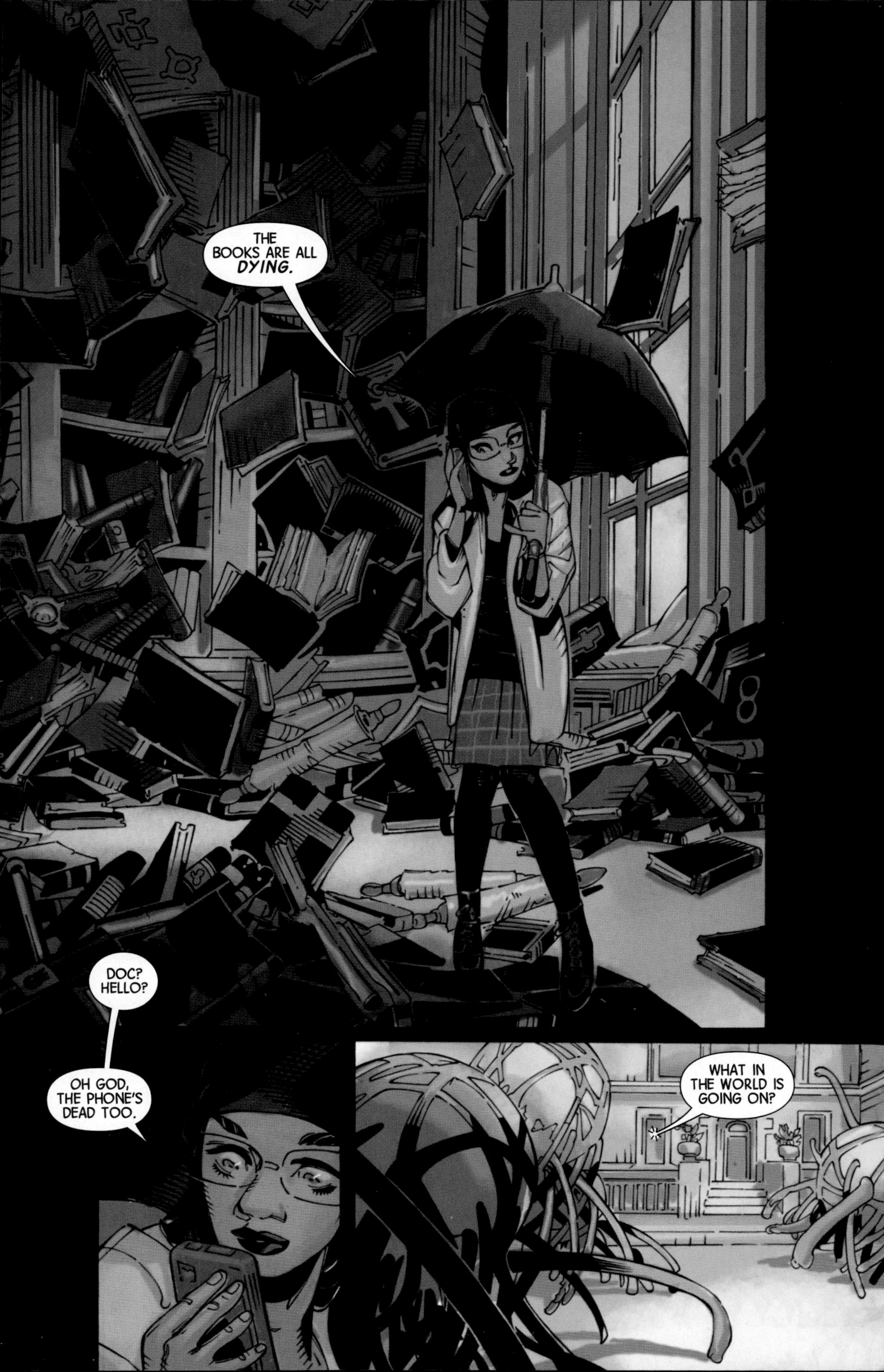
THE BOOKS ARE ALL DYING.
DOC? HELLO?
OH GOD, THE PHONE'S DEAD TOO.
WHAT IN THE WORLD IS GOING ON?

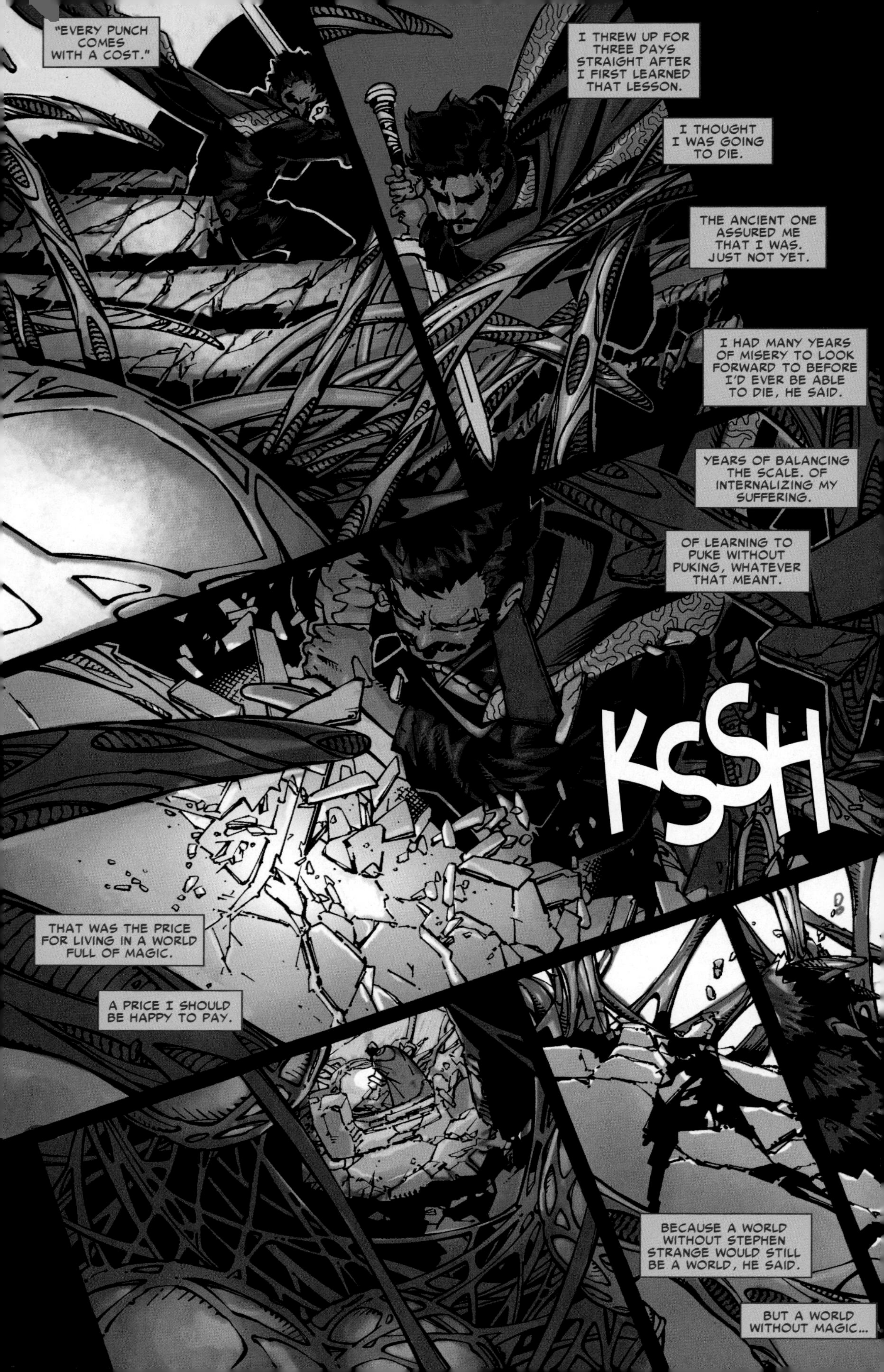
"EVERY PUNCH COMES WITH A COST."
I THREW UP FOR THREE DAYS STRAIGHT AFTER I FIRST LEARNED THAT LESSON.
I THOUGHT I WAS GOING TO DIE.
THE ANCIENT ONE ASSURED ME THAT I WAS. JUST NOT YET.
I HAD MANY YEARS OF MISERY TO LOOK FORWARD TO BEFORE I'D EVER BE ABLE TO DIE, HE SAID.
YEARS OF BALANCING THE SCALE. OF INTERNALIZING MY SUFFERING.
OF LEARNING TO PUKE WITHOUT PUKING, WHATEVER THAT MEANT.
KSSH
THAT WAS THE PRICE FOR LIVING IN A WORLD FULL OF MAGIC.
A PRICE I SHOULD BE HAPPY TO PAY.
BECAUSE A WORLD WITHOUT STEPHEN STRANGE WOULD STILL BE A WORLD, HE SAID.
BUT A WORLD WITHOUT MAGIC...

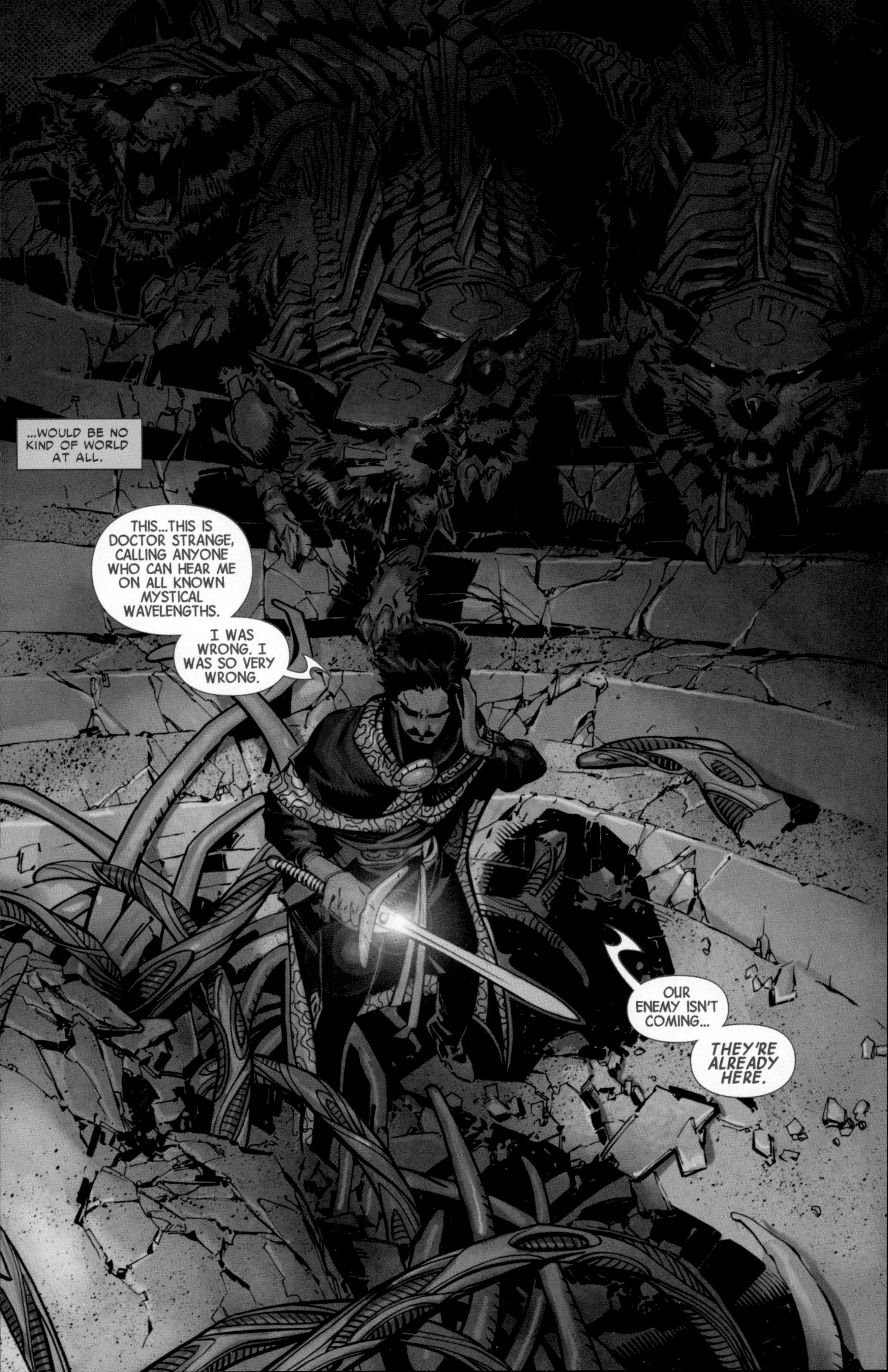
...WOULD BE NO KIND OF WORLD AT ALL.
THIS...THIS IS DOCTOR STRANGE, CALLING ANYONE WHO CAN HEAR ME ON ALL KNOWN MYSTICAL WAVELENGTHS.
I WAS WRONG. I WAS SO VERY WRONG.
OUR ENEMY ISN'T COMING...
THEY'RE ALREADY HERE.

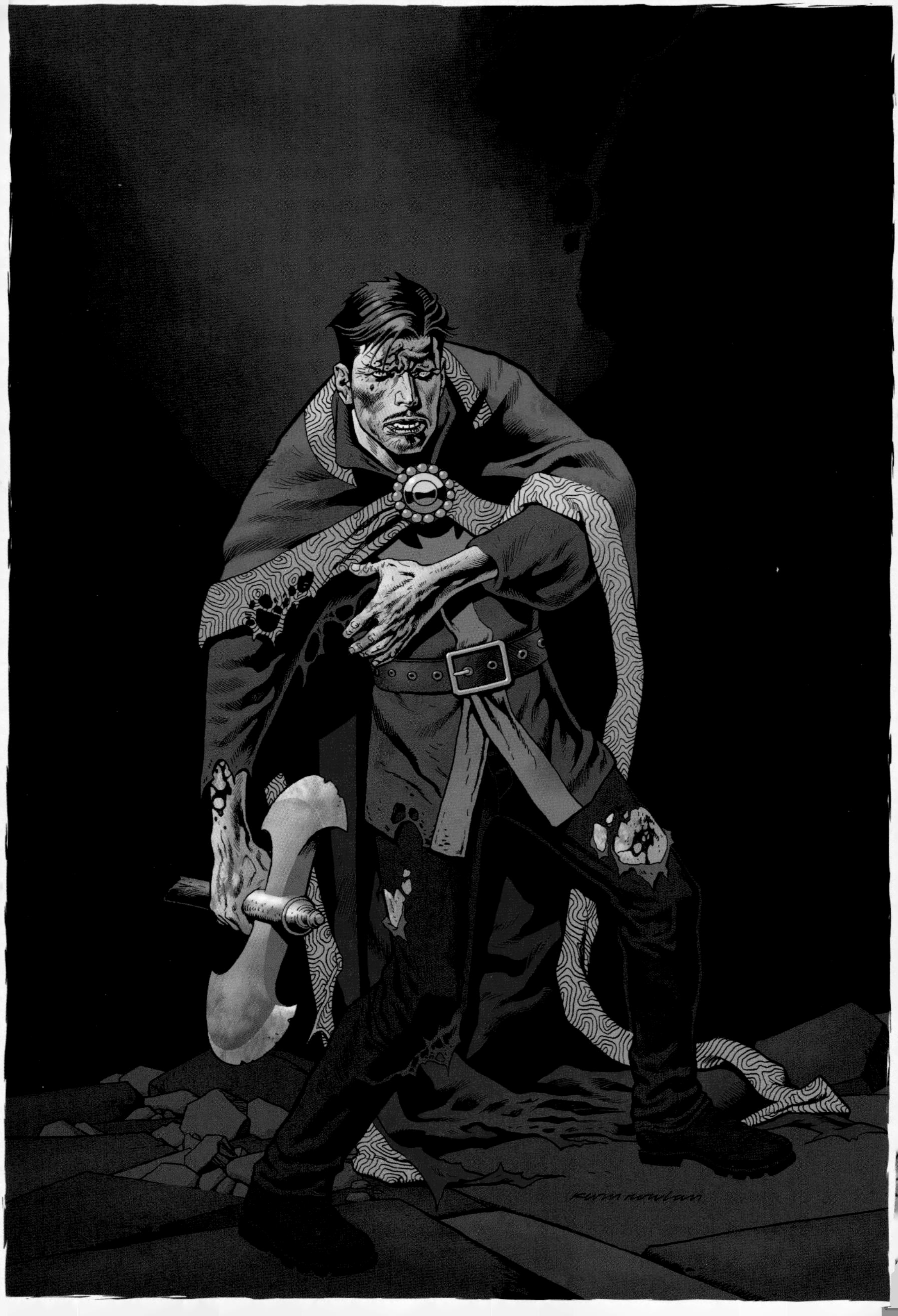

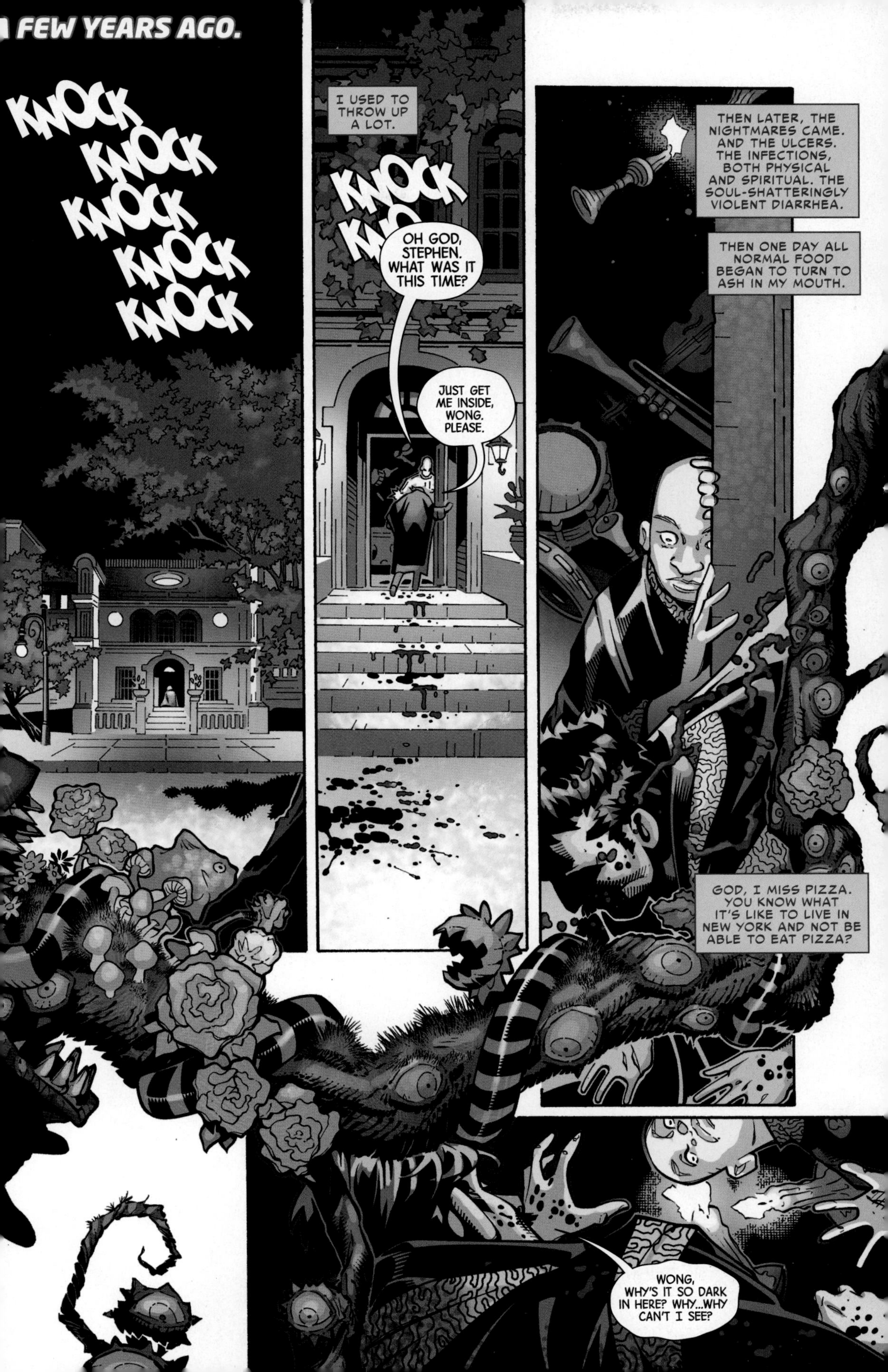
A FEW YEARS AGO.
KNOCK KNOCK KNOCK KNOCK KNOCK
I USED TO THROW UP A LOT.
KNOCK
OH GOD, STEPHEN. WHAT WAS IT THIS TIME?
JUST GET ME INSIDE, WONG. PLEASE.
THEN LATER, THE NIGHTMARES CAME. AND THE ULCERS. THE INFECTIONS, BOTH PHYSICAL AND SPIRITUAL. THE SOUL-SHATTERINGLY VIOLENT DIARRHEA.
THEN ONE DAY ALL NORMAL FOOD BEGAN TO TURN TO ASH IN MY MOUTH.
GOD, I MISS PIZZA. YOU KNOW WHAT IT'S LIKE TO LIVE IN NEW YORK AND NOT BE ABLE TO EAT PIZZA?
WONG, WHY'S IT SO DARK IN HERE? WHY...WHY CAN'T I SEE?

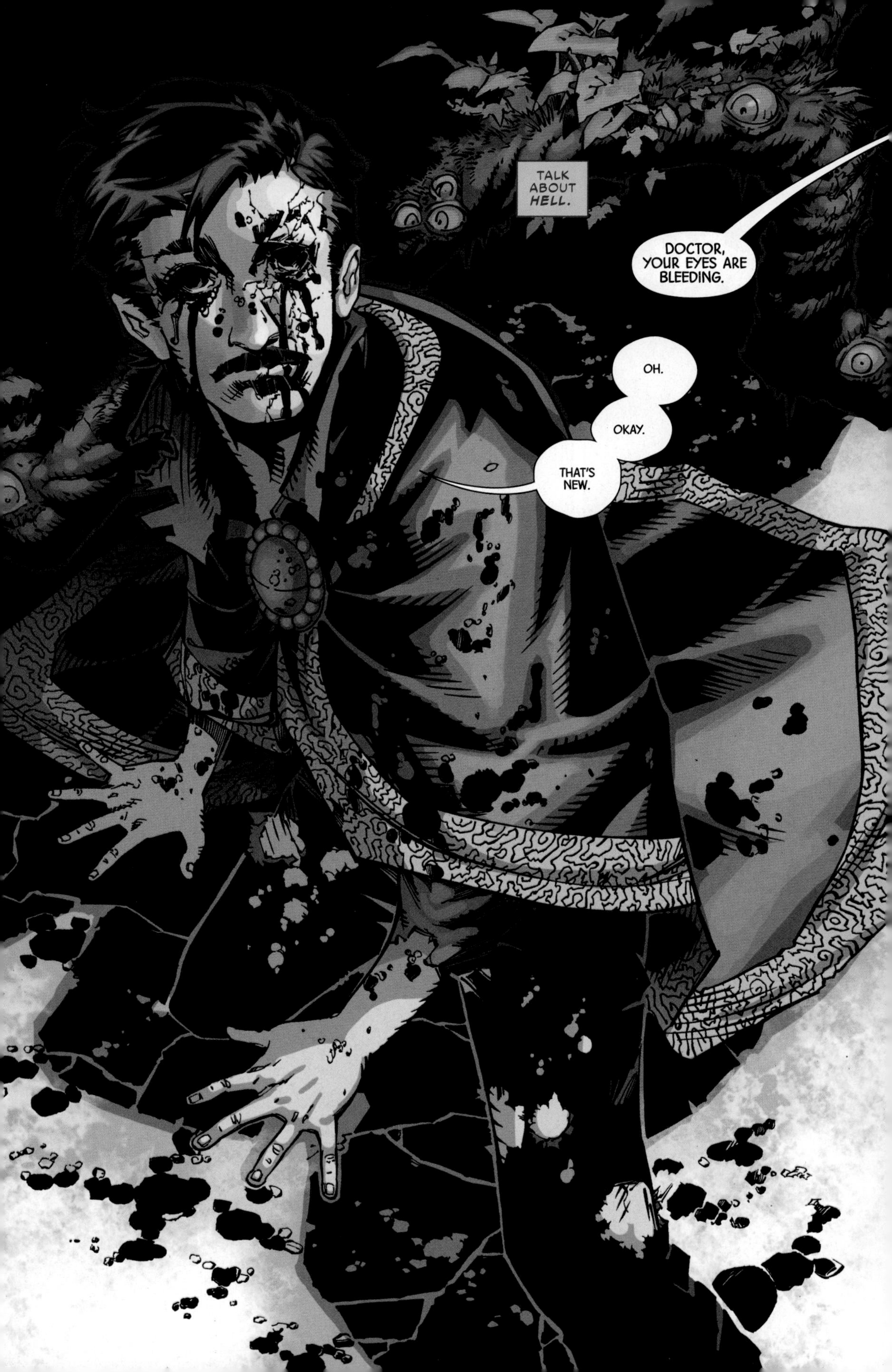
TALK ABOUT *HELL*.
DOCTOR, YOUR EYES ARE BLEEDING.
OH.
OKAY.
THAT'S NEW.

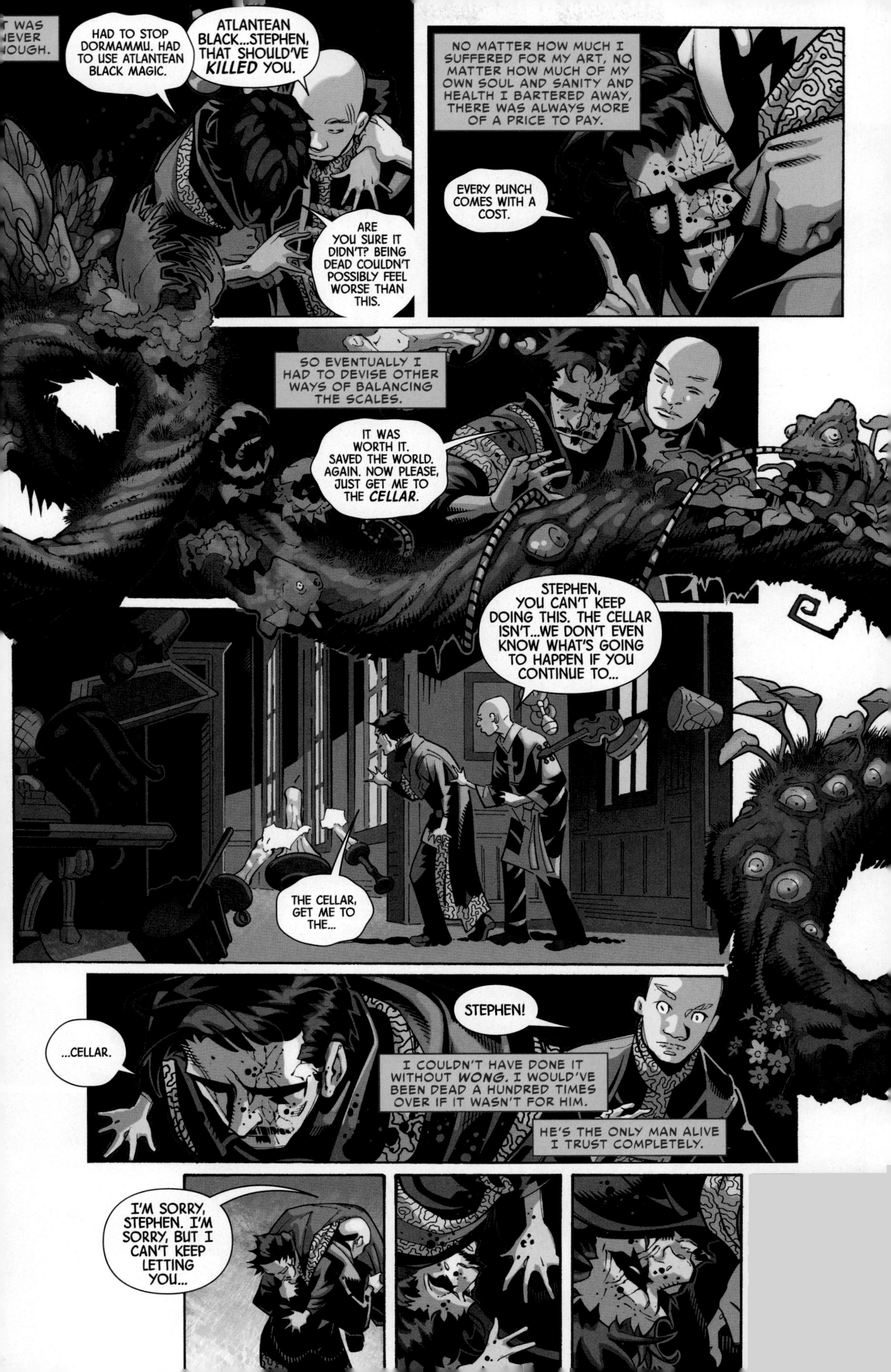

T WAS
NEVER
NOUGH.
HAD TO STOP DORMAMMU. HAD TO USE ATLANTEAN BLACK MAGIC.
ATLANTEAN BLACK...STEPHEN, THAT SHOULD'VE KILLED YOU.
ARE YOU SURE IT DIDN'T? BEING DEAD COULDN'T POSSIBLY FEEL WORSE THAN THIS.
NO MATTER HOW MUCH I SUFFERED FOR MY ART, NO MATTER HOW MUCH OF MY OWN SOUL AND SANITY AND HEALTH I BARTERED AWAY, THERE WAS ALWAYS MORE OF A PRICE TO PAY.
EVERY PUNCH COMES WITH A COST.
SO EVENTUALLY I HAD TO DEVISE OTHER WAYS OF BALANCING THE SCALES.
IT WAS WORTH IT. SAVED THE WORLD. AGAIN. NOW PLEASE, JUST GET ME TO THE CELLAR.
STEPHEN, YOU CAN'T KEEP DOING THIS. THE CELLAR ISN'T...WE DON'T EVEN KNOW WHAT'S GOING TO HAPPEN IF YOU CONTINUE TO...
THE CELLAR, GET ME TO THE...
...CELLAR.
STEPHEN!
I COULDN'T HAVE DONE IT WITHOUT WONG. I WOULD'VE BEEN DEAD A HUNDRED TIMES OVER IF IT WASN'T FOR HIM.
HE'S THE ONLY MAN ALIVE I TRUST COMPLETELY.
I'M SORRY, STEPHEN. I'M SORRY, BUT I CAN'T KEEP LETTING YOU...

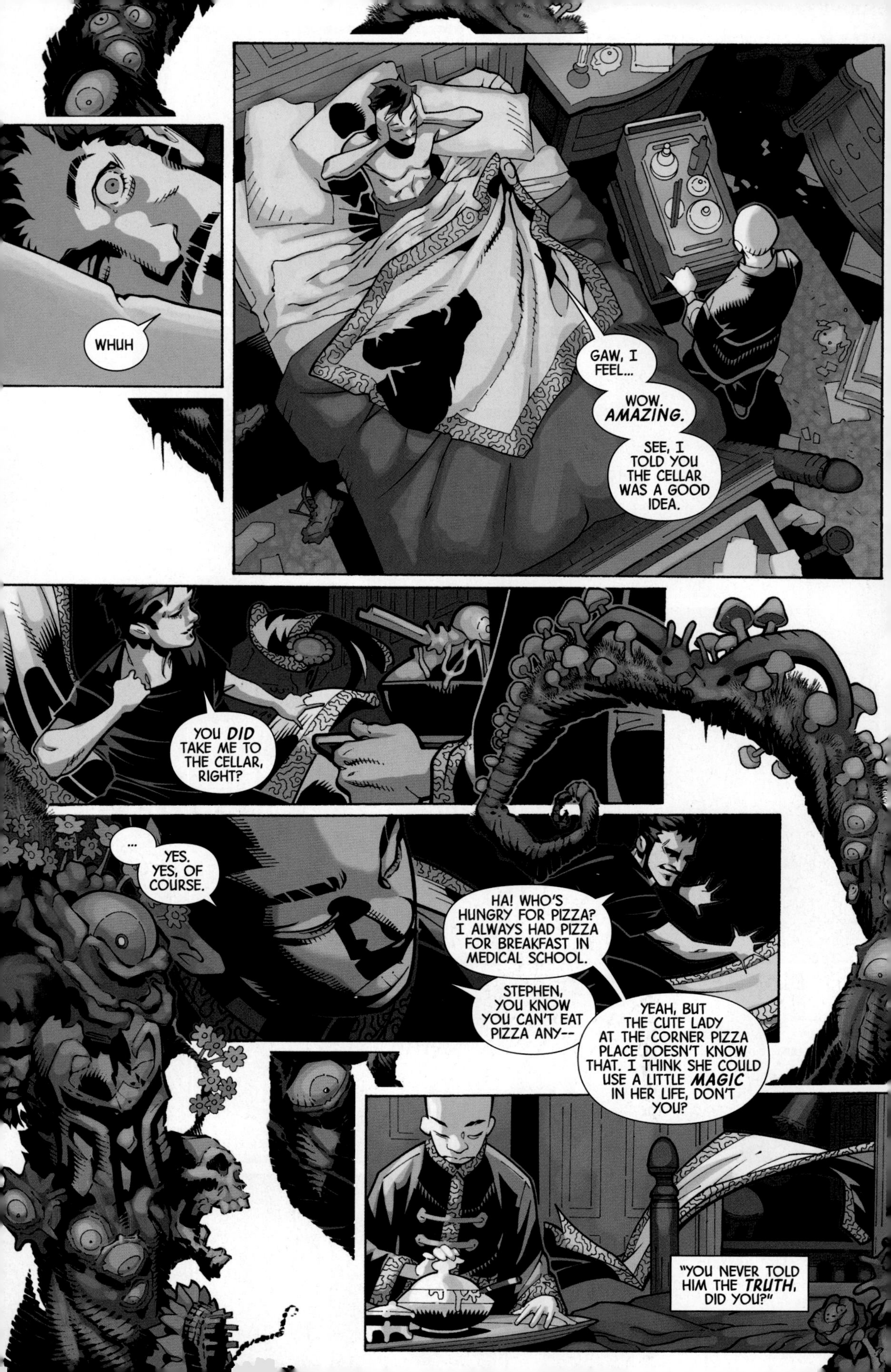
WHUH
GAW, I FEEL...
WOW. AMAZING.
SEE, I TOLD YOU THE CELLAR WAS A GOOD IDEA.
YOU DID TAKE ME TO THE CELLAR, RIGHT?
...
YES. YES, OF COURSE.
HA! WHO'S HUNGRY FOR PIZZA? I ALWAYS HAD PIZZA FOR BREAKFAST IN MEDICAL SCHOOL.
STEPHEN, YOU KNOW YOU CAN'T EAT PIZZA ANY--
YEAH, BUT THE CUTE LADY AT THE CORNER PIZZA PLACE DOESN'T KNOW THAT. I THINK SHE COULD USE A LITTLE MAGIC IN HER LIFE, DON'T YOU?
"YOU NEVER TOLD HIM THE TRUTH, DID YOU?"

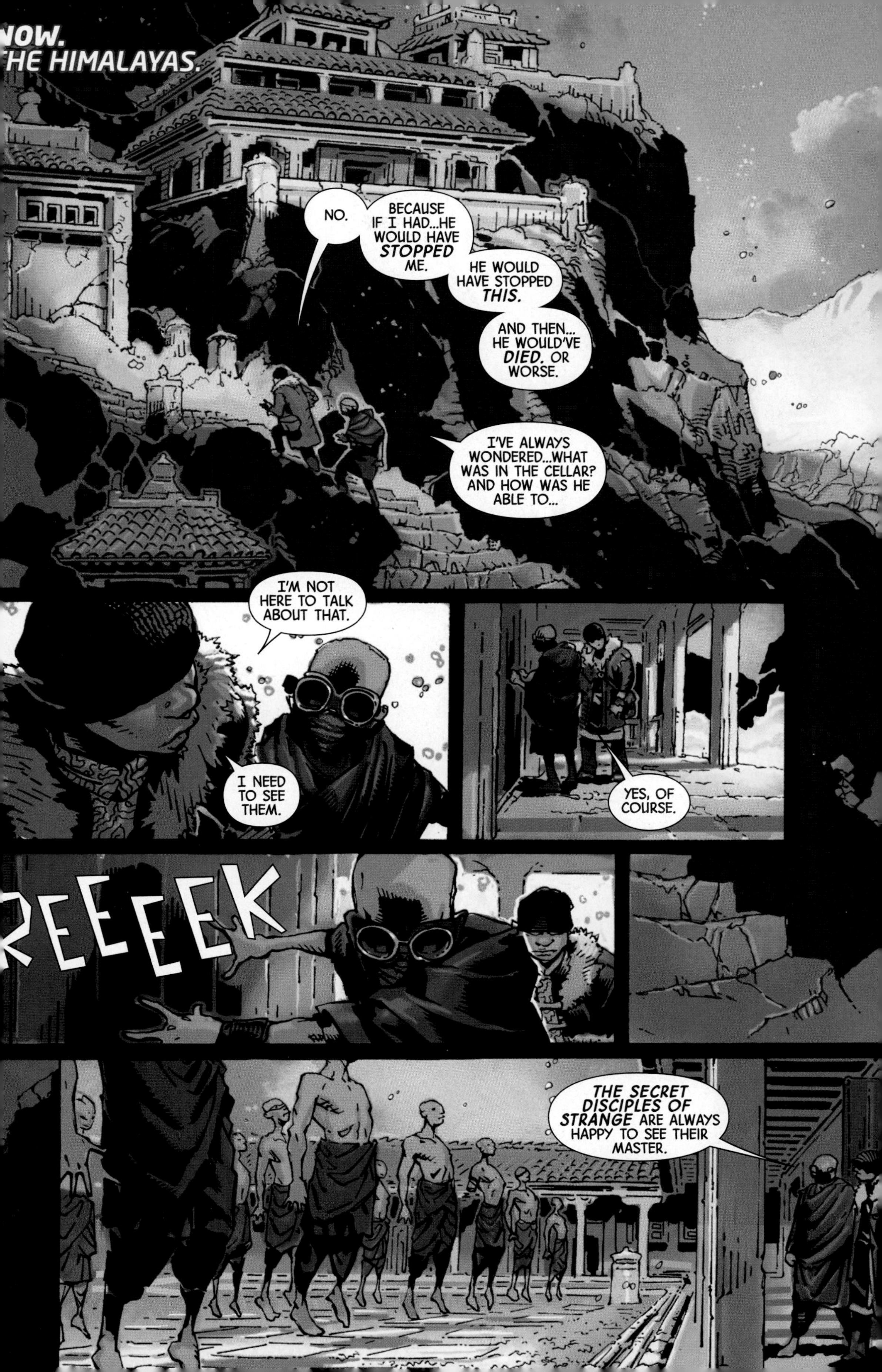
NOW.
THE HIMALAYAS.
NO.
BECAUSE IF I HAD...HE WOULD HAVE STOPPED ME.
HE WOULD HAVE STOPPED THIS.
AND THEN... HE WOULD'VE DIED. OR WORSE.
I'VE ALWAYS WONDERED...WHAT WAS IN THE CELLAR? AND HOW WAS HE ABLE TO...
I'M NOT HERE TO TALK ABOUT THAT.
I NEED TO SEE THEM.
YES, OF COURSE.
REEEEK
THE SECRET DISCIPLES OF STRANGE ARE ALWAYS HAPPY TO SEE THEIR MASTER.

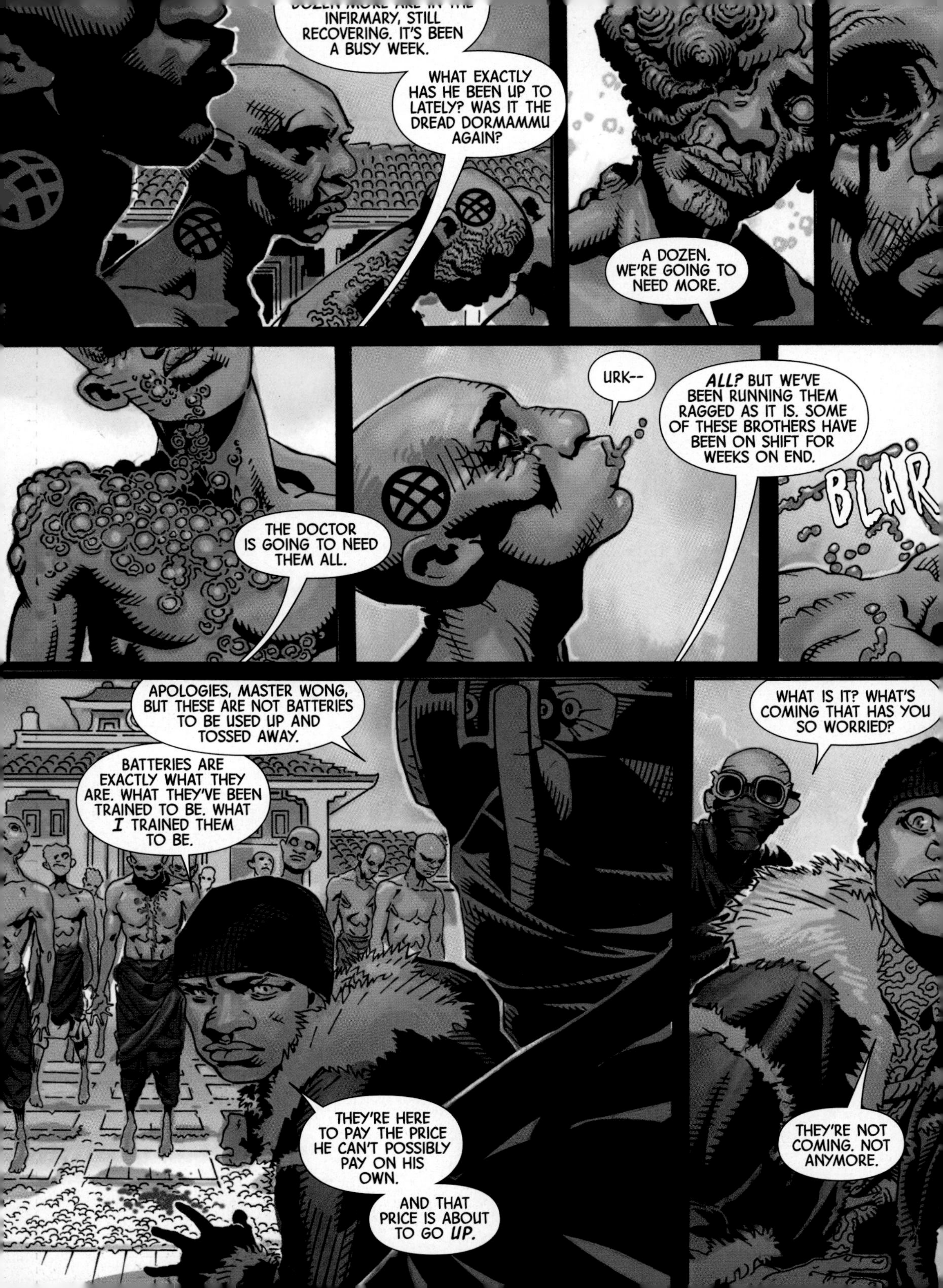
INFIRMARY, STILL RECOVERING. IT'S BEEN A BUSY WEEK.
WHAT EXACTLY HAS HE BEEN UP TO LATELY? WAS IT THE DREAD DORMAMMU AGAIN?
A DOZEN. WE'RE GOING TO NEED MORE.
THE DOCTOR IS GOING TO NEED THEM ALL.
URK--
ALL? BUT WE'VE BEEN RUNNING THEM RAGGED AS IT IS. SOME OF THESE BROTHERS HAVE BEEN ON SHIFT FOR WEEKS ON END.
BLAR
APOLOGIES, MASTER WONG, BUT THESE ARE NOT BATTERIES TO BE USED UP AND TOSSED AWAY.
BATTERIES ARE EXACTLY WHAT THEY ARE. WHAT THEY'VE BEEN TRAINED TO BE. WHAT I TRAINED THEM TO BE.
THEY'RE HERE TO PAY THE PRICE HE CAN'T POSSIBLY PAY ON HIS OWN.
AND THAT PRICE IS ABOUT TO GO UP.
WHAT IS IT? WHAT'S COMING THAT HAS YOU SO WORRIED?
THEY'RE NOT COMING. NOT ANYMORE.

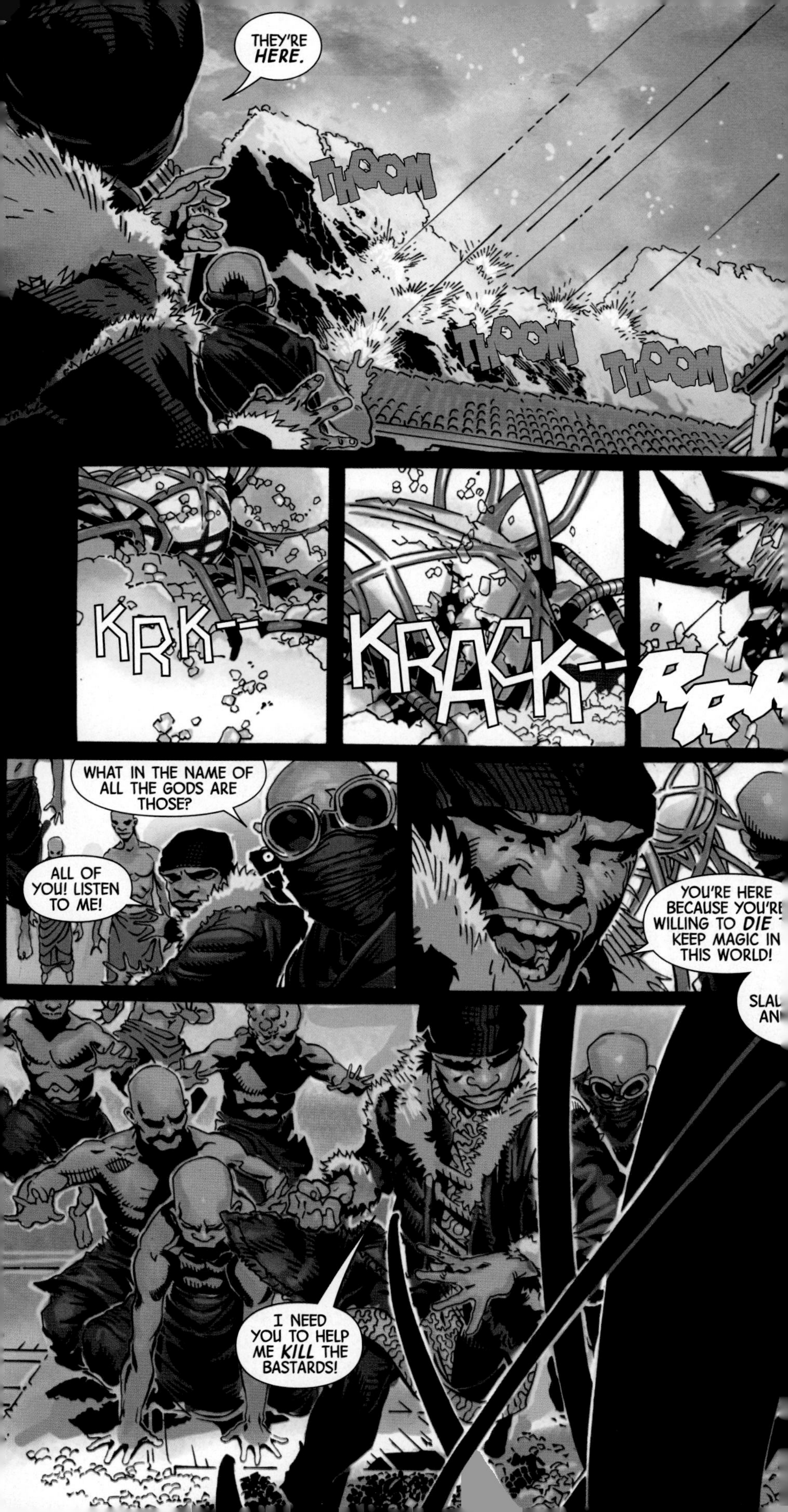
THEY'RE HERE.
THOOM
THOOM
THOOM
KRK--
KRACK--
WHAT IN THE NAME OF ALL THE GODS ARE THOSE?
ALL OF YOU! LISTEN TO ME!
YOU'RE HERE BECAUSE YOU'RE WILLING TO DIE TO KEEP MAGIC IN THIS WORLD!
I NEED YOU TO HELP ME KILL THE BASTARDS!

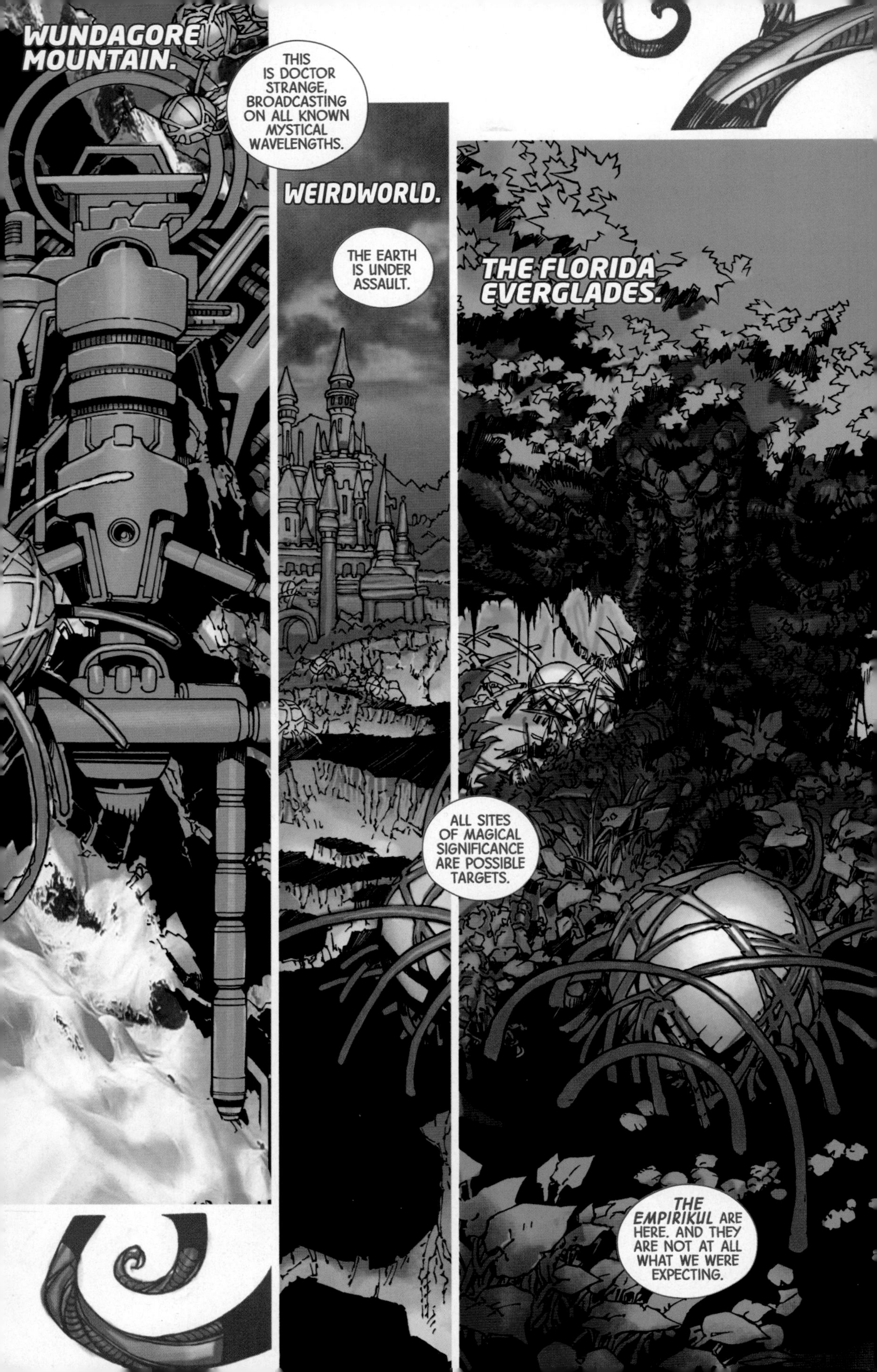
WUNDAGORE MOUNTAIN.
THIS IS DOCTOR STRANGE, BROADCASTING ON ALL KNOWN MYSTICAL WAVELENGTHS.
WEIRDWORLD.
THE EARTH IS UNDER ASSAULT.
THE FLORIDA EVERGLADES.
ALL SITES OF MAGICAL SIGNIFICANCE ARE POSSIBLE TARGETS.
THE EMPIRIKUL ARE HERE. AND THEY ARE NOT AT ALL WHAT WE WERE EXPECTING.

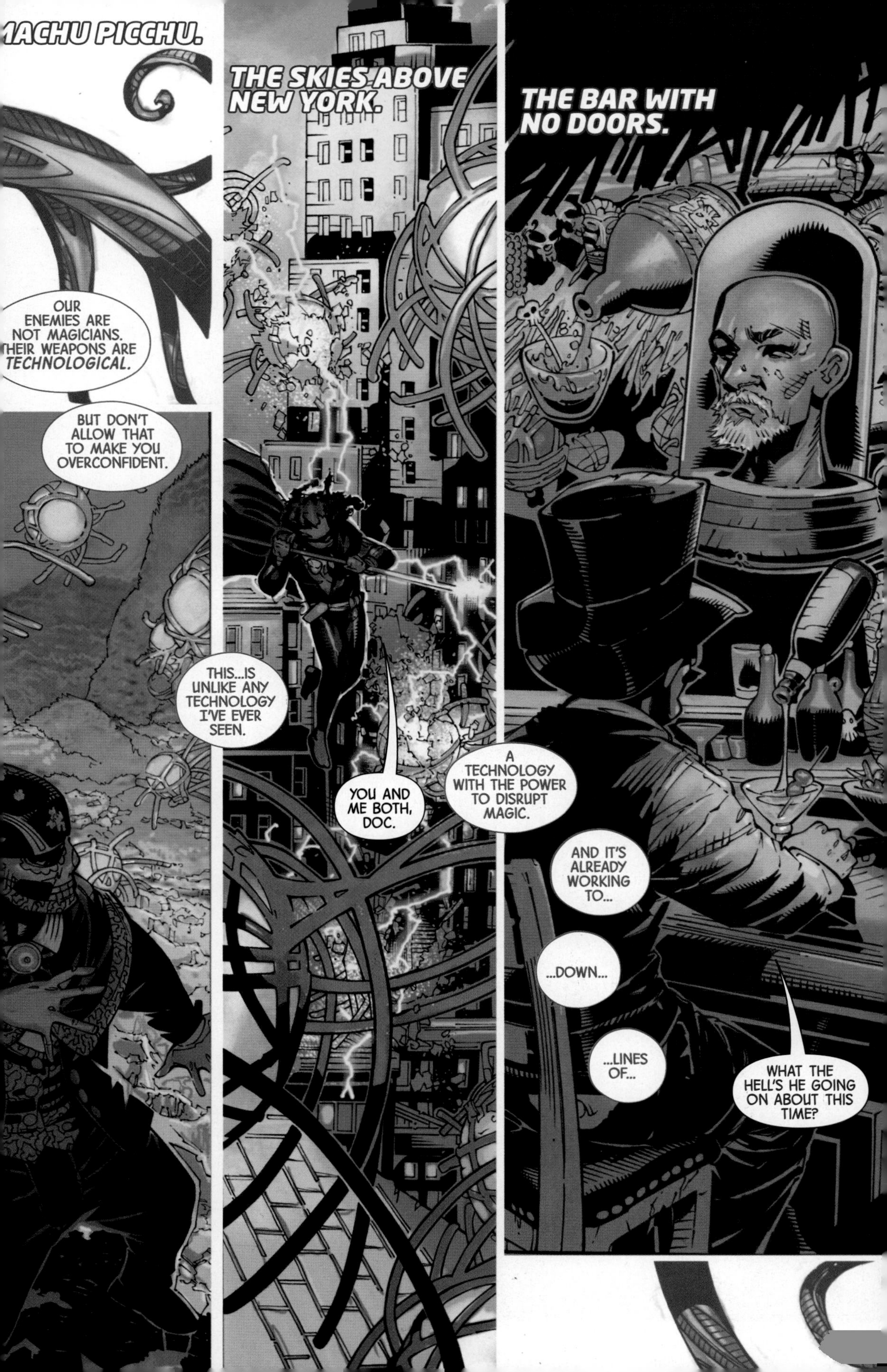
MACHU PICCHU.
OUR ENEMIES ARE NOT MAGICIANS. THEIR WEAPONS ARE TECHNOLOGICAL.
BUT DON'T ALLOW THAT TO MAKE YOU OVERCONFIDENT.
THE SKIES ABOVE NEW YORK.
THIS...IS UNLIKE ANY TECHNOLOGY I'VE EVER SEEN.
YOU AND ME BOTH, DOC.
A TECHNOLOGY WITH THE POWER TO DISRUPT MAGIC.
THE BAR WITH NO DOORS.
AND IT'S ALREADY WORKING TO...
...DOWN...
...LINES OF...
WHAT THE HELL'S HE GOING ON ABOUT THIS TIME?

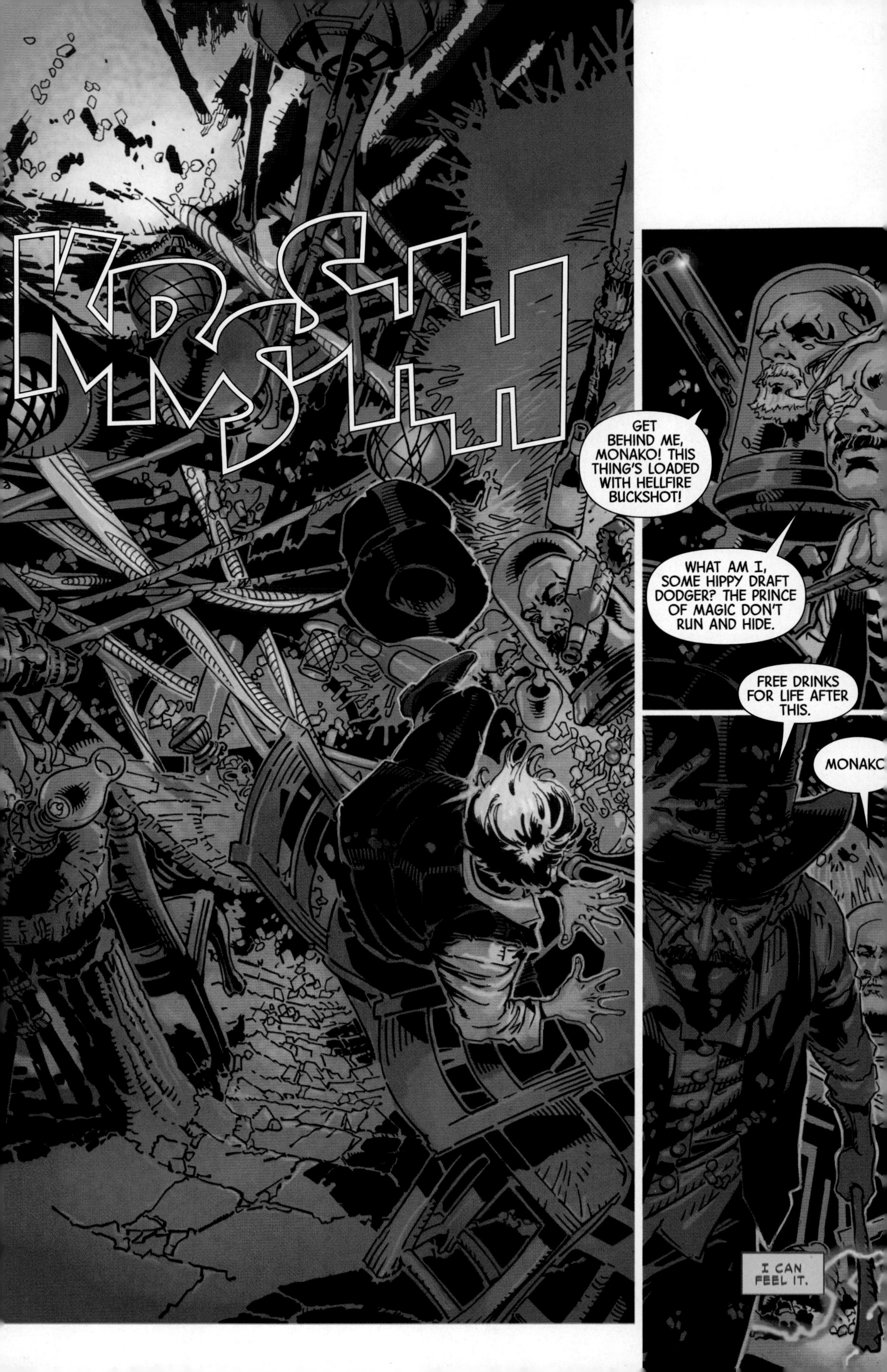
GET BEHIND ME, MONAKO! THIS THING'S LOADED WITH HELLFIRE BUCKSHOT!
WHAT AM I, SOME HIPPY DRAFT DODGER? THE PRINCE OF MAGIC DON'T RUN AND HIDE.
FREE DRINKS FOR LIFE AFTER THIS.
I CAN FEEL IT.

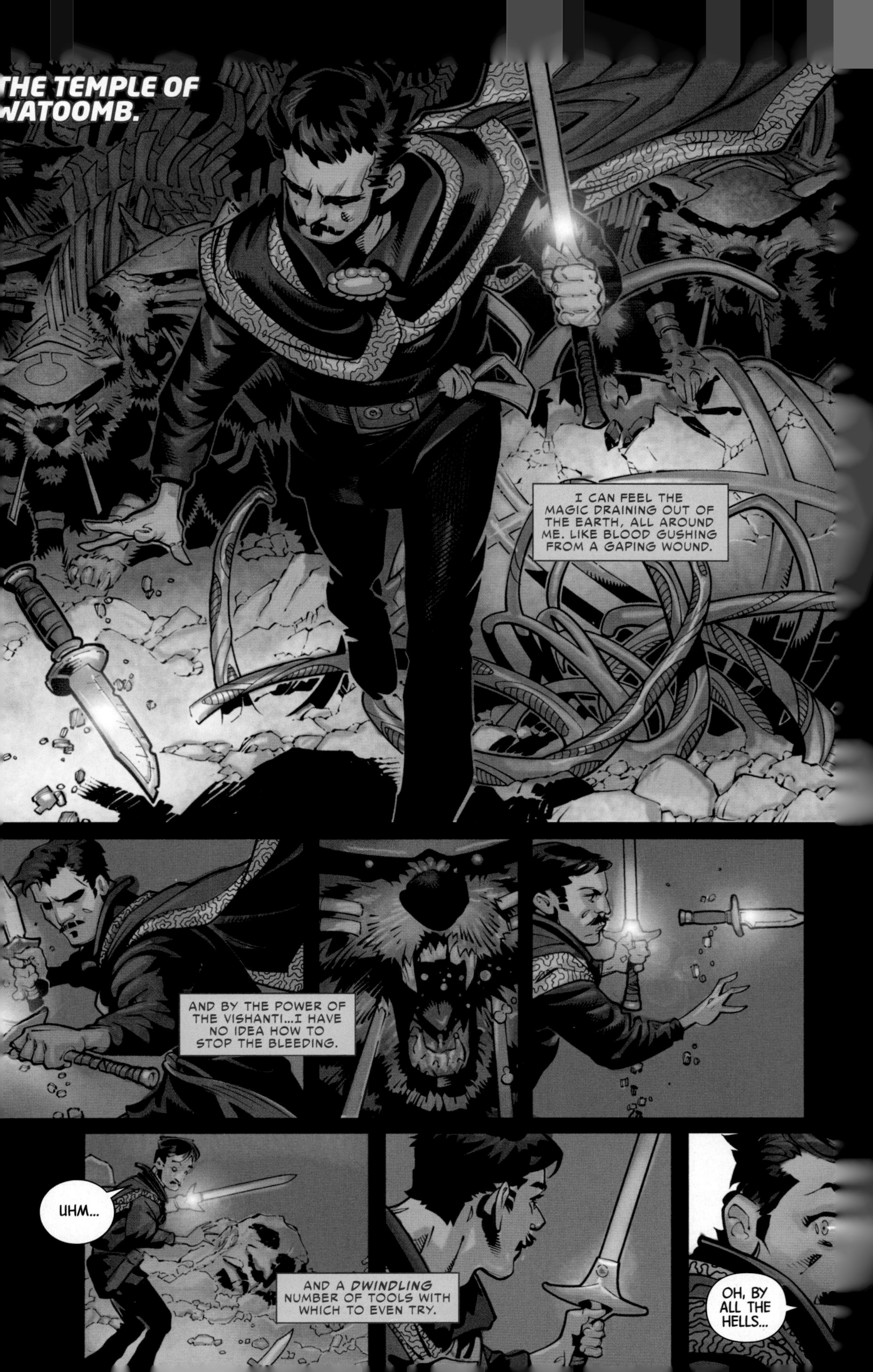
THE TEMPLE OF WATOOMB.
I CAN FEEL THE MAGIC DRAINING OUT OF THE EARTH, ALL AROUND ME. LIKE BLOOD GUSHING FROM A GAPING WOUND.
AND BY THE POWER OF THE VISHANTI...I HAVE NO IDEA HOW TO STOP THE BLEEDING.
UHM...
AND A DWINDLING NUMBER OF TOOLS WITH WHICH TO EVEN TRY.
OH, BY ALL THE HELLS...

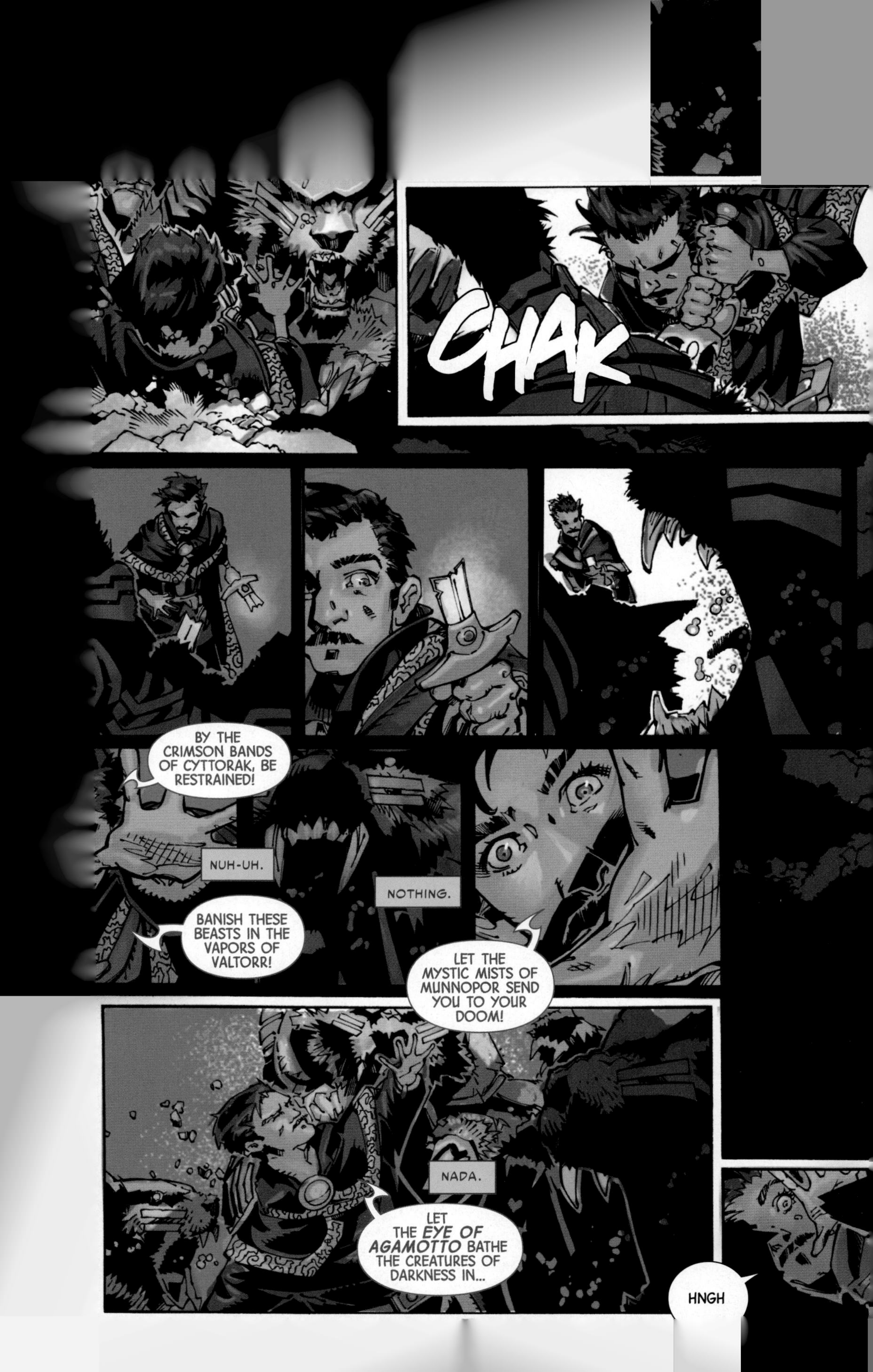
CHAK
BY THE CRIMSON BANDS OF CYTTORAK, BE RESTRAINED!
NUH-UH.
BANISH THESE BEASTS IN THE VAPORS OF VALTORR!
NOTHING.
LET THE MYSTIC MISTS OF MUNNOPOR SEND YOU TO YOUR DOOM!
NADA.
LET THE *EYE OF AGAMOTTO* BATHE THE CREATURES OF DARKNESS IN...
HNGH

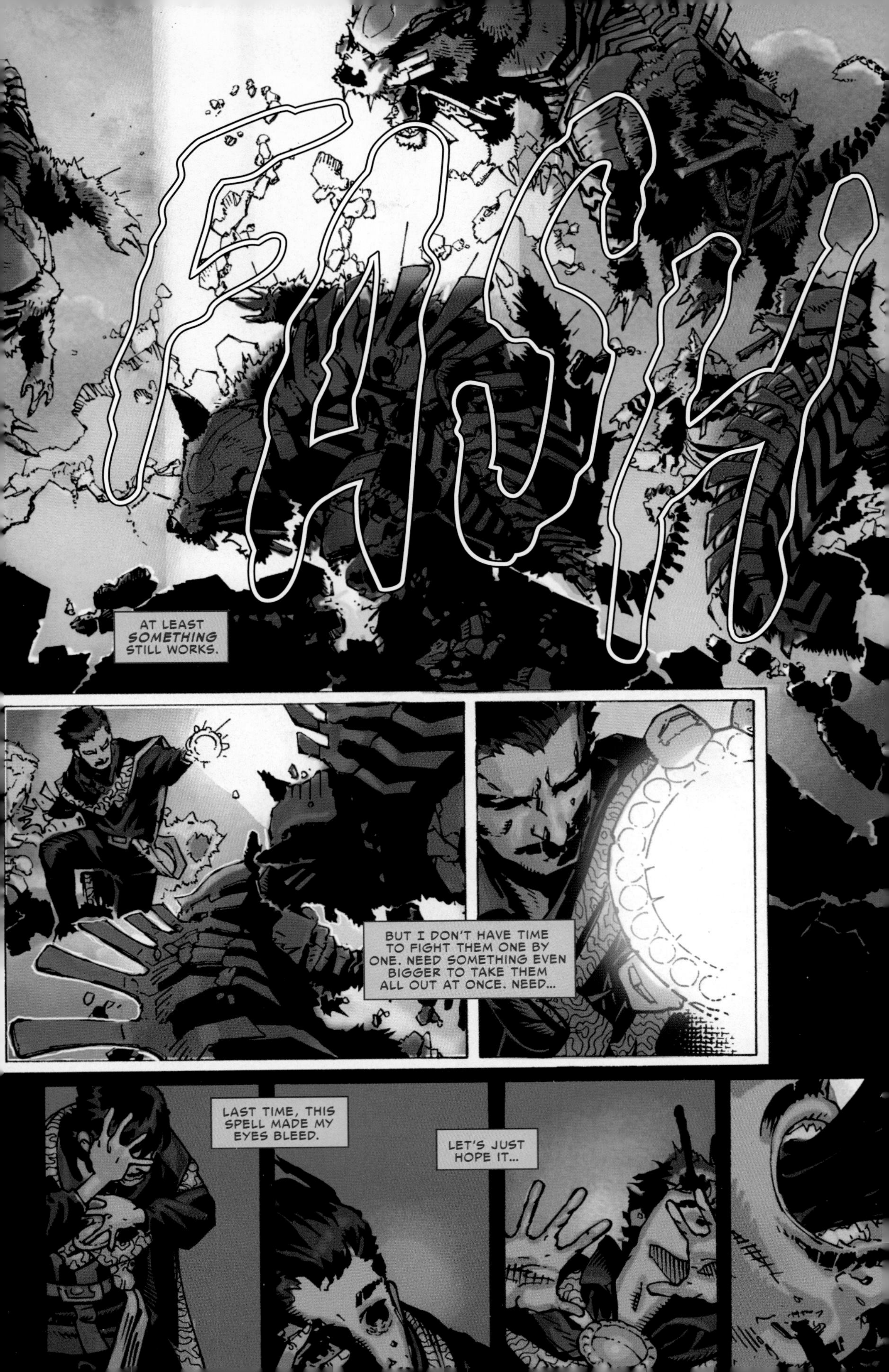
FWOOM
AT LEAST SOMETHING STILL WORKS.
BUT I DON'T HAVE TIME TO FIGHT THEM ONE BY ONE. NEED SOMETHING EVEN BIGGER TO TAKE THEM ALL OUT AT ONCE. NEED...
LAST TIME, THIS SPELL MADE MY EYES BLEED.
LET'S JUST HOPE IT...

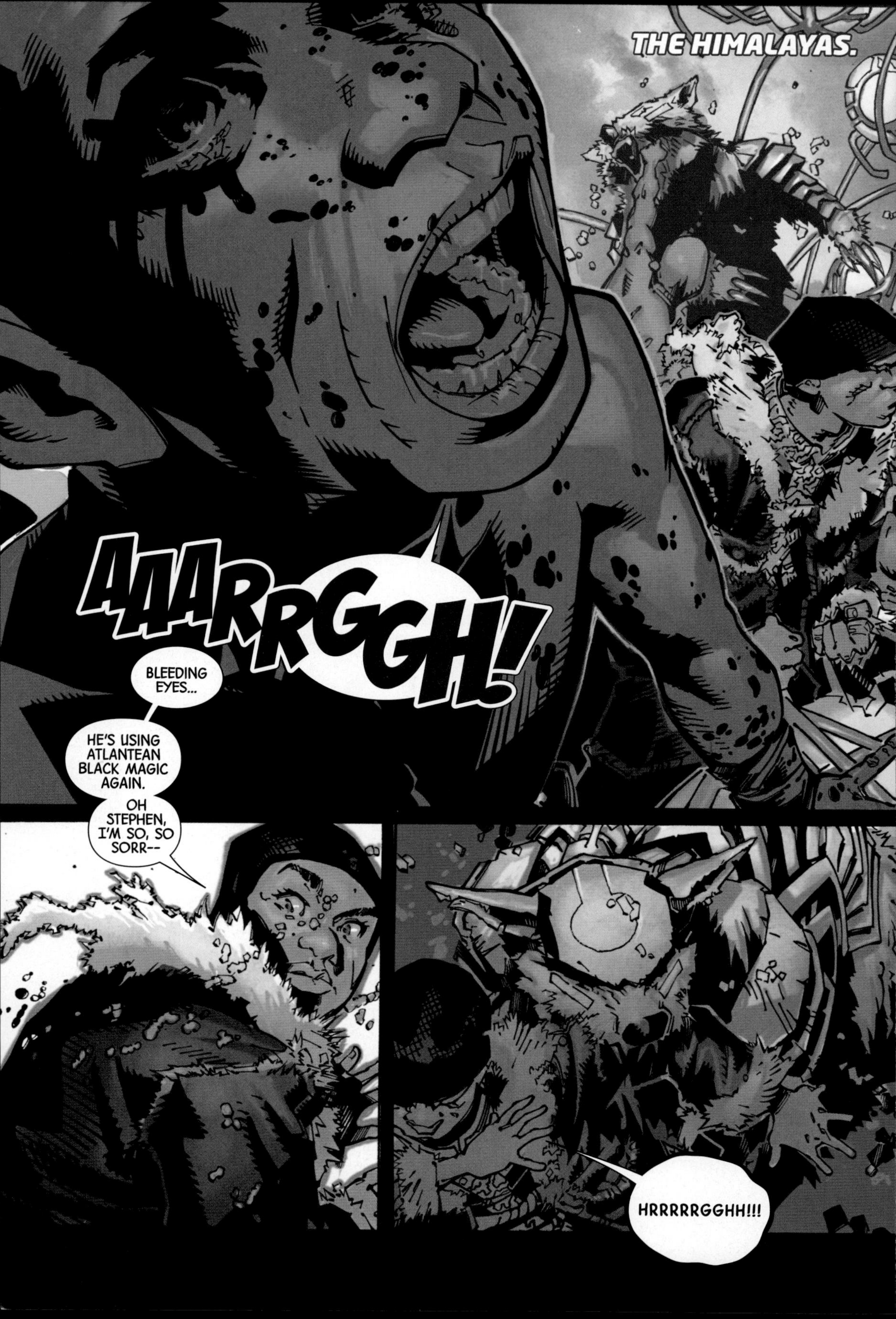
THE HIMALAYAS.
AAARRGGH!
BLEEDING EYES...
HE'S USING ATLANTEAN BLACK MAGIC AGAIN.
OH STEPHEN, I'M SO, SO SORR--
HRRRRRGGHH!!!

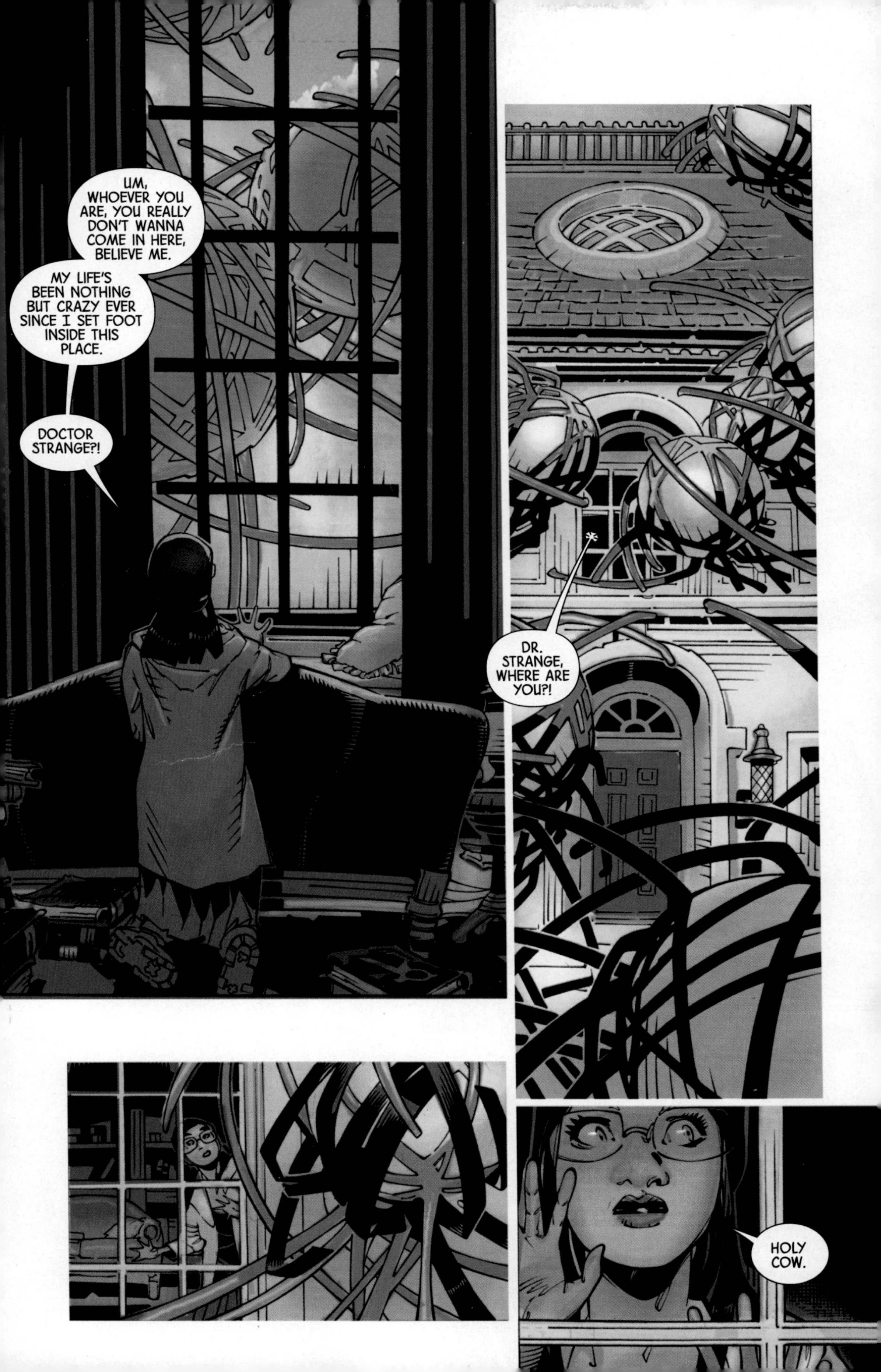
UM, WHOEVER YOU ARE, YOU REALLY DON'T WANNA COME IN HERE, BELIEVE ME.
MY LIFE'S BEEN NOTHING BUT CRAZY EVER SINCE I SET FOOT INSIDE THIS PLACE.
DOCTOR STRANGE?!
DR. STRANGE, WHERE ARE YOU?!
HOLY COW.

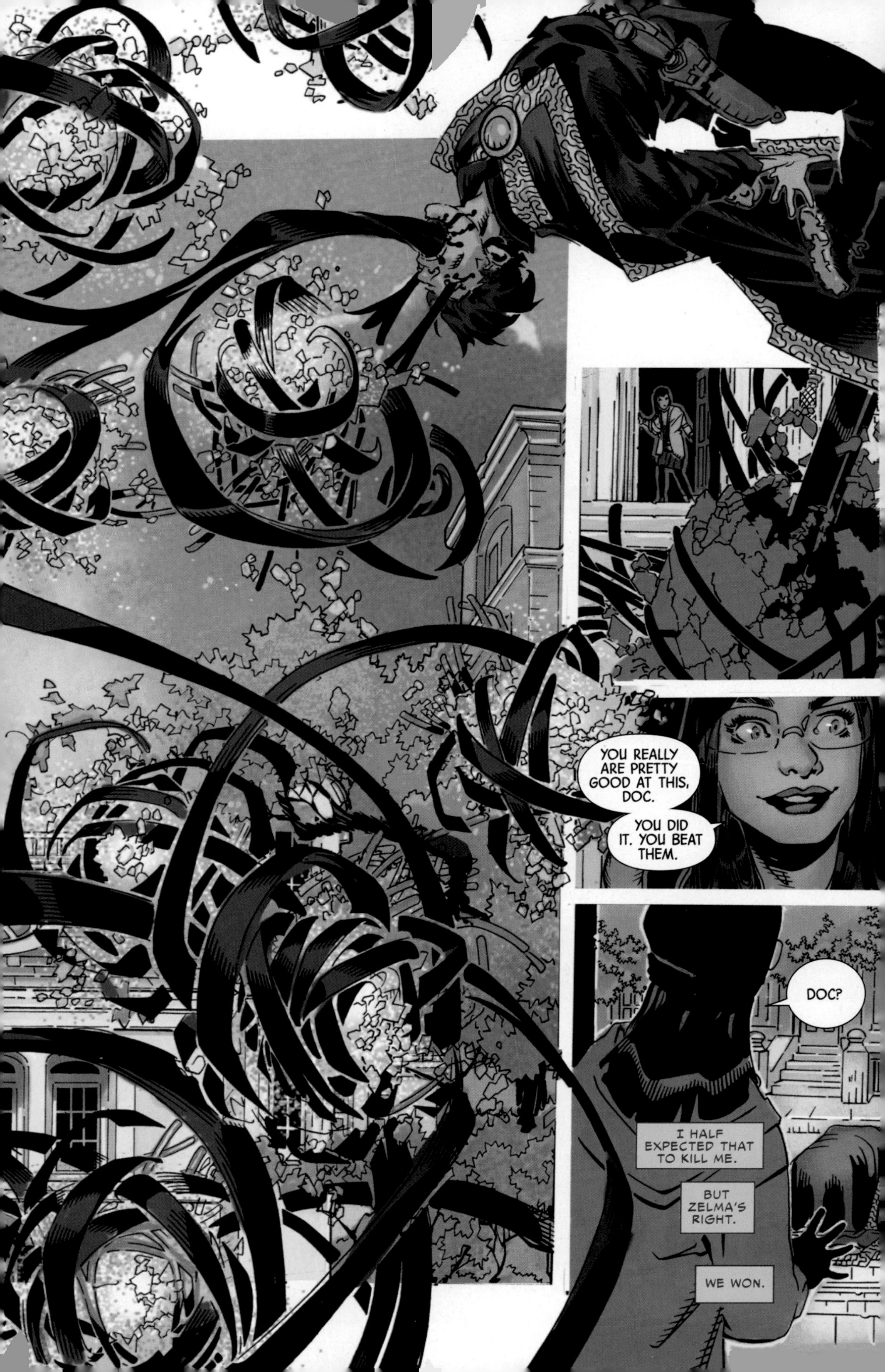
YOU REALLY ARE PRETTY GOOD AT THIS, DOC.
YOU DID IT. YOU BEAT THEM.
DOC?
I HALF EXPECTED THAT TO KILL ME.
BUT ZELMA'S RIGHT.
WE WON.

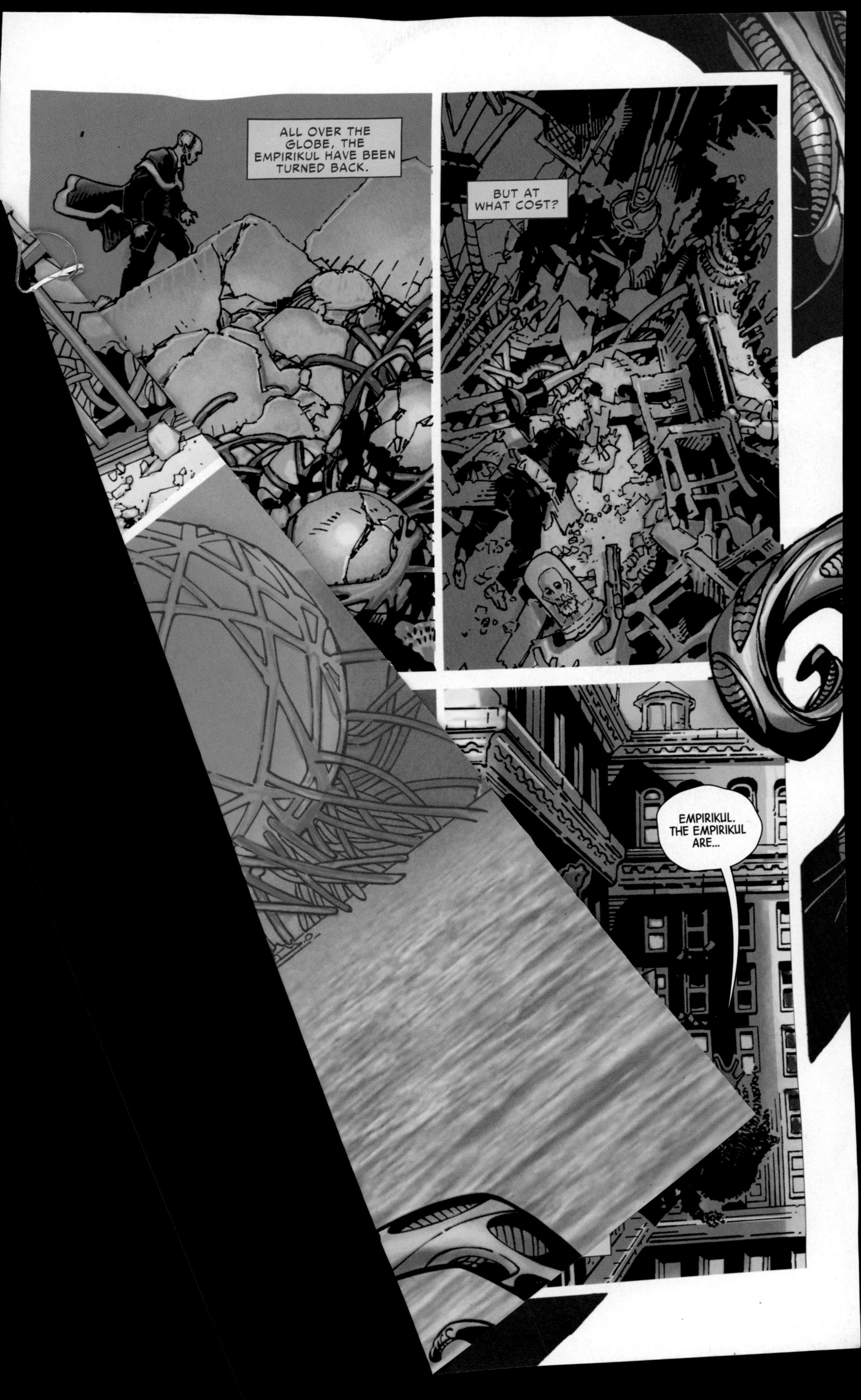

ALL OVER THE GLOBE, THE EMPIRIKUL HAVE BEEN TURNED BACK.
BUT AT WHAT COST?
EMPIRIKUL. THE EMPIRIKUL ARE...

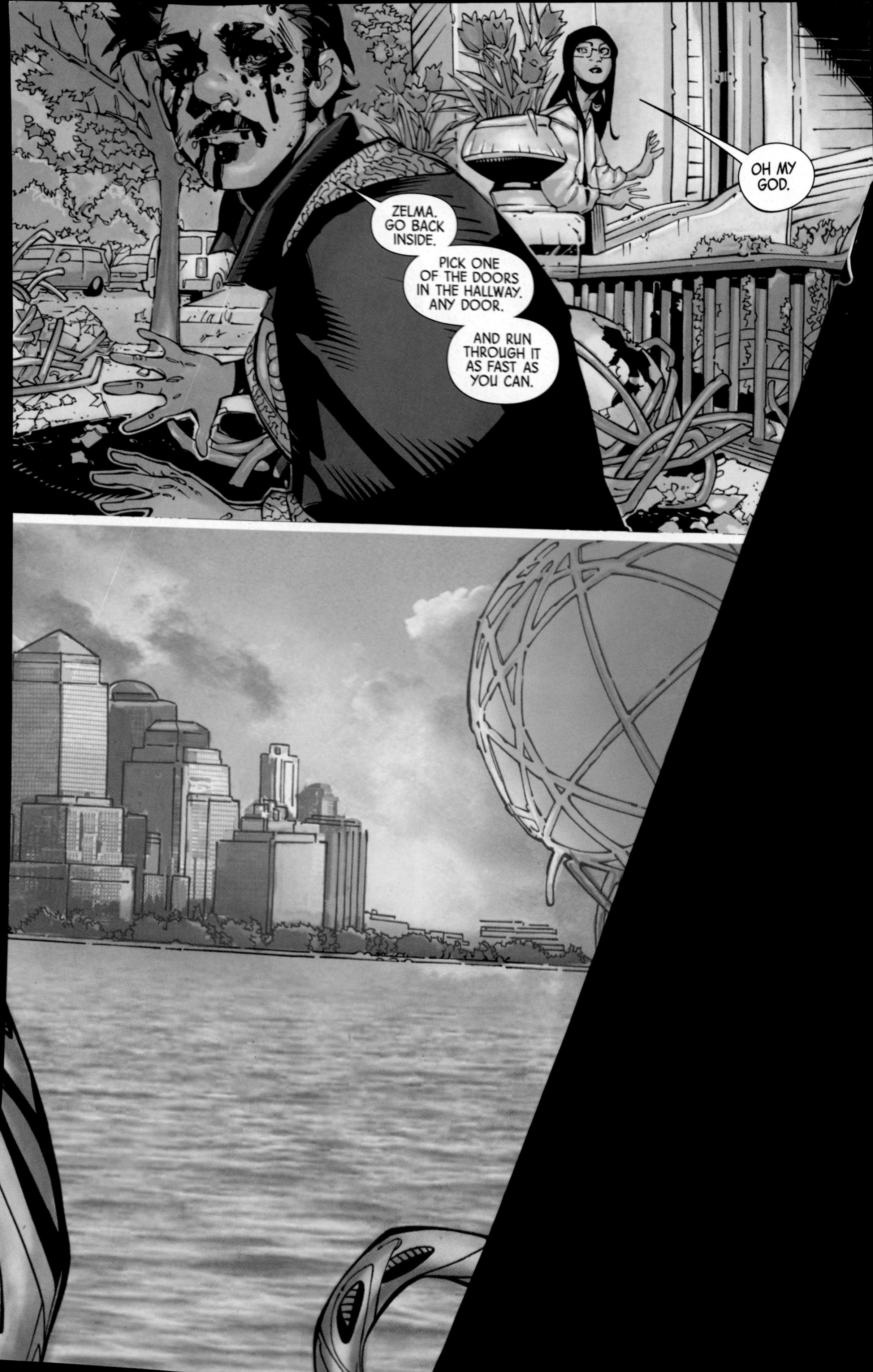
OH MY GOD.
ZELMA. GO BACK INSIDE.
PICK ONE OF THE DOORS IN THE HALLWAY. ANY DOOR.
AND RUN THROUGH IT AS FAST AS YOU CAN.

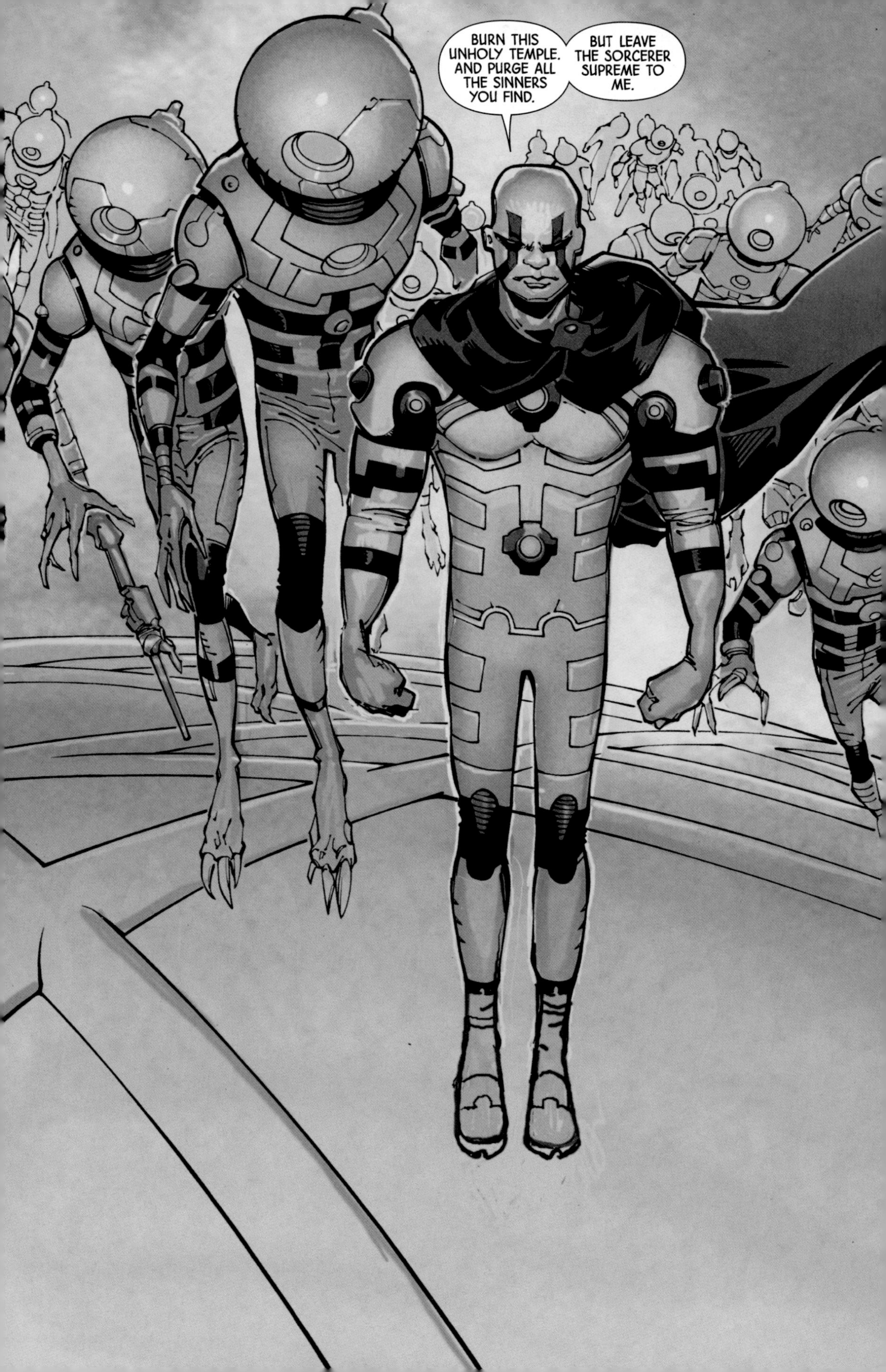
BURN THIS UNHOLY TEMPLE. AND PURGE ALL THE SINNERS YOU FIND.
BUT LEAVE THE SORCERER SUPREME TO ME.

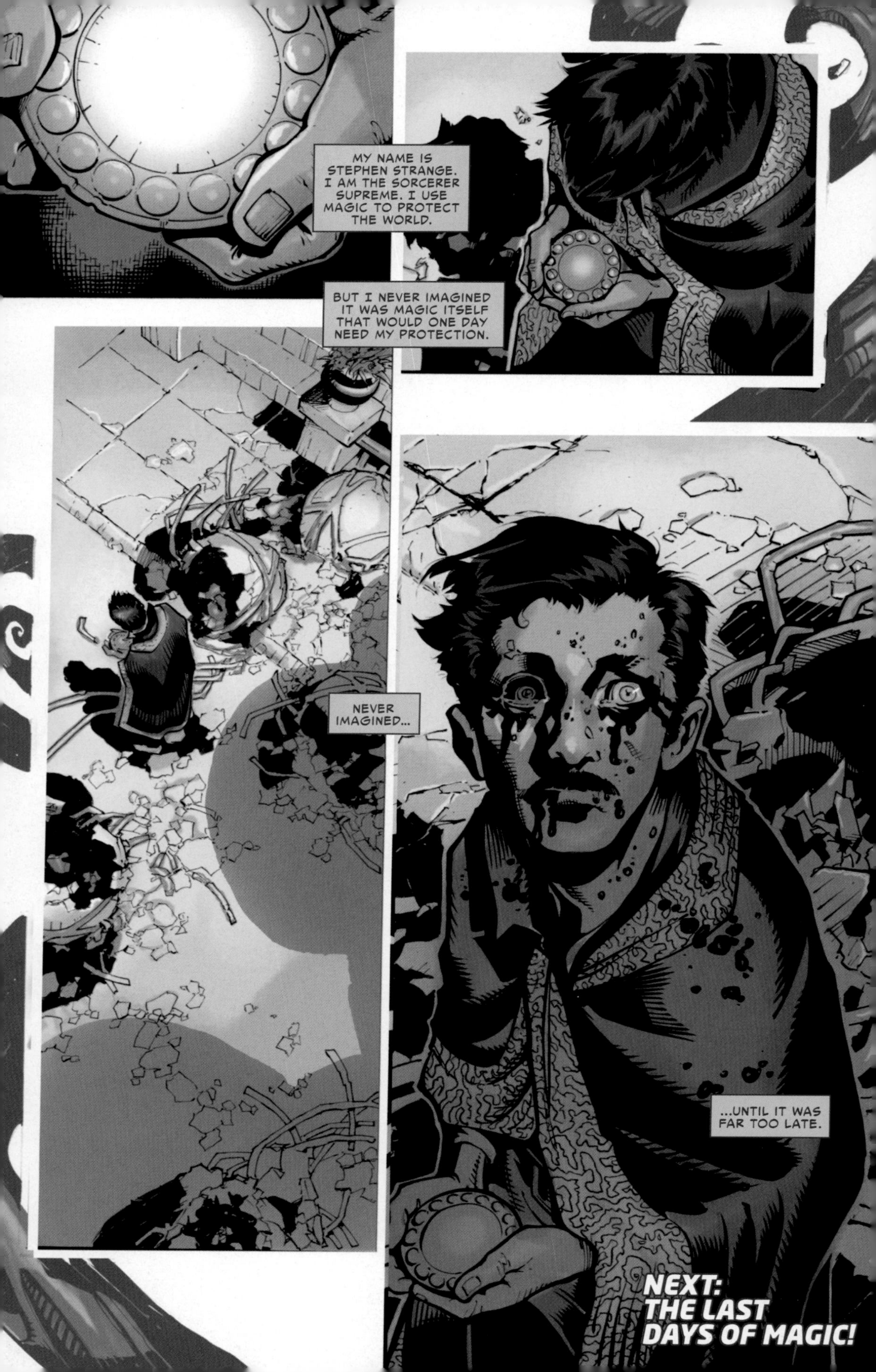
MY NAME IS STEPHEN STRANGE. I AM THE SORCERER SUPREME. I USE MAGIC TO PROTECT THE WORLD.
BUT I NEVER IMAGINED IT WAS MAGIC ITSELF THAT WOULD ONE DAY NEED MY PROTECTION.
NEVER IMAGINED...
...UNTIL IT WAS FAR TOO LATE.
NEXT: THE LAST DAYS OF MAGIC!

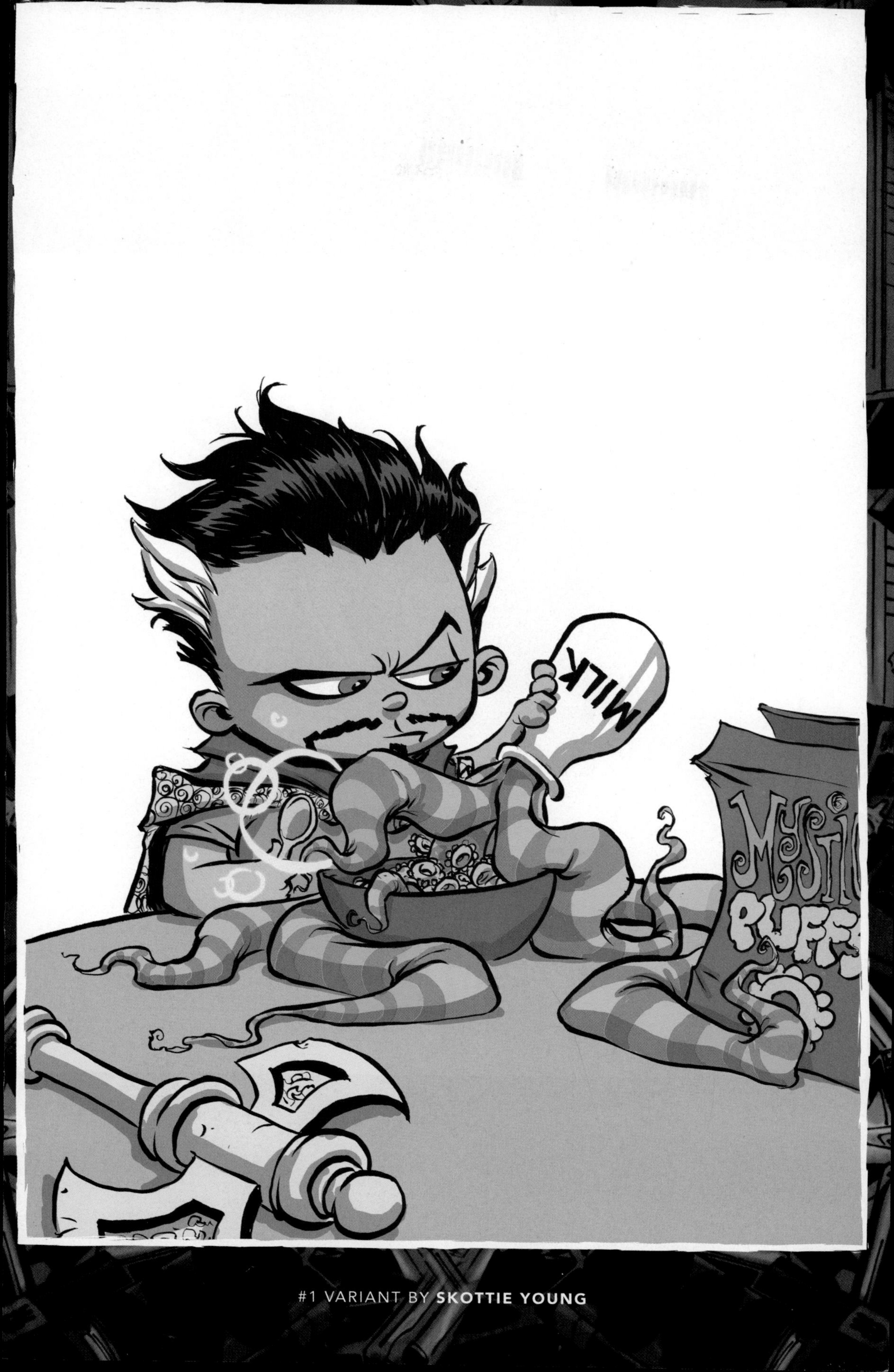
MILK
MYSTIC
PUFFS

#1 VARIANT BY **SKOTTIE YOUNG**

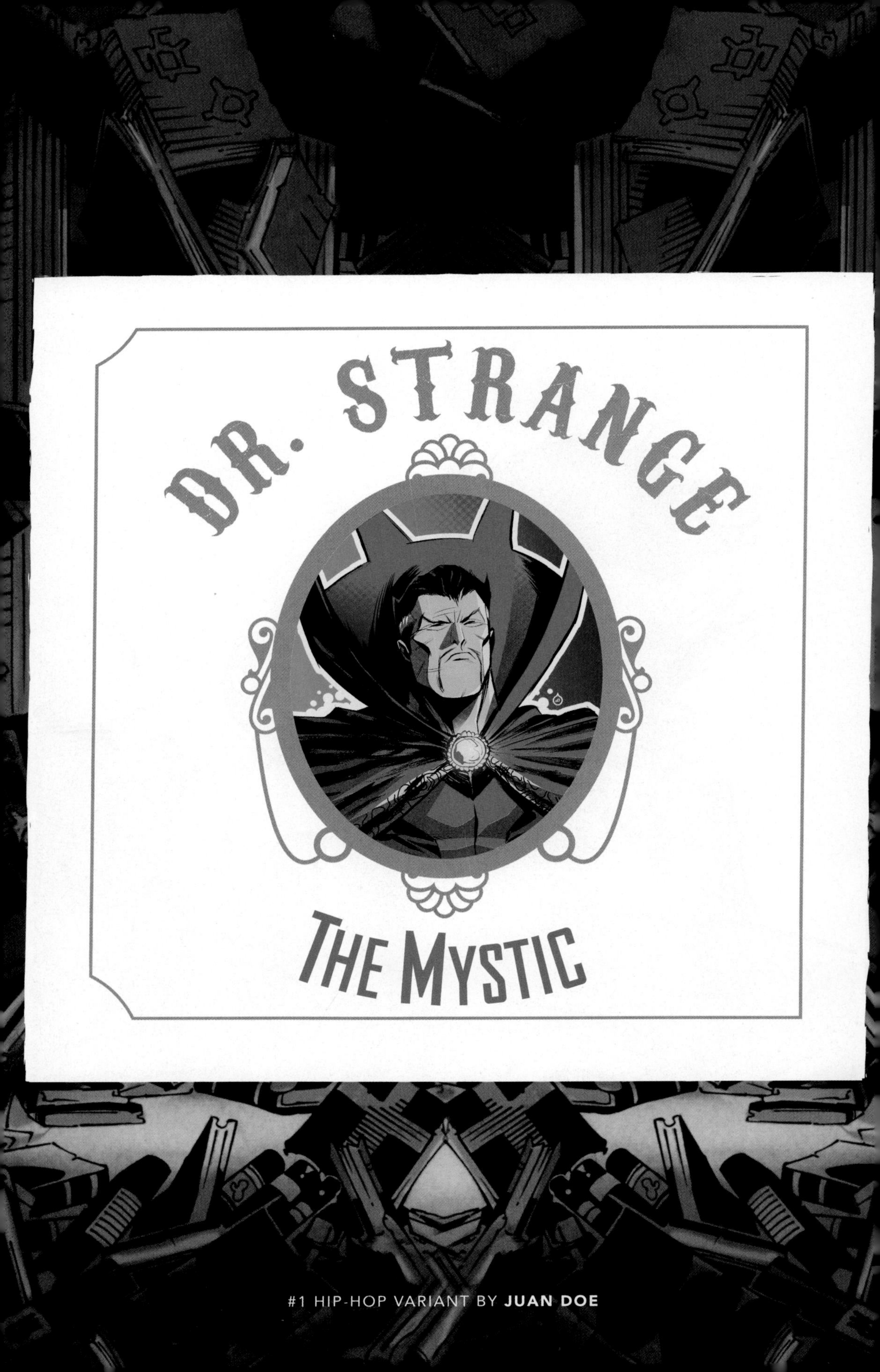
DR. STRANGE
THE MYSTIC

#1 HIP-HOP VARIANT BY **JUAN DOE**

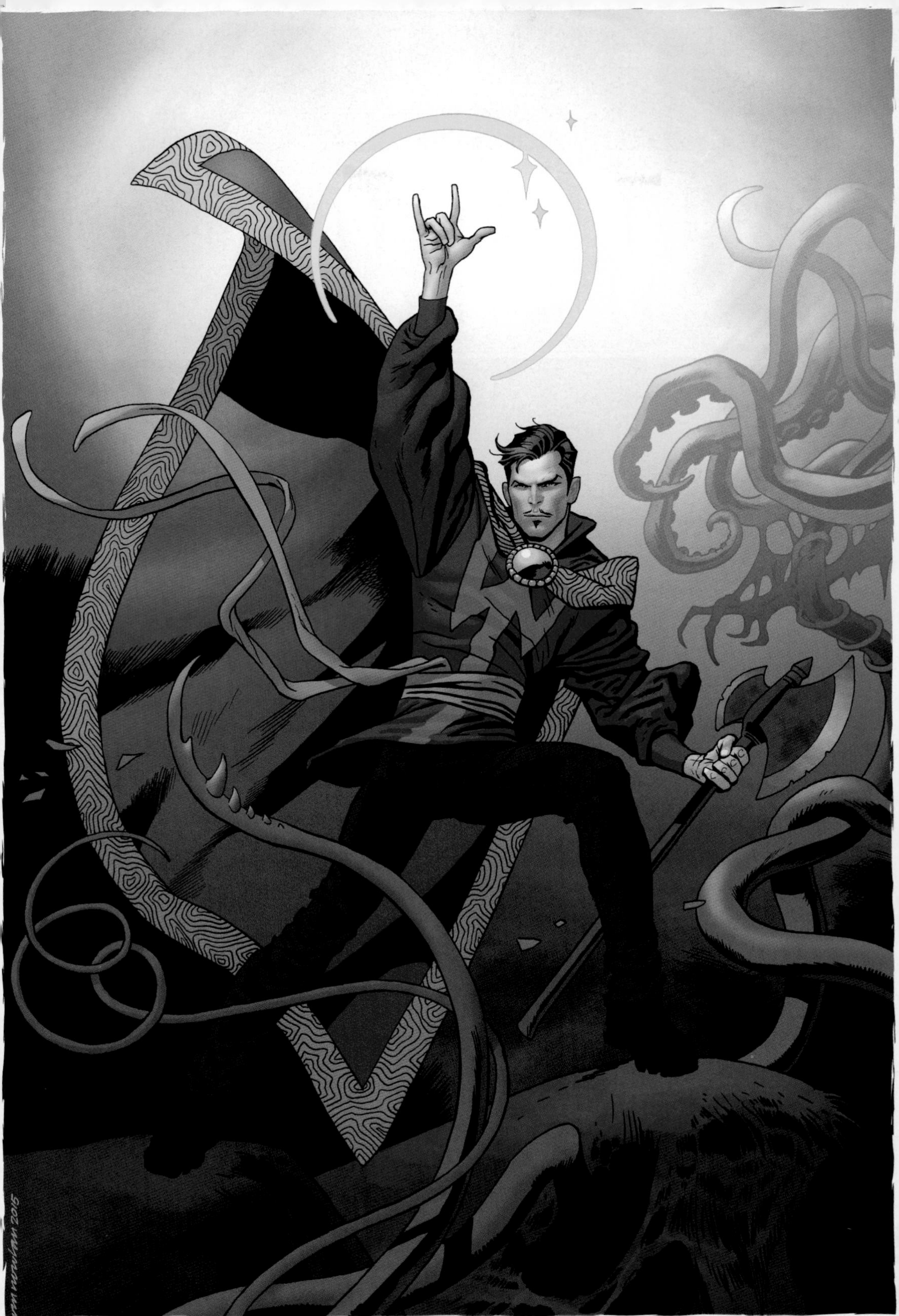

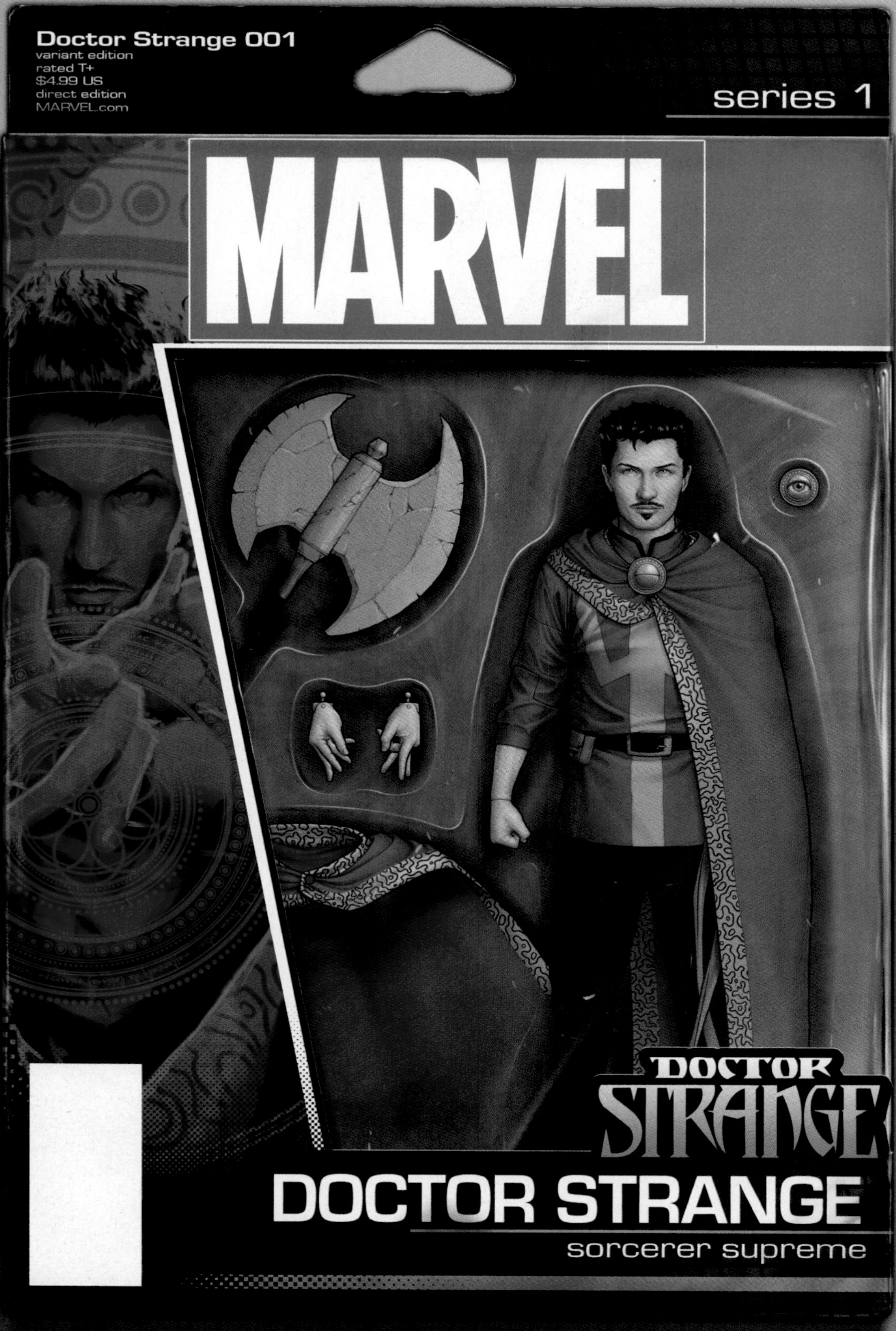

Doctor Strange 001
variant edition
rated T+
$4.99 US
direct edition
MARVEL.com
series 1
MARVEL
DOCTOR STRANGE
DOCTOR STRANGE
sorcerer supreme

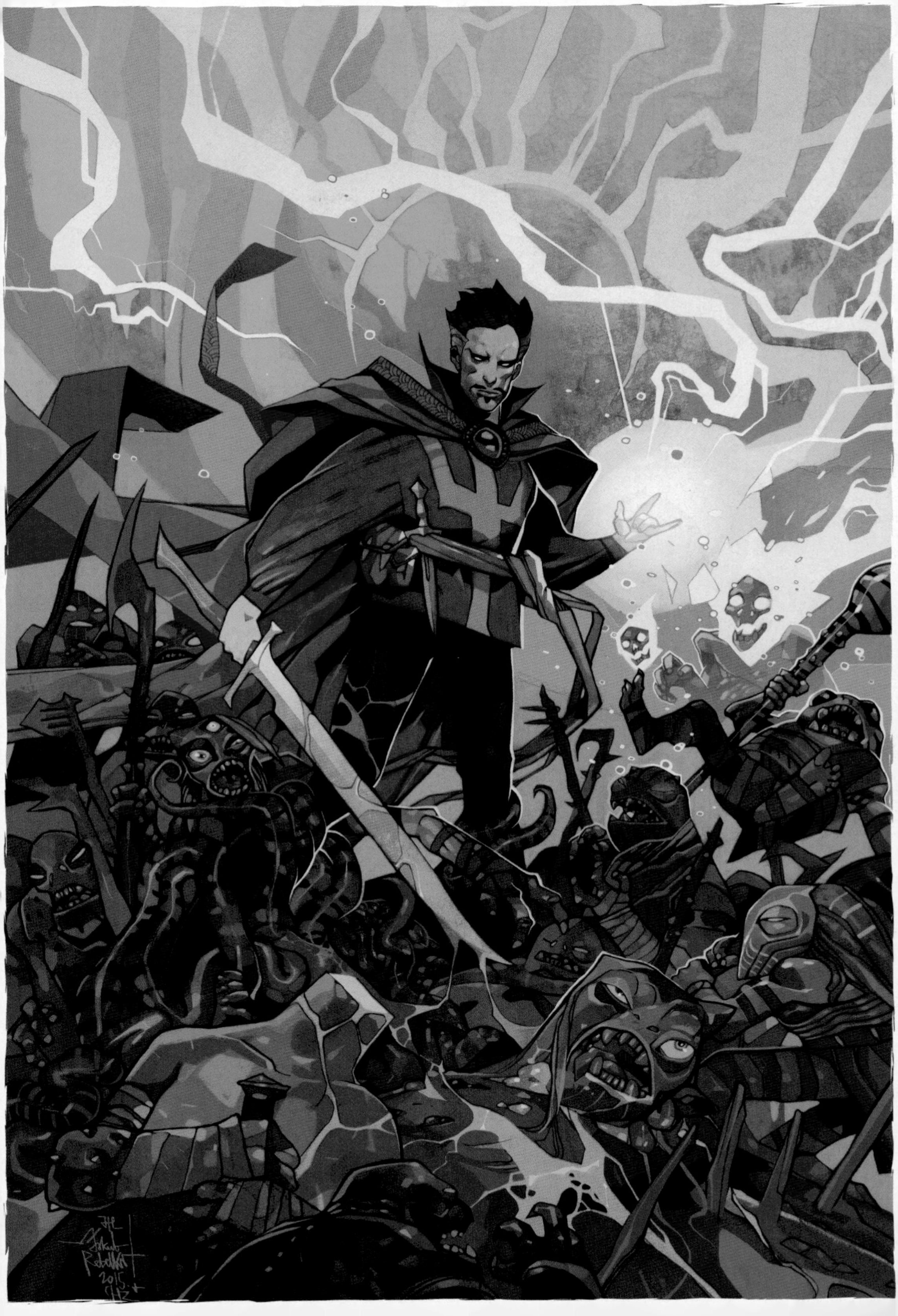

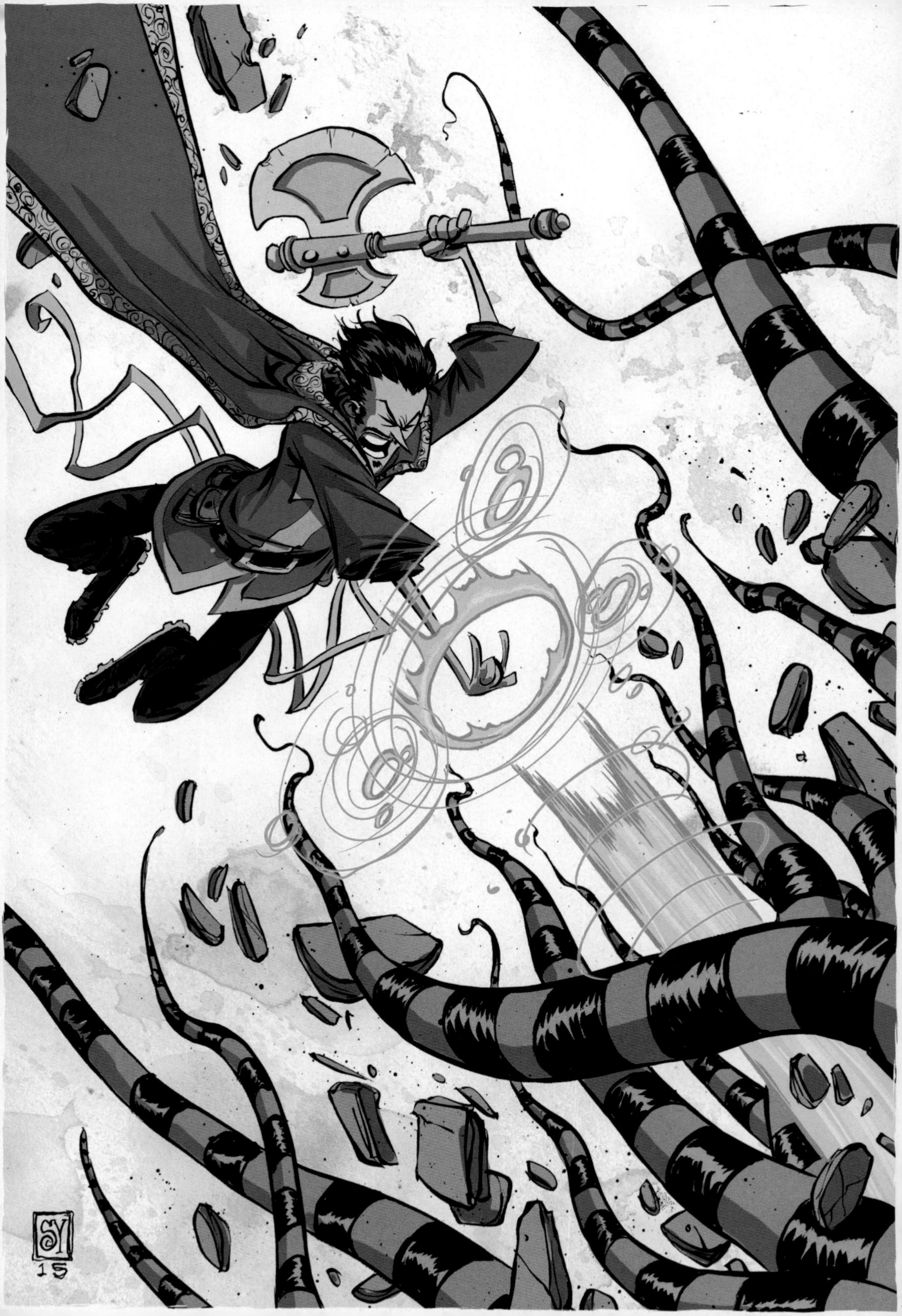

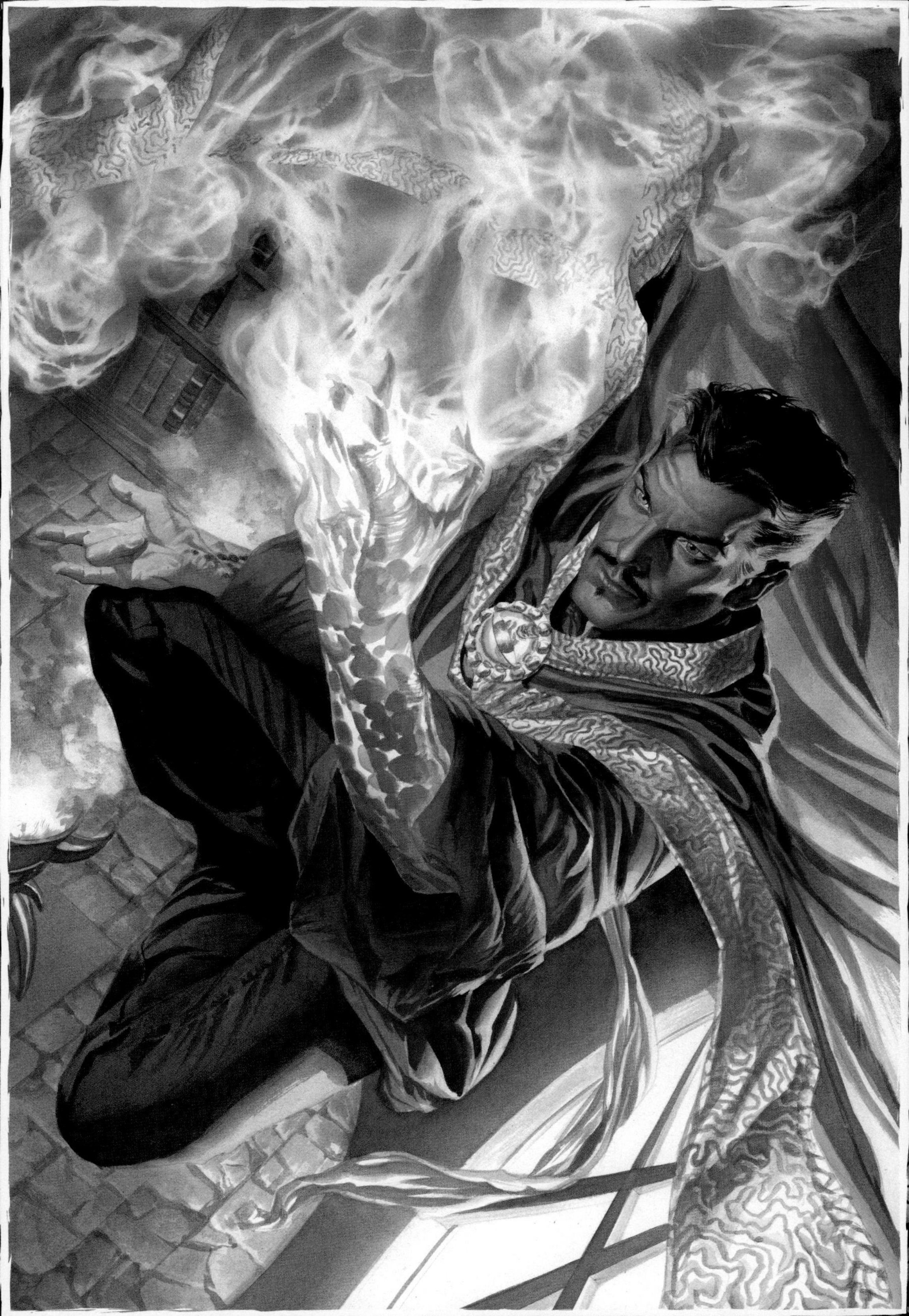

#2 VARIANT BY **ALEX ROSS**

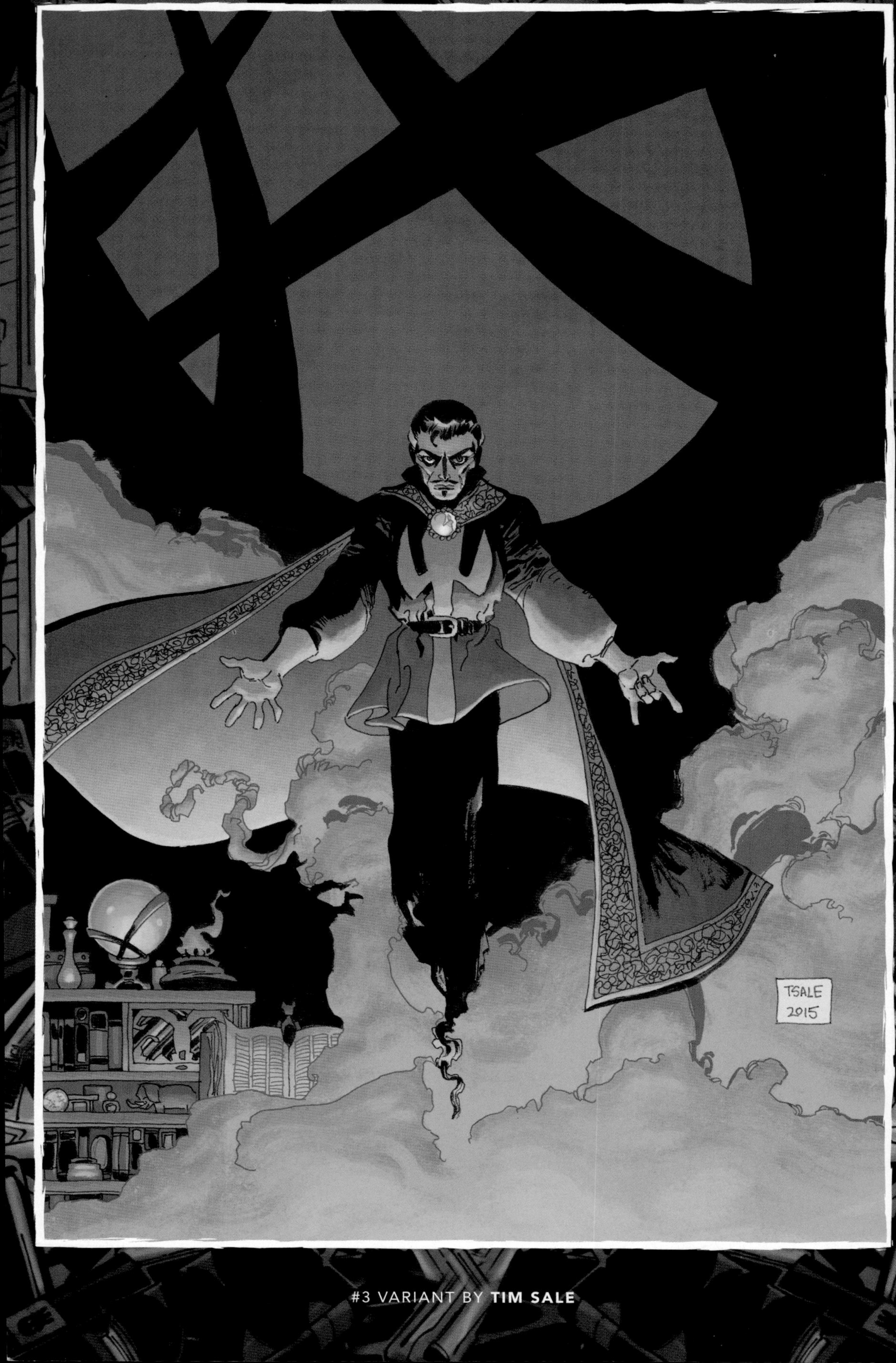
TSALE
2015

#3 VARIANT BY **TIM SALE**

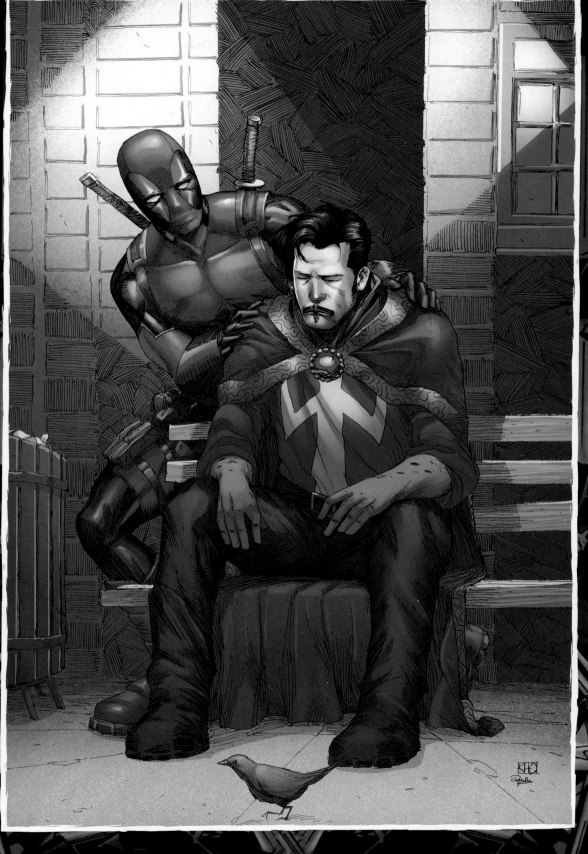

#4 DEADPOOL VARIANT BY **KHOI PHAM** & **RACHELLE ROSENBERG**

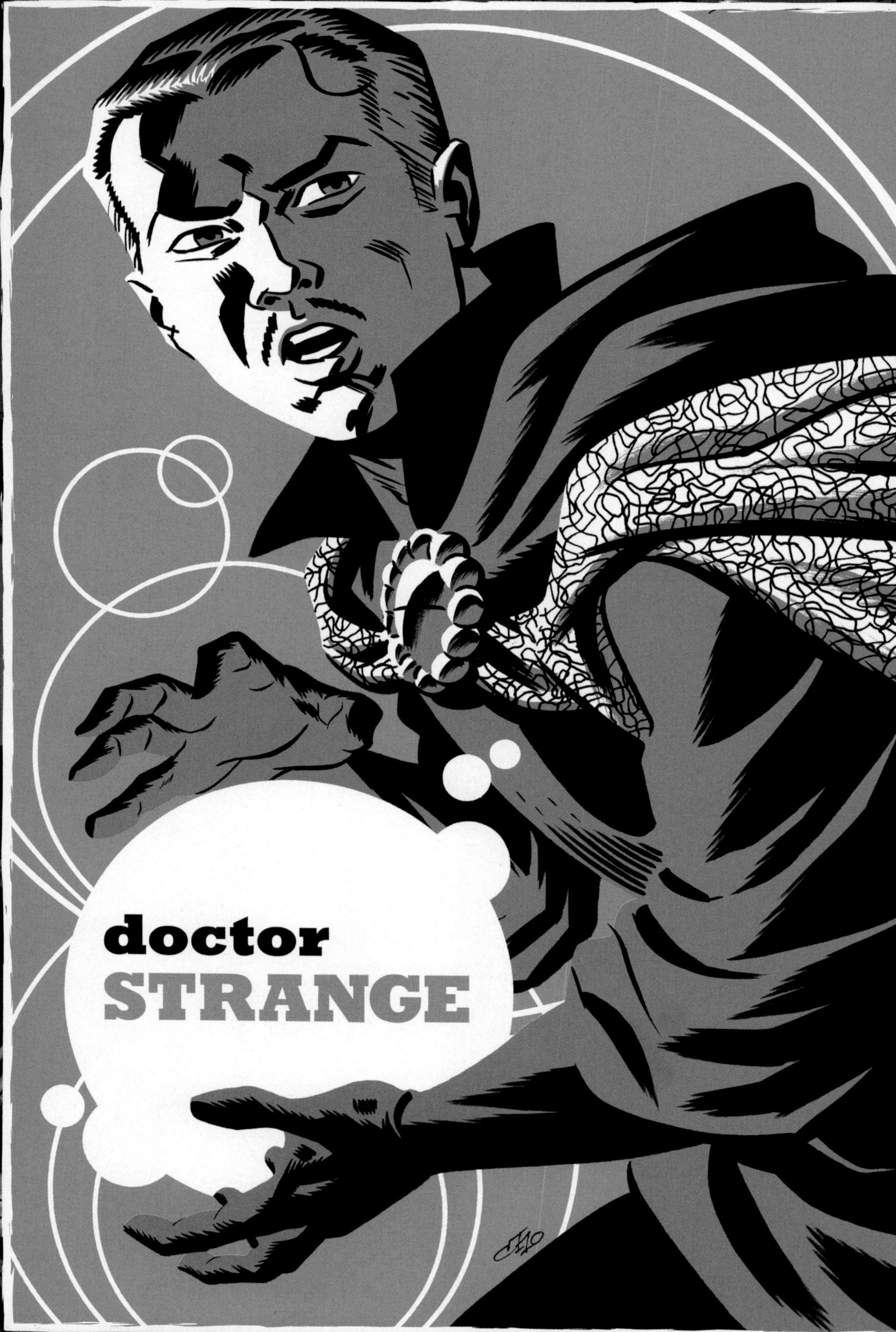
doctor
STRANGE

#5 VARIANT BY **MICHAEL CHO**

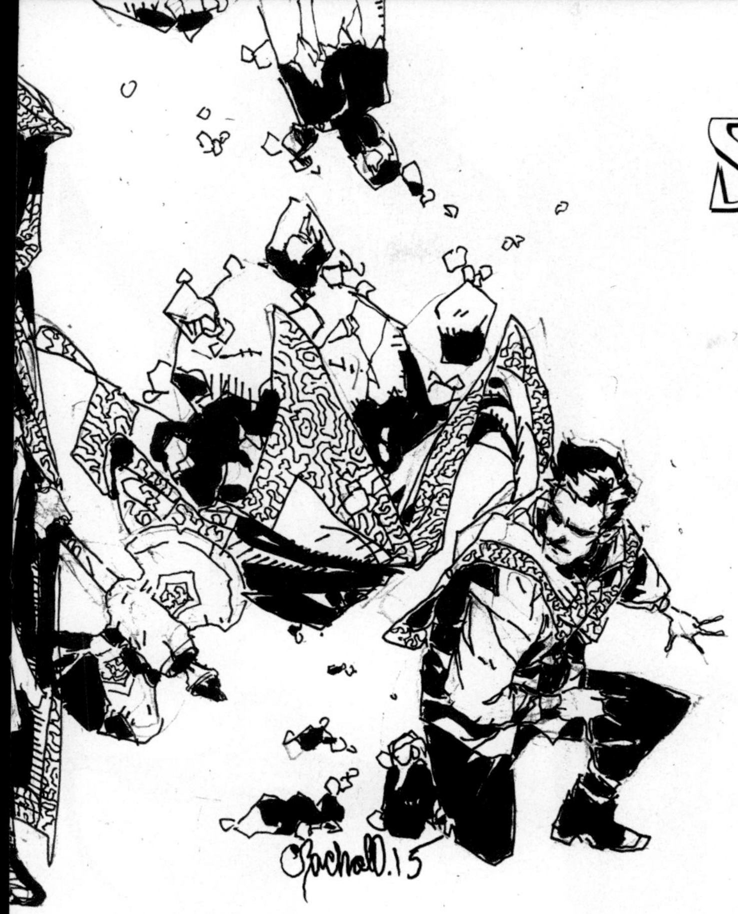

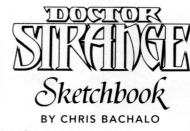

# DOCTOR STRANGE
## Sketchbook
BY CHRIS BACHALO

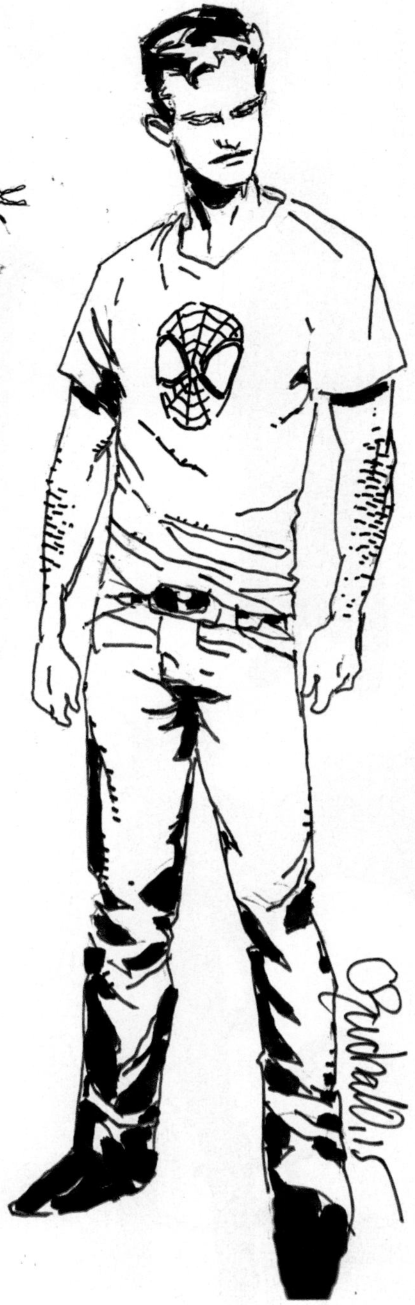

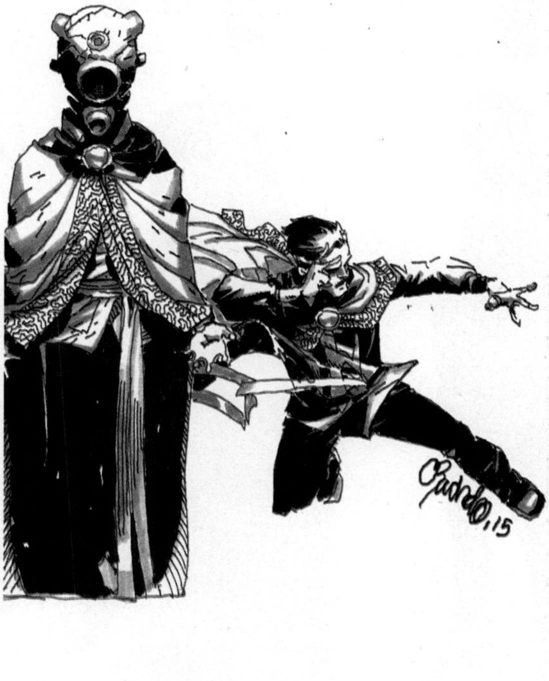

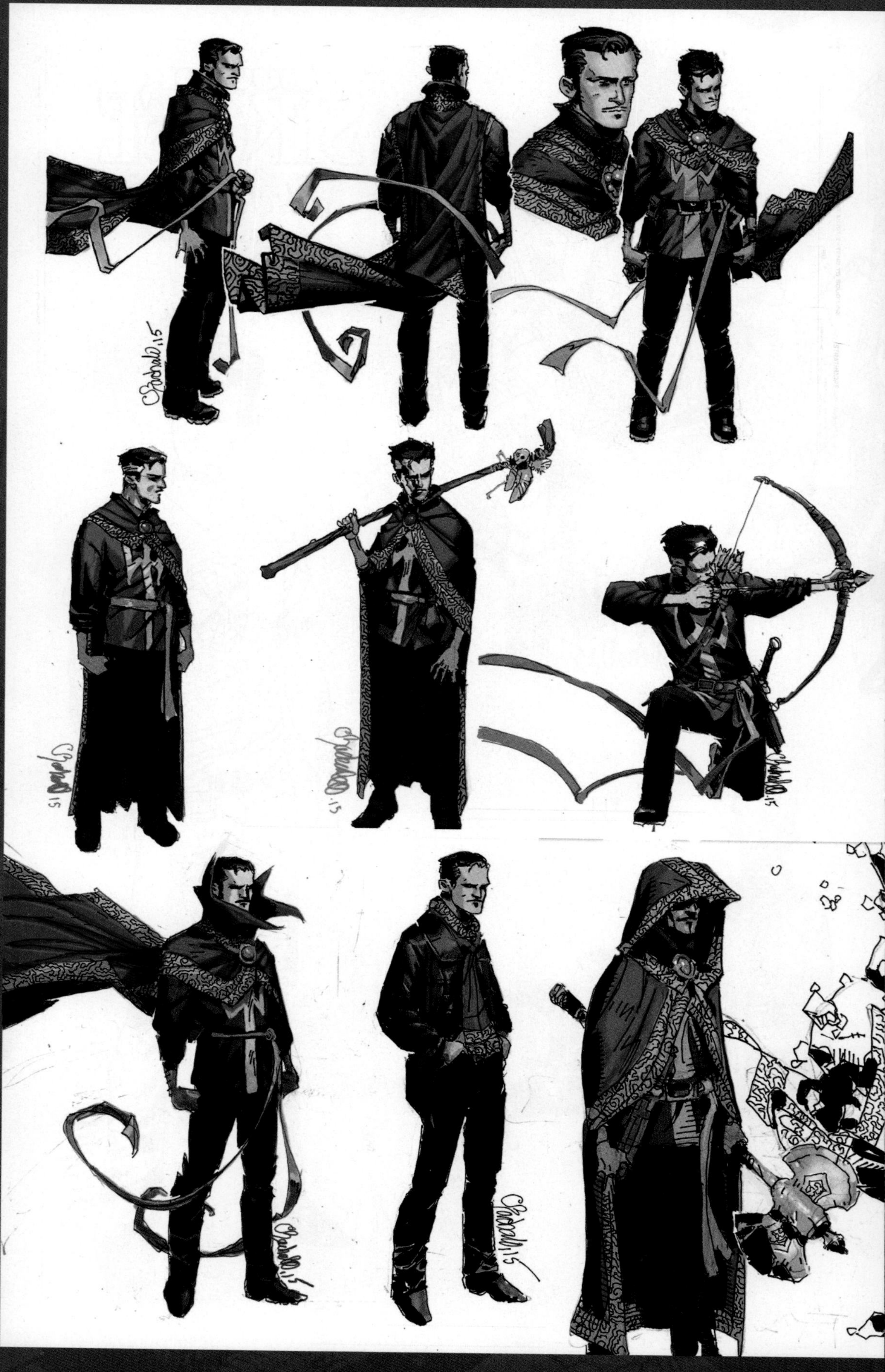

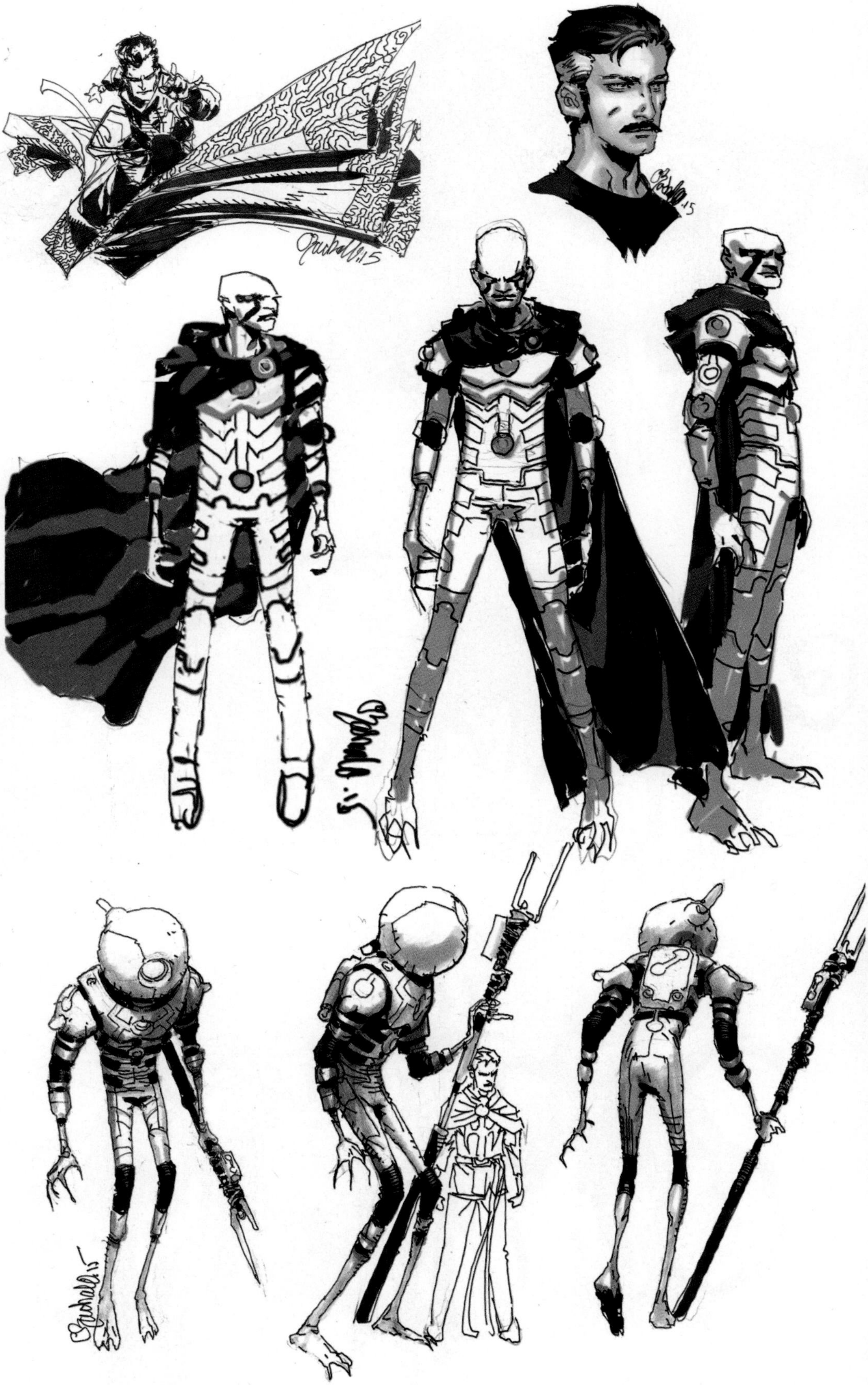

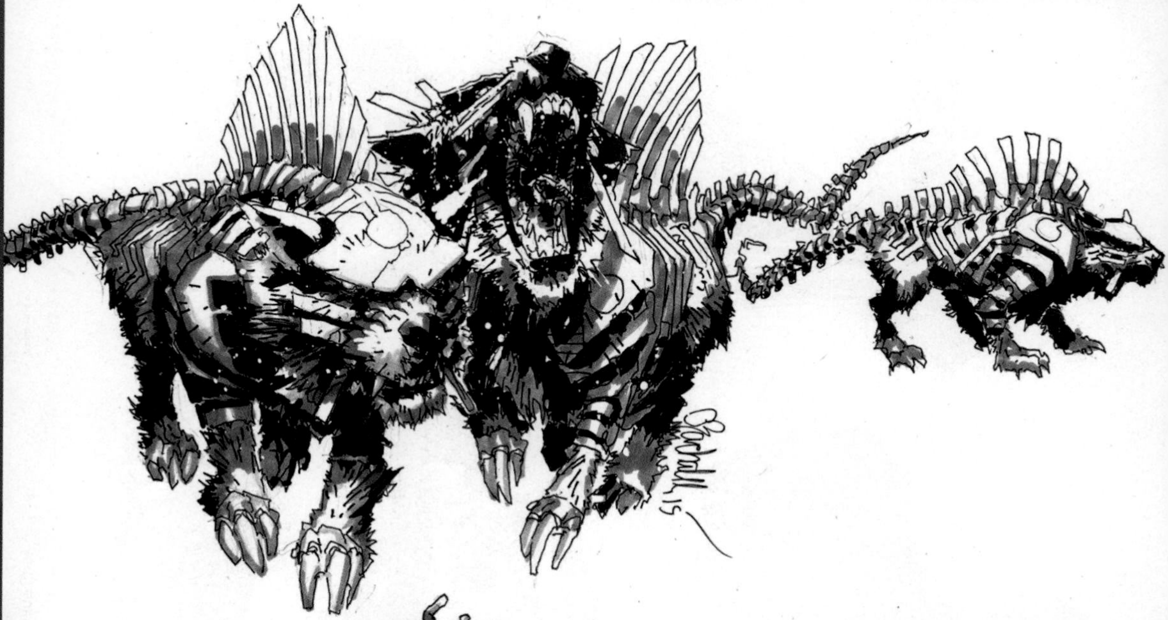

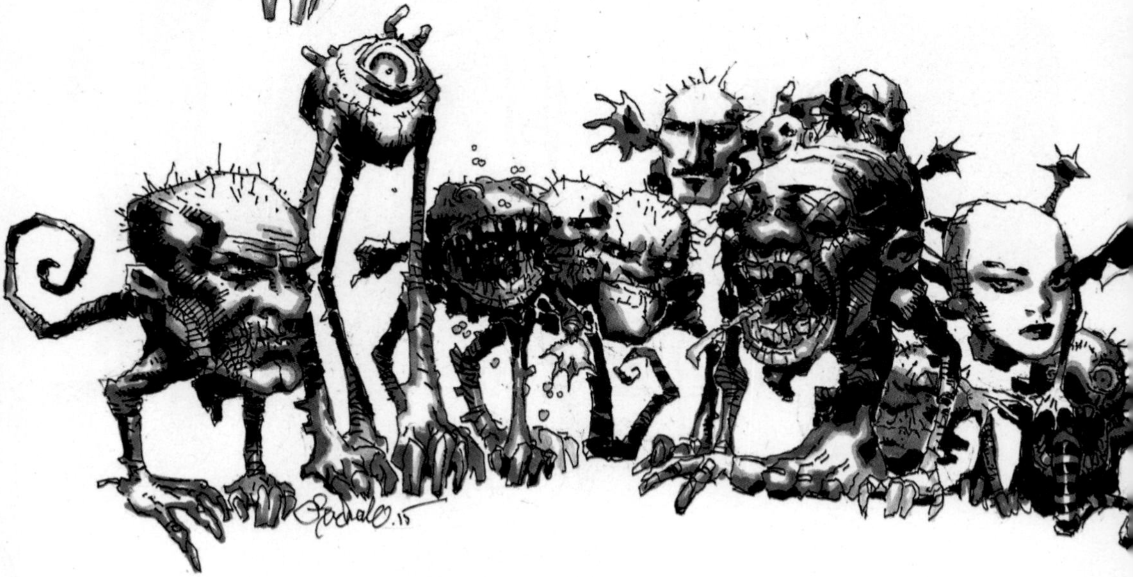

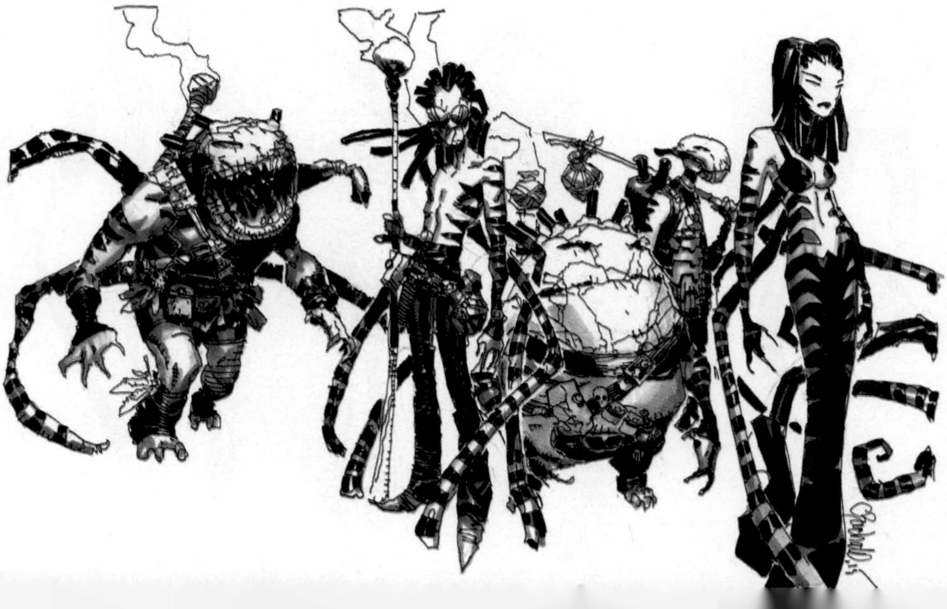

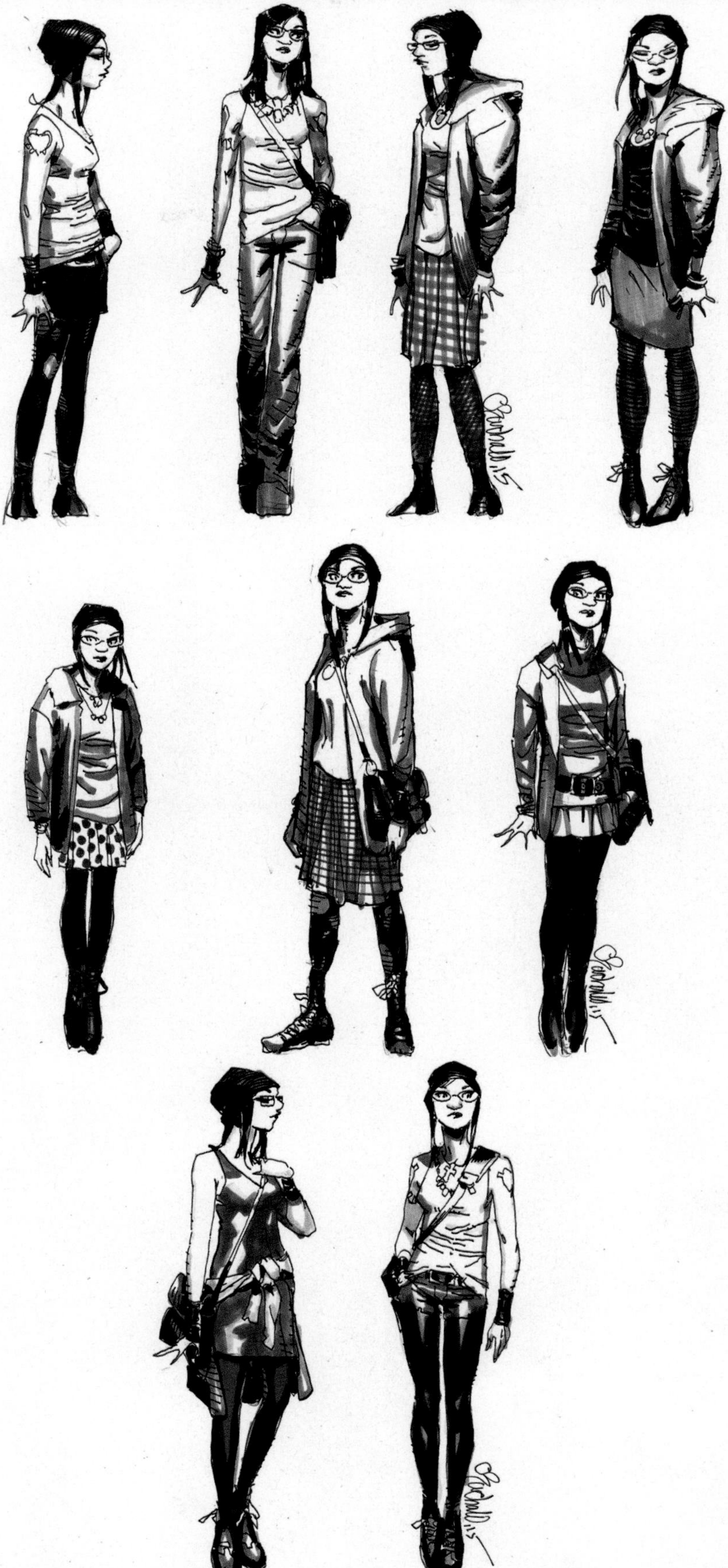

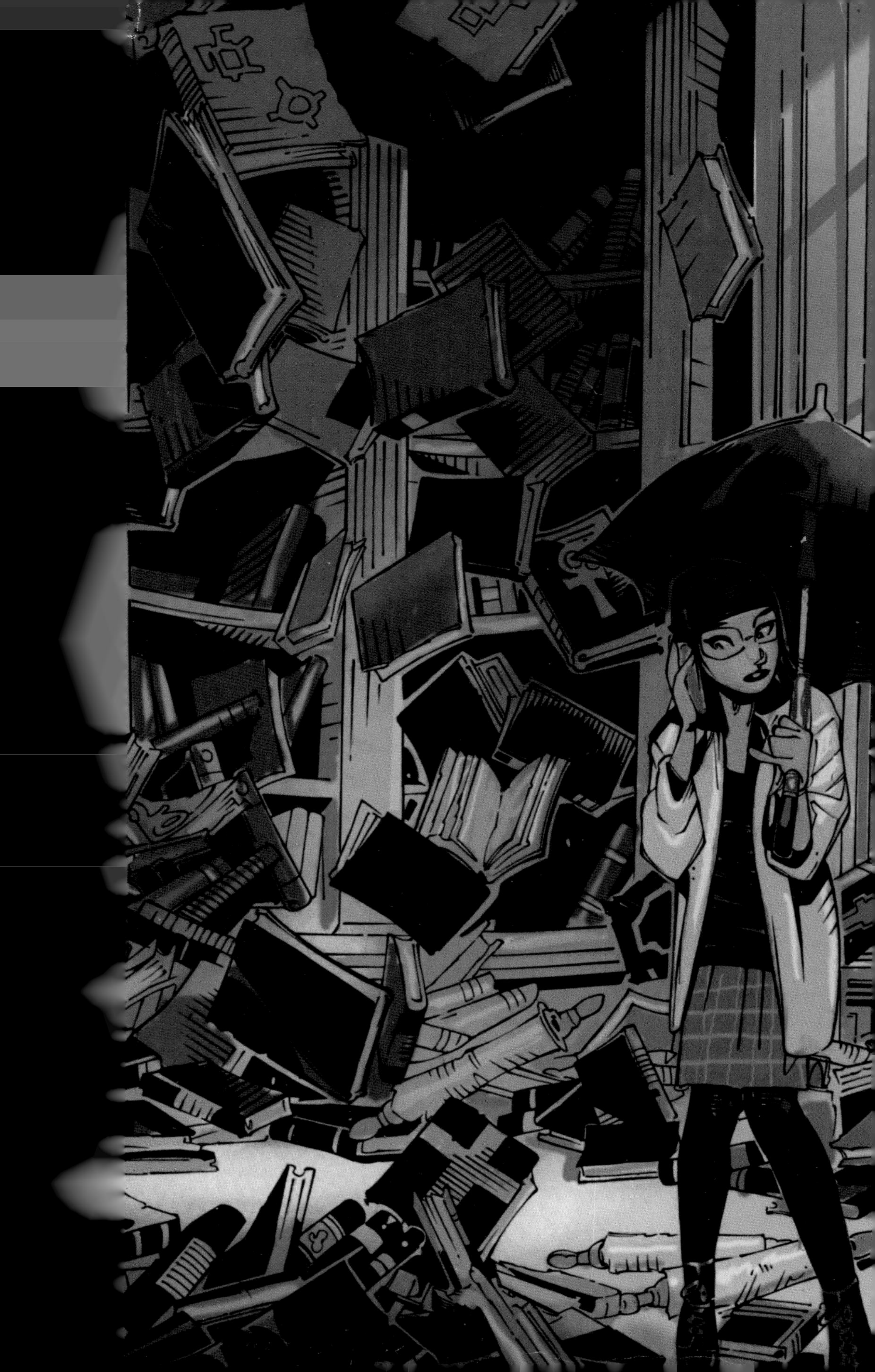